CHURCHILL

Churchill

A PROFILE

Edited by Peter Stansky

WORLD PROFILES

General Editor: Aïda DiPace Donald

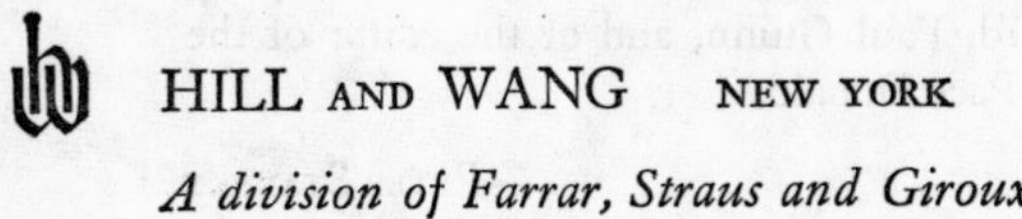

HILL AND WANG NEW YORK

A division of Farrar, Straus and Giroux

ISBN (CLOTHBOUND EDITION): 0-8090-3447-6
ISBN (PAPERBACK EDITION): 0-8090-1404-1
LIBRARY OF CONGRESS CATALOG CARD NUMBER: 70-163576
FIRST EDITION, 1973
PUBLISHED SIMULTANEOUSLY BY DOUBLEDAY CANADA LTD., TORONTO
MANUFACTURED IN THE UNITED STATES OF AMERICA
1 2 3 4 5 6 7 8 9 10

I am grateful to the friends and colleagues who have taken the time to discuss with me writings about Churchill. I would like particularly to mention my deep gratitude for the suggestions of A. F. Thompson, Shirley Hazzard, Paul Guinn, and of the editor of the series, Aïda DiPace Donald.

—PETER STANSKY

Contents

Introduction vii

Winston Churchill, 1874–1965 xv

PART ONE

Young Churchill 3
JOHN GIBSON LOCKHART

The Youngest Man in Europe: Churchill at Twenty-four 17
G. W. STEEVENS

At the Colonial Office, 1905–8 21
RONALD HYAM

Historian of the Great War 36
PETER WRIGHT

Genius Without Judgment: Churchill at Fifty 48
A. G. GARDINER

The Family Man and Writer in the 1930s 54
ROBERT RHODES JAMES

A Man of First Principles: Churchill in 1940 67
ISAIAH BERLIN

Churchill in War 91
B. H. LIDDELL HART

Churchill as Prime Minister 110
JOHN COLVILLE

In Parliament After the War 152
WOODROW WYATT

PART TWO

The Power Politician and Counterrevolutionary 173
ARNO J. MAYER

Churchill on Balance 188
CLEMENT ATTLEE

Churchill: A Minority View 207
GORONWY REES

The Inner Man 222
ANTHONY STORR

Bibliographical Note 263

Contributors 267

Introduction

IN MARCH, 1965, the American periodical *The Atlantic Monthly* dedicated a special number to Churchill under the heading: "The Greatest Englishman." The exaggeration is understandable, coming only a few months after his death. But enough time has now passed for the fact of his greatness, if not the degree of it, to be beyond argument. Yet if Churchill had died in 1940, in his sixty-sixth year, he would have been remembered chiefly as a fascinating but ultimately unsuccessful political figure in the first four decades of twentieth-century Britain.

Even, perhaps, if he had died sometime after the Second World War—having at the war's end returned with characteristic over-commitment to partisan politics and to attacks on his former Labour colleagues in the national government—his claim to greatness might not have been so readily or universally granted. There, all too palpably, was the intemperate political chieftain, blurring the recollection of the great unifying wartime leader. And in the early days of the Cold War—which, with his gift for finding a striking phrase, he helped along in his "Iron Curtain" speech at Fulton, Missouri, in 1946—he appeared to some a difficult, even a senile old man, who was participating in politics beyond his time. His postwar political activity was motivated at least in part by determination to wipe out the insult of his rejection by the electorate in 1945. Power had to be regained, and indeed was, but not even his most devout admirers would claim that these were his great years.

It was not until 1955, at eighty-one, that he finally retired. Then, no longer a mercurial force in the play of British politics, he could safely be moved into myth, and became a figure whom all Britain and the Western world could venerate now that his days of activity were over.* The tributes that had poured out on the occasion of his eightieth birthday were renewed at the time of his death a decade later. The funeral itself was an extremely moving ceremony, watched by the world on television and film, and recorded in countless words and photographs. Not since the death of the Duke of Wellington was the nation so moved.

It is characteristic of Churchill, with his instinct for pomp and circumstance, that he should have given some thought years earlier to the ceremonial to be followed at the time of his death. It is unlikely, though, that he would have foreseen the dual symbolic aspect of the funeral itself when the time came for it: a farewell to a great Englishman, and a farewell to the greatness of England. The decline of British influence on the world had been tacitly if not overtly acknowledged in the realignments of the postwar power structure. Now even the illusion of imperial grandeur had ended; this was as clear to the man in the street as to the men in Westminster.

Churchill began his political career at a time when Great Britain was the most powerful country in the world. His first period of

* His heroic stature and its early introduction into popular consciousness is marked, I believe, by the great number of books for children written about him: an image of extraordinary force is impressed upon the young at a time when it is likely to remain in their memories for life. In this respect at least, he may well prove to be "the greatest Englishman"; certainly no other twentieth-century political figure approaches him. [ed.]

importance, treated here by Ronald Hyam, was during the heyday of empire, from the turn of the century to 1914. He moved steadily forward as undersecretary of state for the colonies, president of the Board of Trade, home secretary, and first lord of the Admiralty. But from 1915 to 1939 his life was a succession of comparative failures, all on a grand scale. He was war secretary, colonial secretary, and chancellor of the exchequer, but his aggressive stands against those he considered enemies of the state—Bolsheviks and workers—and his increasingly critical attitude toward his colleagues isolated and weakened him, despite his high offices. Then, at the time of the Second World War, he achieved the premiership and led Britain alone against Hitler.

In his eightieth-birthday speech he stated modestly, "It was the nation and the race dwelling all round the globe that had the lion's heart. I had the luck to be called upon to give the roar." But "to give the roar" required a genius that was peculiarly his, and a dauntless tenacity of a sort that in the past frequently had led to his undoing, for he would not see the possibility of an attitude toward a problem other than the one he himself adopted. So, in 1940, after the fall of France, he did not waver in his conviction of an ultimate British victory over the Nazis. Adapting a phrase of Rupert Brooke's in a sonnet of the First World War, one can say that now, as the Second World War began, Churchill was matched with his hour.

He did, as he intended, lead Britain to victory, and paradoxically —as discussed by Liddell Hart—he led her grandly off the main stage as he made concessions to her eventual allies, the United States and the Soviet Union, concessions that helped assure the defeat of Germany but also resulted in Britain's decline to a second-class power. And though the United States and Russia were the dominant partners in the alliance in the sheer accumulation of power, Churchill, as the spokesman for embattled Britain, caught the imagination of people everywhere.

This culmination as prime minister and war leader makes Churchill a figure whose position is secure in the world's history. Although his importance in the war years can make the rest of his life seem like little more than a long prologue and a brief epilogue to those heroic years, in fact all of Churchill's life is of interest. The object of the present collection is to try to suggest as many facets of it as possible, without pretending to completeness and without touching on every one of his activities or all aspects of his personality. The biographies of him are legion; some are satisfactory but most are in differing ways inadequate to the challenge their subject presents.

The mammoth official life—which at this time consists of three thick volumes of text bringing the story up to 1916 and three companion volumes of documents—has been delayed by the death of its original author, his son Randolph. For any student of Churchill it is an invaluable source, but it holds too closely to the motto that Randolph Churchill set himself, "He shall be his own Biographer," and tends to present too many unassimilated documents, even in the main volumes. But whatever its faults, it will continue to be indispensable.

Apart from formal biographies, there are also innumerable studies, some of which I mention in the bibliography, of various parts of Churchill's career; and he is a compelling figure in almost any political memoir, biography, or autobiography of the period. But to extract bits and pieces from such books—with some exceptions, where the effect is self-contained—would result in a confused picture and would not do justice to either author or subject. Rather, I have attempted here to select, on the whole, essays complete in themselves that suggest aspects of Churchill—a "profile"—and will give the reader some feeling and appreciation for his strengths and weaknesses.

Every facet of Churchill's life is marked by controversy and drama, even his very entry into life prematurely during a ball at Blenheim, the seat of the head of the family, his grandfather, the Duke of Marlborough. Since he was a masterly writer, he has been able to present his own version of events, with an overpowering rhetoric of assurance. (His lack of self-doubt most of the time was balanced by periods of black depression, about which Anthony Storr writes in his psychoanalytical study.) Accordingly, his own books, while they afford a great deal of pleasure, must be read with care. His coparticipants in events, and historians, are continually attempting to set the record straight. But in many cases, most particularly in his accounts of his own and Britain's role in the two world wars—it is frequently hard to distinguish between them—he has been able to set the terms of the debate, and to convey his story first. As Noel Annan, the intellectual historian, has remarked in a review of a recent group of Churchill books:

> In a curious way Churchill may impose upon historians in the future his own vision of history. They may be able to discern some broad principle which reconciles some of the more startling changes in policy, but apart from his brief spell in the field of social insurance (before the First World War) it is hard to associate him with any of the movements of change in this country. But they will never be able to convey the true sense of British politics in the first half of this century without often referring to this astonishing phenomenon who, almost totally ignorant of how the rest of his countrymen lived, exhibited so many of their characteristics in a most memorable form, and was hailed in his old age, after a lifetime of unfulfilled promise, as the saviour of his country.*

He was clearly motivated at the beginning of his career by an effort to prove himself worthy of his father and more deserving of affection and regard than parental neglect would seem to indicate. Like his father, he was intensely ambitious, but he failed to show any early promise and was shunted off into the military. He was intent on fame, and on fortune as well. As a member of the upper classes, but as the son of a younger son, he had the tastes of the very rich, but not the income, and he was determined to succeed. He had that assurance—as pointed out by G. W. Steevens—that goes with being a member of the British ruling classes, the conviction that he belonged to the best group in the world. Along with this went bravado and arrogance: he would risk his life in order to make a grand show. At the same time he was able to speak generously and selflessly: to speak for the downtrodden (whose misery he never experienced) and for those in prison when he was home secretary before the First World War; and to "speak for England" during the Second World War.

He did not question the social order or his own place in it, but he was determined to make himself as important as he felt he deserved. Early on, the thought may well have occurred to him that he might someday be prime minister. He was probably surprised that the premiership took so long in coming. Yet there must have been moments, particularly during his growing estrangement from his own Tory Party, in the late 1920s and 1930s over

* *The New York Review of Books,* July 10, 1969, p. 30. [ed.]

India and in the later 1930s over rearmament, when he felt that his ambitions would never be realized. (Churchill had changed allegiances twice before, from Tory to Liberal and back again, which hardly created confidence within party organizations.)

The conventions of upper-class life meant that children need not be much trouble to their parents, but Winston was unusually ignored. Still, he was able to forgive his parents their neglect, perhaps because he was sustained for years by the overflowing love of his nurse, Mrs. Everest, and later by a very happy marriage and family life. He had to make his own career, and in a way he could be unconventional about procedures, because so little was expected of him. He did not do well at school, although he enjoyed in later life exaggerating these failings, but Harrow, his public school, helped instill in him a respect for, and a knowledge of, English prose. If he had not been the extraordinary human being he inherently was, he might have turned out simply another Edwardian "gent," an officer on half-pay, who would have served his country in India and in France during the First World War, and perhaps have figured in the Harrovian lists of those who had died for King and Country. That was not enough for him, and it was an act of will that made him into the "glow-worm," as he described himself at thirty-two.

In his early years he was always pushing himself forward, for medals, for office, as an observer at the front for any war. He began by making his way as a correspondent, but journalism was to serve him as an entrance to politics, and his flamboyant escape from the Boers made him a hero. (Whether he violated the terms of his imprisonment as a correspondent is one of the many disputed points about his life.) It meant, in practical terms, that his defeat as Parliamentary candidate in 1899 was turned into a victory in 1900.

His precipitousness, his excitement about any possibility that offered itself, his frequently excessive commitment to the cause of the moment continued as his style in politics. He began to be enjoyed as someone who was colorful, and about whom stories could be told but who was not trusted. Asquith, the leader of the Liberal Party, whose ranks he joined over the issue of free trade in 1904, felt he was incapable of discrimination and loyalty, and explicitly predicted that he would not be prime minister. A. G. Gardiner, in his discussion here, points out that Stanley Baldwin, the Tory leader between the wars, who shared some of the sobriety of Asquith's views while granting many of Churchill's gifts, felt that since Churchill lacked judgment and wisdom, his opinions need not be taken seriously.

In a sense, these eminent critics were right; but another way of putting it would be to say that Churchill lacked caution, and perhaps balance. He would devote himself single-mindedly to the immediate question at hand, whether it was how to solve the problems of the poor or how best to unload a truck. (Whatever the case, he was highly methodical, and believed that administration should not be sloppy and that all suggestions and orders should be conveyed in writing or, if first discussed orally, should then be written out.) During the Second World War, as John Colville reminds us, his memoranda, accompanied by the red tags he had printed up saying ACTION THIS DAY, were the terror of his staff, but they helped produce the efficiency that was essential to winning the war. His Edwardian high spirits were too much for many of his political contemporaries, and frequently they served *him* badly as well—could make him curt and unfeeling—but they were also what gave him his gifts of imagination, those extraordinary phrases that leaped to his lips or pen, his fantastic enthusiasm. When the combination of man and circumstance was in tune, as happened at certain points in his career, he was exactly right, and the price was worth paying for all his mistakes and gaffes.

Since he committed himself completely to the cause of the moment, it is hard to be sure of the depth of a particular commitment: how much, for example, did he believe in the causes of the Left when he and Lloyd George, in the Asquith government before the First World War, were the chief architects in creating what has come to be regarded as the twentieth-century foundation of the welfare state in Great Britain? He was deeply involved in such revolutionary concepts as unemployment insurance, even though he was moved not by radical ideology but simply by a desire to do his best for his country. He recognized the wastefulness of the Edwardian social system, the needlessly high price in unrest and suffering down below that was paid for the opulence the rich enjoyed, and he hoped to make Britain a better place for all. But his aim was to strengthen, not to upset, the status quo, and this was one reason for his near-hysterical hatred of "Bolshevism" between the wars, as Arno Mayer points out. What he wanted was England "as she was, only more so," with some degree of contentment for all. He was a pragmatist in the service of an ideal of a traditional England. With that the paramount consideration, he could adapt to the needs of circumstance and appear to change his mind and principles—as when he welcomed Stalin enthusiastically as an ally during the Second World War.

His independence, his imagination, his ability to see ways that were obscure to others, seemed to go off the track from the second year of the First World War to shortly before the outbreak of the Second World War.* But in 1940 he felt that it was he, of all English politicians, who was best qualified to wage the defense of England, and it would appear that he was right. This overriding achievement should be kept in mind as successive stages of his career are considered in the pages that follow. I have attempted to bring together some of the most telling views of Churchill, in various styles and guises, at various points in time—some admiring, some critical—in order to illuminate a man who, with all his faults, did heroic service for his own country and for the Western world.

PETER STANSKY

Stanford in Britain
Cliveden
June, 1971

* Since it would require other books of documents to discuss them adequately, it has seemed wisest not to touch directly on the debates among historians over, for example, the value of Churchill's unsuccessful attempts to save Antwerp in October, 1914: did the few days' delay caused by the attempt mean that the nearby coast was saved for France? The controversy is much more intense over the question of the Gallipoli campaign of 1915: if the British had persisted, would it have succeeded? Churchill was largely responsible for the campaign; did its failure lead to his being dropped from power during the war? Consideration of these issues would involve complex discussion of details, essential if one were concerned with trying to determine the precise nature of specific events, but obscuring the lineaments of a man's personality and importance. Similar limitations affect the much-debated question of the various strengths and deficiencies of Churchill's policies during the Second World War. [ed.]

Winston Churchill, 1874–1965

WINSTON CHURCHILL was born on November 30, 1874, in Blenheim Palace, the home of his grandfather, the Duke of Marlborough. He was the eldest son of Lord Randolph Churchill (1849–1895) and Jennie Jerome (1854–1921), a rich, beautiful American of less exalted background. Lord Randolph was a prominent and imaginative Tory politician whose career reached its height in 1886 when he was chancellor of the exchequer; it collapsed that same year when his resignation over the military budget was accepted. He had little faith in the intelligence and future of his son, who was to write Lord Randolph's biography in 1906 and who, throughout his life, was motivated to some degree by a desire to prove his father had been wrong in his estimate.

He was educated at private schools from 1882 to 1888; then, from 1888 to 1892, at Harrow. From 1893 to 1894 he was a cadet at the

Royal Military Academy at Sandhurst; in February, 1895, he was commissioned in the 4th Hussars.

He had his first taste of war as an observer of the conflict between Spain and Cuba in 1895. It was there, too, that he began his career as a journalist. In 1896 he went to India with his regiment, in 1897 fought on the northwest frontier, and in March, 1898, published his first book, an account of that campaign—*The Story of the Malakand Field Force.* During his time in India he deepened his political knowledge through extensive reading of the *Annual Register*; a close reading of Gibbon and Macaulay helped form his style. In 1898 he managed to attach himself to the campaign in the Sudan, and he published *The River War* in 1899. In July, 1899, he ran unsuccessfully for Parliament as a Conservative candidate from Oldham. In October he went to South Africa as a war correspondent during the Boer War; he was captured while defending an armored train, but escaped from prison. The exploit made him famous. He wrote two volumes on the war: *Ian Hamilton's March* and *London to Ladysmith via Pretoria.* That same year, 1900, he published his one novel, *Savrola.*

In 1900 he was elected to Parliament from Oldham, as a Tory. He became increasingly discontented with his party, particularly its policy to expand the army and its growing commitment to tariffs. In 1904 he "crossed the floor" of the House of Commons and became a Liberal. When the Liberals formed a government in December, 1905, he was appointed undersecretary of state for the colonies; in the general election of 1906 he was elected for northwest Manchester as a Liberal. After Asquith became prime minister in 1908, Churchill was made president of the Board of Trade, with a seat in the Cabinet. That same year he was very happily married to Clementine Hozier. In February, 1910, he became home secretary and in 1911 first lord of the Admiralty. In all his posts he was known for his imagination—he was thought to be somewhat radical—and for his willingness to try new ways. As first lord he helped to strengthen the navy, so that it was in a state approaching preparedness when war came in 1914.

His own career during the war was not successful. At the time the government was reorganized in May, 1915, he was demoted to being chancellor of the duchy of Lancaster, in large part because of the already evident failure of the Gallipoli campaign that brought the British to the Dardanelles. Churchill was largely responsible for the adventure. The hope was to knock Turkey out of the war, but the terrain, the number of Turkish troops, and an insufficiency of British forces and supplies doomed the campaign and Churchill's reputation. He resigned from the government in November, 1915. From then until the following June he served on the front in France.

Lloyd George, who had succeeded Asquith as prime minister, called him back into the government as minister of munitions in 1917. He became secretary of state for war in 1919 and was a firm supporter of the unsuccessful Allied campaign against the Bolsheviks in Russia that year. From 1921 until 1922 he was colonial secretary, and was active in negotiating the treaty creating the Irish Free State in December, 1921. He was defeated in the general election of 1922, and was not successful in returning to Parliament until November, 1924, at which time he rejoined the Tory party. He was appointed chancellor of the exchequer in the Baldwin government of that year. He led England back onto the gold standard in 1925, in the hope of restoring economic confidence. But the effect of the move was to damage Britain's international economic position. During the general strike in 1926 he edited the government paper, the *British Gazette,* and allowed his enjoyment of a fight to make him excessively vehement against the workers.

Throughout these years, even while active as a politician, he continued to write, publishing *The World Crisis* in four volumes (1923–29), his account of the First World War. Labour came into power in 1929, and Churchill went out of office. Before the national government was formed in 1931 he had already dissociated himself to a considerable degree from his party over what he regarded as its too indulgent attitude toward India.

During most of the 1930s he was in the political "wilderness." But it was a productive period for his writing: most notably *My Early Life* (1930); *Marlborough,* his biography of his great ancestor in four volumes (1933–38); and *Great Contemporaries* (1937). He became increasingly alarmed about the international situation, the growing strength of Germany, and the need for rearmament. When war broke out in 1939, he was brought back into the government as first lord of the Admiralty. On May 10, 1940, he became prime minister, and during the next five years he led his country to victory.

In July, 1945, a majority of the electorate would not trust him in peace as they had in war, and a Labour government was elected. From 1948 to 1954 Churchill published his six-volume history, *The Second World War*. He returned to power as prime minister from 1951 to 1955; he then retired as leader of his party, but remained as a member of Parliament until 1964. From 1956 until 1958 his *History of the English-speaking Peoples* appeared; much of it had been written before the Second World War. In 1953 he was made a Knight of the Garter, and received the Nobel prize for literature. He died on January 24, 1965, received a state funeral at St. Paul's, and was buried in Bladon Churchyard near his birthplace at Blenheim.

PART ONE

JOHN GIBSON LOCKHART

Young Churchill

WINSTON SPENCER CHURCHILL was born on November 30, 1874. The Churchills were a West-country family, which rose meteorlike to fame and fortune in the person of the great Duke of Marlborough. Thereafter, for one hundred and fifty years, they lived chiefly on their laurels, until the second son of the seventh duke began to write a new chapter in the family history. The story of Randolph Churchill has been superbly told. Today he is remembered as the man who gave a fresh impetus to the Tory Party in the humdrum eighties, when its leadership was respectable rather than dynamic, who fell out with Lord Salisbury and "forgot Goschen," and while still a comparatively young man was struck down by a terrible and incurable disease.

From *Winston Churchill,* by J. G. Lockhart. London: Gerald Duckworth & Co. Ltd., 1951, pp. 9–25.

In January, 1874, he married Jennie Jerome, a lovely and fascinating American girl, one of the famed Jerome sisters, daughters of Leonard Jerome, a picturesque man who made and lost and remade a fortune. Two years later the young couple, with their baby Winston, moved to Dublin, where Randolph's father, the Duke, had been appointed viceroy and governor-general by Mr. Disraeli, during his famous last administration.

The Churchills lived in Little Lodge. Lord Randolph was naturally much occupied with his work as unpaid private secretary to his father, and his wife inevitably became a leader in Dublin society; so that in their little boy's world nurses, and later governesses, loomed most large. Of these, Mrs. Everest was first, both in time and in his affections. When he was too old for a nurse, she continued to share his secrets and frame his early opinions. Later still, as housekeeper, she remained his chief confidante, to whom he told his troubles, sometimes by telegram, and when she visited him at Harrow he kissed her in the presence of his companions—an act of courage that any schoolboy will appreciate.

Years afterward he would recall a few stray memories of those early days in Dublin—of the time when he was kicked off his donkey in Phœnix Park, of a glimpse of a grim concourse of men who might have been Fenians, but were probably soldiers; of how once he ran away into the woods, which were really shrubberies, and hid from authority; and of a Mr. Burke, later the victim of a famous murder, who gave him a drum. His father was a remote godlike person; his mother was a "fairy princess," especially when she was dressed for an evening party. "I loved her dearly—but at a distance." Winston himself was an active, affectionate, and mischievous child. "He's not much yet," was an early verdict delivered by Lord Randolph on his son, "but he's a good 'un, a good 'un!" The goodness was less evident to those who had charge of the child, for, by his own later admission, he was a very naughty little boy.

It all ended in 1879, when the Conservatives went out and their successors appointed a new viceroy. Lord Randolph returned to England to enter on his Parliamentary career; and two years later Winston went to his first school, fortified by the possession of three half-crowns, which he nearly lost in the cab. The school was not good and he hated it. The headmaster believed in frequent flogging, and doubtless Winston, aged seven, came in for a full share. After a while he fell seriously ill, and when he recovered, his parents, probably suspecting that a mistake had been made, sent him to an establishment at Brighton, kept by two ladies. Here he stayed, not unhappily, until it was time for him to go to Harrow. He did not learn very much from the ladies, but he edited a paper, acted in a play, and discovered with delight *Treasure Island* and *King Solomon's Mines*.

For the Harrow entrance examination he submitted a Latin paper that contained a blot, several smudges, and a complete absence of written matter; so that he must have been passed by the headmaster's faith rather than by his own good works. Not altogether unexpectedly, he started as two from bottom of the whole school. His later progress was almost equally undistinguished. To his early days at Harrow belongs the often-told tale of his encounter with a future colleague, the Right Hon. L. S. Amery. When Winston had been at school for a month, he visited the swimming bath, where he happened to see a boy, apparently of his own size, standing meditatively on the brink. The temptation was too strong, and Winston pushed him in, a moment later to discover to his horror that his victim was none other than Amery, a pocket Hercules, head of his house and gym champion. Retribution followed, but ended when Winston, apologizing for his error, remarked: "My father, who is a great man, is also small."

Neither then nor subsequently did Winston show any appreciation of the advantages of a classical education. Greek to him was Greek. His Latin was a little better, although the difficulties of syntax were insuperable, and in the end he formed a working alliance with a boy in the sixth form. The partner did the Latin translations, and Winston, who already wrote with ease and fluency, did the English essays. All that Winston extracted from a classical education was a stock of well-worn tags, of doubtful value to his later oratory. Sometimes, when he was a Cabinet minister, he would bring out one of them and observe the pained surprise of his chief, Mr. Asquith, himself a brilliant scholar. English, far more than Latin, was Winston's subject, and while still in the Lower School at Harrow—from which indeed he never emerged—

he surprised everybody by winning a prize for reciting, without a single mistake, twelve hundred lines from Macaulay's *Lays of Ancient Rome.*

But this was a solitary distinction. The truth is that at Harrow he was a dunce. Lord Randolph would have liked to send him to the bar, but reluctantly decided he had not the brains. The army, of course, was intellectually a less exacting vocation—or so men thought in those easier days. Besides, Winston had accumulated an impressive collection of soldiers—fifteen hundred in all—supported by eighteen field guns and transport supplied by Lord Randolph's old colleague in the Fourth Party, Sir Henry Drummond Wolff. One day the commander-in-chief's father appeared to review the troops. Afterward he asked Winston if he would like to go into the army, and the boy, who saw himself in a flash as one of the great captains, at once said that he would. So it was settled for him, and it must be owned that aggressiveness and troublemaking were both qualities which looked like being more useful in the army than elsewhere.

In the back of his mind the boy already had other plans for the future. His father was still a remote Olympian. Later his son was to say that he could recall only three or four intimate conversations with him. Lord Randolph, besides his preoccupation with politics, was a shy, reserved person, always portrayed by the cartoonists as a very little man with a very large moustache. But already he was the young hope of the Tories, the man who did not hesitate to challenge Gladstone and Chamberlain and the paladins of the Liberal Party, and gave as good as he got in the exchanges. He was an annoyance not only to the enemy but to his own leaders, whom he irreverently nicknamed "the Goats." In Winston he had a furious partisan; and the boy had daydreams of the time when he would take his place at his father's side in the forefront of the battle. For Randolph fell into deep trouble. Twice he had threatened resignation and won his point. The third time, when he was chancellor of the exchequer, he was unlucky. He went out and never came back. His son longed to join him in his lonely struggle. So, although the army would be all right for a while, already there were thoughts of politics.

Still, he had to get into Sandhurst, a process of daunting difficulty. Twice he tried and failed, before he was taken from Harrow and sent to a crammer in the Cromwell Road. His career at school had been inglorious and not very happy. Afterward he was to describe his time there as "one of discomfort, restriction and purposeless monotony." He shone neither at work nor at games, his solitary athletic achievement being the winning of the public schools fencing championship. He was not a popular boy, but made a few friends and collected a few experiences, which were to entertain him more afterward than they entertained him at the time. He was surprised and a little touched when on his departure, Welldon, the headmaster and a perspicacious man, predicted that his pupil would make his way in the world all right.

The crammer, who held an impressive record for getting unpromising boys through a not very testing examination, was to succeed where Harrow had failed. He knew all the answers and most of the questions. But before Winston could profit by this more professional treatment, for the first of many times he nearly lost his life. While playing in the country with his brother and a young cousin, he jumped off a bridge on to some fir trees. For three days he was unconscious and for three months he was in bed. The year was 1892, when Lord Randolph had had his breach with the Conservative leader. "I hear that Randolph's son has met with a serious accident," was the quip that went round the Carlton Club. "Playing a game of 'Follow my leader'—well, Randolph isn't likely to come to grief in that way."

During convalescence Winston became absorbed in political events, his interest being quickened by the talk of men like Balfour, Chamberlain, Rosebery, Asquith, and Morley, who were in and out of his father's house. His partisanship was fiercer than ever, the Conservatives, who owed his father so much and had practically driven him from office, being little better in the son's eyes than those old enemies, the Liberals. At about this time he had one of his rare intimate talks with his father. "Do remember," Lord Randolph had said, "things do not always go right with me. My every action is misjudged and every word distorted. . . . So make some allowances." Winston never forgot. In 1892, when the Conservatives went into Opposition again, a new opportunity seemed to open; but mortal illness intervened, and even so blind an admirer as Winston began to notice a failing in the quality of his father's speeches. The knowledge made him all the more anxious to be of an age to stand at his father's side.

But first that dreadful examination had to be passed. Once again the crammer triumphed, and Winston qualified for a cavalry cadetship at Sandhurst. His father, who thought the cavalry needlessly expensive, and had had in mind the 60th Rifles for his son, was displeased, and wrote him a long and severe letter. He had only just scraped into Sandhurst, Lord Randolph complained, and was in danger of becoming a "social wastrel." Winston was pained, but impenitent, and went off to order the costly outfit of a gentleman-cadet.

Before entering Sandhurst he had a holiday in Switzerland with his brother and a tutor. He and the tutor went up the Wetterhorn and Monte Rosa. Winston begged to be allowed to climb the Matterhorn too, but the tutor, a prudent man, was obdurate. Nevertheless, during the Swiss tour Winston contrived to have his second narrow escape, this time from drowning. He was having a swim in the Lake of Geneva and the boat from which he was bathing was nearly carried away by the wind.

Sandhurst proved more congenial than Harrow. Winston did not like the drill and was a familiar figure in the Awkward Squad, but life was freer than it had been at school, games were not compulsory, and military history was a much more exciting study than Latin, French, and mathematics. He liked the practical work, too, thoroughly enjoyed riding school, and when he was at home was treated almost as a grown-up. Yet his queer relations with his father continued, for at the slightest hint of comradeship the older man seemed to take offense, and once, when his son offered to help the private secretary, he "froze me into stone." But Lord Randolph had become a very sick man, and in 1894, after a vain journey round the world in search of his lost health, he came home to die.

Meanwhile, Winston was living the ordinary life of a gentleman-cadet. He rode a great deal and worked reasonably hard, but not so hard as to exclude an occasional escapade, as when, during his last term, he played a leading part in an anti-prudery riot at the old Empire. After a number of canvas screens had been pulled down, he made his first public speech. As a result, he and his companions missed the last train back to Camberley and had some difficulty in getting there in time for early parade the next morning.

So the weeks at Sandhurst slipped by, and in 1894 he passed out very creditably as eighth in a batch of one hundred and fifty. Besides mastering the elements of his future profession, he had learned other lessons of even greater value for his after life. He had learned to ride the hard way, with many tumbles. He had begun to find out how to get the last ounce of experience and enjoyment out of life, which at Harrow had seemed a dull business. He had acquired some discipline, though not, perhaps, very much, and developed a love of adventure which was to stay with him all his days.

While Winston was still a cadet at Sandhurst, the 4th Hussars arrived at Aldershot. Their commanding officer was Colonel Brabazon. An old friend of Lord Randolph, he asked young Churchill to dine with him in mess. Winston's hankering for the cavalry was nourished by this glimpse of the splendors of uniform and plate, by the excellent food and music, and by the welcome he was given; and having conducted himself, as he believed, "with discretion and modesty," the invitation was repeated more than once. Finally, the Colonel intimated a wish that Winston should join the regiment. Lord Randolph demurred. He still thought the 60th Rifles more suitable, and was a little cross with Brabazon, who "had no business to go and turn that boy's head." But Randolph was dying. He did not or could not press his point, and one of his last remarks to his son was "Have you got your horses?"

He died on January 24, 1895, and with him ended Winston's dreams of political comradeship. Henceforward he would fight his own battles, unassisted except by his mother, who at forty was still a very beautiful woman. She was to give him her support without stint, and to be, he would say, more like a sister than a mother to him.

So in March Winston joined his chosen regiment, enduring cheerfully the subaltern's routine of riding school, stables, and the barrack square. Before his training he had thought himself an accomplished horseman; presently, with many misadventures, he discovered his error. His discomfort was much increased when he tore a muscle, and since to cry off even for a day was to offend against an unwritten code, he continued, although in great pain, to appear in riding school. Such mishaps apart, he enjoyed his training, the riding, the comradeship, and the pageantry of the great parades, as when twenty-five thousand men, in the brilliant uniforms of those days, passed before Queen Victoria, sitting in her carriage at the saluting point.

Early in that first year his old nurse, Mrs. Everest, died. As soon as Winston heard she was ill he hurried to London to see her, and sat by her bed while she worried because the rain had soaked his jacket. He went out for a specialist and then returned by the midnight train to Aldershot, so as not to miss the early parade next day. When that was over, he hastened back to London and sat by the old woman's side until she died. She had been a dear and intimate friend, and to such he was then, as he was always to be, the most faithful of friends in return.

Aldershot was all very well for a time, but to be a soldier was to fight, and at the moment Britain was in a lull between those little distant wars which kept her professional army occupied in Victorian days. Winston's restless eye, wandering round the map of the world, presently settled upon Cuba, where the Spaniards were making their last serious effort to quell an insurrection. Here, if no promotion was to be won, at least a young officer could discover what it was like to be under fire. He began to pull the necessary strings. Colonel Brabazon was sympathetic, Sir Henry Drummond Wolff, then Ambassador at Madrid, was helpful, and the required permission having been obtained, in November, 1895, Winston took ship for New York on the first of his adventures overseas.

On arrival in Cuba, he joined a Spanish mobile column operating against rebels in the interior. The operations were indecisive, for the Cubans knew all the tricks of guerrilla warfare. Winston saw some skirmishing and came under fire, before the column marched back to the coast. Then he went home, with three reminders of his first sight of active service. The first was the Spanish Order of Military Merit (First Class). The second was a taste for cigars. The third was the habit of the siesta.

He returned to a London at perhaps the most spectacular moment in its history, on the eve of the Diamond Jubilee. As a young Hussar and the cadet of a famous family, he had his full share of the splendid entertainments of the season of 1896, remembering as perhaps their highest point the Duchess of Devonshire's fancy dress ball. Long after the captains and the kings of the following year had departed and the pomp of yesterday was "one with Nineveh and Tyre," that short Augustan age—its magnificence, its sense of security, and its opulence—loomed large in the background of his life. It was the world as he had first known it, and with all its imperfections he thought it good. He certainly enjoyed it. He was a gay, though not always a very dependable, guest. On one occasion by sheer carelessness he was late for a dinner at which the Prince of Wales was present. Without Winston the company numbered thirteen, and in the circumstances no one would sit down. "Don't they teach you to be punctual in your regiment, Winston?" inquired the prince severely; and Colonel Brabazon, who was one of the company, was noticeably displeased.

But the festive days passed. The 4th Hussars were under orders for India, and in the next trooping season they sailed. Winston celebrated his arrival by an accident that seemed trivial enough at the time but was to have lasting consequences. Getting out of the boat that was taking him ashore at Bombay, he dislocated his shoulder. The injury was to cripple him at polo and to prevent tennis; while, after the accident, whenever he made a special effort, and sometimes when he was making none, he might easily put his shoulder out again.

Life in India enchanted him. Those were the spacious days when a subaltern, with a small supplement to his pay, could fare sumptuously and enjoy all the sport he wanted. Bangalore, whither the 4th Hussars went, was one of the most delectable of stations. Polo, of course, was the ruling passion. The officers of the regiment were secretly determined to win the Inter-Regimental Cup, an ambition they could hardly hope to realize in a hurry. They began well by establishing a record, for they won a first-class tournament within fifty days of landing in India. Winston played with enthusiasm and, despite his uncertain shoulder, with some proficiency.

But polo and parades did not exhaust his energy. He had been reflecting on the obvious gaps in his education. There was so much he did not know and had not read. India, and in particular the Indian hot weather, offered opportunities and he took them. Someone had spoken of ethics: what were they? Someone else had talked of the Socratic method: who was Socrates? One inquiry led to another, and from philosophy he turned to history and economics. Aided by his mother, who sent him parcels of books, he did a course of serious reading. Gibbon's famous work fascinated him, as it had fascinated his father. Macaulay (despite some adverse judgments on the great Duke of Marlborough, which a later Churchill would one day try to correct) became his model in prose. Plato, Schopenhauer, Malthus, Darwin, and Winwood Reade were other authors whom he read with absorbed interest, though not always with entire understanding. In these months of self-imposed education he may have laid the foundations of his own literary style. At any rate, at this time he tried an unpracticed pen on his first literary work. This was *Savrola,* an heroic novel, which subsequently found a publisher.

He was an unusual young officer. A slim, freckled youth, quick to resent a real or fancied slight, and as quick to respond to a friendly overture, pugnacious, generous, argumentative, awkward, irrepressible, and impatient, as yet he scarcely gave promise of what was to come. His brother officers liked him but thought him bumptious and held it their duty to keep him in his place. This was not easy. There is a story of an evening in mess when young Churchill laid down the law on polo until the other subalterns decided they had had enough. They took him and put him struggling under an immense divan. Then they all sat on it; but, as they piled themselves up, a disheveled figure crawled from underneath, remarking: "You can't keep me down like that."

In 1897 he went home on leave. He was at Goodwood when news arrived of trouble on the northwest frontier. The tribesmen of the Swat Valley were up, and a field force of three brigades, under the command of Sir Bindon Blood, was being formed to deal with them. It was a very small war, to be merged presently in a rather less small war, but such as it was, Winston was determined not to miss it. A year earlier at Deepdene, the home of Lord William Beresford, he had met Blood and wheedled out of him a promise that if ever the General commanded another expedition on the frontier, he would take Winston with him. A telegram of reminder was at once sent, and, since time pressed, Winston caught (as usual after nearly missing) the train for Brindisi.

At Bombay he found an encouraging answer waiting. At the moment there were no vacancies, but the young man could come up as a war correspondent. Arrangements were rapidly made, and, confronted with commissions from the *Daily Telegraph* and the *Pioneer,* the commanding officer of the 4th Hussars could not refuse the necessary leave. So Winston hurried north to Nowshera, railhead of the Malakand Field Force, finishing his journey to the front by tonga. Into the details of that little war it is superfluous to enter. The story was to be sufficiently told in *The Malakand Field Force,* Winston's first serious essay in literature. The book had flashes of a style that was forming, of satire, and of a sense of prose. It was a shadow of things to come, and a little more, for when it appeared a kindly reviewer mentioned Napier. "It may be doubted," the author wrote, "whether an historical record gains or loses value when described by an eye-witness." The doubt was to linger over the years.

Actually, the fort at Chitral, which the tribesmen were besieging, had been relieved, and a surprise attack on Malakand camp had been repelled before Winston arrived. But he was consoled by a day of hand-to-hand fighting, for which he was mentioned in dispatches as "having made himself useful at a critical moment." A little later he was posted to the 31st Punjab Infantry, but he continued to act as war correspondent, giving satisfaction to his editors not merely by the vigor and color of his reports but by his ingenuity in getting them back quickly.

Meanwhile, although the Malakand had quieted down, along the frontier the tribes were rising, inflamed by the fighting and by rumors of success, and the government of India determined upon a larger expedition, to be commanded by Sir William Lockhart. Once again Winston began to pull strings, but this time fate was against him. Sir Bindon Blood did his best, but new Punjabi officers were arriving, and at Bangalore a long-suffering colonel had begun to demand the return of his missing subaltern. So Winston went back unwillingly to the south and the old routine of army life. In his leisure moments he finished *Savrola* and wrote *The Malakand Field Force,* but his heart was in the north with that formidable army, which was to march magnificently up to Tirah Maidan and less magnificently to march back again. His chance came at last in March (1898), when he was at Meerut with the regimental polo team. The Hussars lost their match, but Winston got his way. His leave was expiring in three days, but he posted off to Peshawar, where, largely through the good offices of Ian Hamilton, he somehow persuaded Sir William Lockhart to add an extra orderly officer to his staff. If Winston's persuasiveness had failed, he would have broken his leave and been in serious trouble.

Tirah was an unsatisfactory little war—for the Afridis, who saw their fastnesses invaded; for the troops, who suffered heavily on their return journey; for the government of India, which had to foot the bill; and for Winston himself, whose duties as an extra orderly officer did not allow him many of the opportunities he coveted. He got some fun, after his fashion, exchanging shots with enemy snipers and relieving hard-pressed pickets, but soon his restless mind was ranging about seeking for some fresh adventure.

The Sudan, he decided quite rightly, was coming into the news again. Kitchener was preparing an expedition to destroy the Dervish empire and, belatedly, to avenge the death of Gordon. Here was something more like a real war. Once again he set to work. "But now," he was to write later, "I began to encounter resistance of a new and formidable character." His technique had become a little too well known, himself notorious as a pushing young fellow who would worm himself in anywhere. His brother-officers, many of whom had never been under fire, were envious of a comrade who had already seen three campaigns, and not one of them with his regiment. The Orderly Room was inclined to think he ought to be busy learning the elements of his profession, while the higher authorities, tired of being first bypassed and then criticized in books and articles, thought a certain junior subaltern should be taught his place. "Influence" is never popular, even when it cannot be ignored; and Winston had worked his way by mobilizing in his support everyone, beginning with his mother, whose word might weigh with the men who counted. So in this new venture he met rebuff after rebuff. The War Office was not unsympathetic, but Kitchener, the all-important Sirdar, was adamant, perhaps because he disliked soldier-journalists. He was not, he declared, going to have Winston in the Sudan. The irresistible force, it seemed, had met the immovable mass.

Somehow, Winston got leave home, where his faithful ally, Lady Randolph, was busy in his cause with luncheons, dinners, and persuasive letters to the great. All was in vain. Then the interest of the prime minister, Lord Salisbury, was engaged. He had read *The*

Malakand Field Force; he had followed Winston's dispatches in the *Daily Telegraph*; he remembered—not happily, but perhaps a little guiltily—the young man's father. He sent for the son, they had a talk, and presently the desired telegram was on its way to Kitchener. Back came a bleak, forbidding answer. Winston was blocked again.

His next approach was through Sir Evelyn Wood who, as adjutant-general, had some say in appointments to the British contingent. At last fortune smiled. Thanks to the good offices of Lady St. Helier and a certain impatience at the War Office over Kitchener's arbitrary methods, Sir Evelyn was converted; and soon Winston was notified of his attachment as a supernumerary lieutenant of the 21st Lancers. He was to pay his own expenses to Egypt and back and, if killed, was not to be a charge upon public funds. He was to report at once at Cairo. Only pausing to contract with the *Morning Post* for a series of letters from the front, he was off; and from Cairo he hurried by train and steamer to Wady Halfa, where the Anglo-Egyptian army was preparing for its last spring.

Once more he had won, but he was not happy. What would the Sirdar do when he encountered the young man he had vowed he would not have? Probably he would send him back to kick his heels in Cairo. So Winston surmised, but fortunately for him Kitchener had other preoccupations, and when he learned that he had been overruled, merely shrugged his shoulders and thought about something else. Accident or a more local prejudice was probably the explanation when, at the end of Winston's journey, he was put in charge of the lame horses and brought up the rear of a limping procession many miles behind the rest of the regiment.

The sequel is history, told by Winston himself in *The River War*. He had the luck to take part not only in the last of the old battles, in which armies fought in close order and full view of each other, but in a famous cavalry charge, which, too, was the last, or almost the last, of its kind. The Anglo-Egyptian Army, after destroying Mahmoud's force at the junction of the Nile and the Atbara, advanced without opposition to the threshold of the Dervish capital. On September 1 [1898], Winston, whose squadron was part of the advanced screen, had his first sight of the enemy, massed in defense of Omdurman, and was sent to report their presence to Kitchener. All was ready for the battle next day. That evening, wandering by the river, Winston exchanged chaff with the gunboat officers, one of whom good-naturedly tossed him a bottle of champagne. The donor was David Beatty.

In the battle next day 60,000 Dervishes succumbed to the weapons and discipline of Kitchener's force. There were some anxious moments when the desperate attacks nearly reached the advancing columns, but the issue was never in serious doubt. Winston's time came when the 21st Lancers were ordered to charge a line of Dervishes on a flank. The Lancers trotted, wheeled, galloped. They overran the line they had seen and charged into and through a larger body of the enemy they had not seen. On they went, tumbling into a dry watercourse full of Dervishes, who flung themselves on the ground and slashed savagely at the horses with their curved swords. Many fell, but many more, including Winston, clambered out on to the other side. Dervishes were running in all directions and fighting fiercely as they ran. Winston pistoled two of them and pulled up. The charge, a picturesque but futile exploit, was over; the Dervishes were rallying to fall upon the scattered Lancers; and Winston, crouching low in the saddle, galloped out of the melee. He discovered his troop, shot another Dervish, and so finished his part in the Battle of Omdurman.

That afternoon his troop was sent to try to intercept the Khalifa, who was in flight from his capital. It missed its man, but Winston found a baby a few hours old, which he salvaged inexpertly from the battlefield. Going on to the Sirdar's tent, he saw some men knocking the chains off Charles Neufeld, a prisoner of the Dervishes for thirteen years, and heard him say, "I have forgotten how to walk!" Next day he revisited the battlefield with Lord Tullibardine. Wounded men, half dead with thirst, were still crawling about it, and Winston emptied his water bottle. In Omdurman itself the destruction of the Mahdi's tomb and the dismemberment of his corpse stirred him to indignation. Magnanimity toward a defeated foe was an abiding article of his faith.

G. W. STEEVENS

The Youngest Man in Europe: Churchill at Twenty-four

WINSTON SPENCER CHURCHILL is the youngest man in Europe. A gallery of young men's pictures could not possibly be complete without him, for there is no younger.

In years he is a boy; in temperament he is also a boy; but in intention, in deliberate plan, purpose, adaptation of means to ends he is already a man. In any other generation but this he would be a child. Anyone other than he, being a junior subaltern of Hussars, would be a boisterous, simple, full-hearted, empty-headed boy. But Churchill is a man, with ambitions fixed, with the steps toward their attainment clearly defined with a precocious, almost uncanny judgment as to the efficacy of the means to the end.

He is what he is by breeding. He is the eldest son of Lord Randolph Churchill, and his mother is American. Lord Randolph was

---

From *Churchill by His Contemporaries,* edited by Charles Eade. London: Hutchinson Publishing Group Ltd., 1953, pp. 34–38.

not so precocious as he was popularly supposed to be, but they begin early in America. From his father he derives the hereditary aptitude for affairs, the grand style of entering upon them, which are not the less hereditary in British noble families because they skip nine generations out of ten. Winston Spencer Churchill can hardly have seen much of government and Parliament and forensic politics at twenty-four, but he moves in and out among their deviations with the ease, if not with the knowledge, of a veteran statesman. But that inheritance alone would not give him his grip and facility at twenty-four; with us hereditary statesmen and party leaders ripen later. From his American strain he adds to this a keenness, a shrewdness, a half-cynical, personal ambition, a natural aptitude for advertisement, and, happily, a sense of humor.

At the present moment he happens to be a soldier, but that has nothing whatever to do with his interest in the public eye. He may and he may not possess the qualities which make a great general, but the question is of no sort of importance. In any case, they will never be developed, for, if they exist, they are overshadowed by qualities which might make him, almost at will, a great popular leader, a great journalist, or the founder of a great advertising business.

He will shortly leave the army; in the meantime his brief military career is interesting, mainly as an illustration of the versatility, the pushing energy, and—its complement—the precocious worldly wisdom of the man. Educated at Harrow, he passed, like anybody else, into Sandhurst, at eighteen, in 1893, passed out with honors in 1894, joined the 4th Hussars in 1895. From then until now is less than four years; yet in that time he has seen something of three campaigns—not an ungenerous allowance for a field-officer of more service than Winston Spencer Churchill counts years of life. He saw his service, it is true, more in the irresponsible way of war correspondent than of the plodding grind of a subaltern with his regiment; but then that is the only way—bar miracles—in which a man can see three campaigns in four years. Having to give the first years of his manhood to war-making, he characteristically gave them in the way that was likely to prove most fruitful of experience for use afterward.

Before he had been a year in the army he was in Cuba, traveled over much of the island, saw a certain amount of service, got the

Order of Military Merit from Marshal Martinez Campos, and wrote letters to the *Daily Graphic*. In the last frontier war in India he started as the correspondent of the *Daily Telegraph* and *The Pioneer*—to what other subaltern of twenty-two would it have occurred to syndicate himself thus fruitfully?—went on to the 31st Punjab Infantry, was mentioned for "courage and resolution" by Brigadier-General Jeffreys, and wound up as orderly officer to Sir William Lockhart. What other subaltern of twenty-two would have gone through so many phases? To top all he was author of the first book published on the series of campaigns—*The Story of the Malakand Field Force*—and the book was a decided success.

How many men had the combination of merit, energy, and luck to combine the Tirah clasps with Khartoum? Very few, but among the few duly appeared Winston Churchill. He got up just in time to march from Fort Atbara with the 21st Lancers, to which he was attached—missed them, indeed, by a day, but rode out confidently at night, missed the track, lit matches and found it, had to turn miles out of his way for water, overtook the force next day. He finished the march, scouted in the reconnaissances, rode in the charge. Now—you will have guessed—he is writing a book. And yet he found time on his way home to prepare three political speeches.

It was not possible that a man who has done so much so well at twenty-four would be altogether popular. Enemies he has probably none, but precocious success is not the way to win facile friendship—even when joined with modesty—and Winston Churchill is, outwardly, not modest. In the army especially, where the young are expected not to know better than their elders—or, at least, to keep their knowledge to themselves—his assurance has earned him many snubs. One general will delight in his lighthearted omniscience, the next, and the next, and the next will put a subaltern in his place. But Winston Churchill cannot be snubbed. His self-confidence bobs up irresistibly, though seniority and common sense and facts themselves conspire to force it down.

After all, he is hardly to be charged with any but outward immodesty. Chaff him about his self-satisfaction, and he laughs and says, "I'm young." He knows he is not omniscient; but he knows it will pay to pretend to be.

He is ambitious and he is calculating; yet he is not cold—and that saves him. His ambition is sanguine, runs in a torrent, and the calculation is hardly more than the rocks or the stump which the torrent strikes for a second, yet which suffices to direct its course. It is not so much that he calculates how he is to make his career a success—how, frankly, he is to boom—but that he has a queer, shrewd power of introspection, which tells him his gifts and character are such as will make him boom. He has not studied to make himself a demagogue. He was born a demagogue, and he happens to know it.

The master strain in his character is the rhetorician. Platform speeches and leading articles flow from him almost against his will. At dinner he talks and talks, and you can hardly tell when he leaves off quoting his one idol, Macaulay, and begins his other, Winston Churchill. A passionate devotion to the matter in hand, an imperturbable self-confidence, a ready flow of sonorous, half-commonplace, half-lofty English, a fine faculty of striking imagery —we shall hear more about this in the course of ten years. Out of the perfect stump orator's wallet he has taken everything but humor; his humor he is likely to keep for private moments; he is not yet the man who, like Lord Rosebery, will feel he can afford to smile at himself in public.

His face is square and determined rather than delicate; his body fitter for the platform than for the saddle; his color reddish and sanguine. He looks a boy. As yet, naturally, he knows little more than many clever boys, whether of faces or of men. But for all that, he has put himself in the directest way of learning. At present he calls himself a Tory Democrat. Tory—the opinions—might change; democrat—the methods—never. For he has the twentieth century in his marrow.

What he will become, who shall say? At the rate he goes there will hardly be room for him in Parliament at thirty or in England at forty. It is a pace that cannot last, yet already he holds a vast lead of his contemporaries. Meanwhile he is a wonder: a boy with a man's ambitions and—more wonderful yet—a very mature man's self-appreciation—knowledge of his own powers and the extent to which each may be applied to set him forward on his road.

RONALD HYAM

At the Colonial Office, 1905–8

IT HAS GENERALLY BEEN SUPPOSED that the relationship between Elgin and Churchill was a difficult one. Edward Marsh, who had good opportunities for observing things from Churchill's side as his private secretary, described Elgin, none too sympathetically, as "a rugged old thane of antique virtue." Winston regarded him, Marsh thought, with "impatient respect, recognising his four-square stability and his canniness, but desiderating initiative and dash." What Elgin thought of Churchill Marsh was never able to discover, but he conjectured that "their qualified esteem was mutual."

Undoubtedly, Churchill sorely tried Elgin's patience. Like Gulliver, he found "by experience that young men are too opinionative

---

From *Elgin and Churchill at the Colonial Office,* by Ronald Hyam. London and Basingstoke: Macmillan and Company Ltd., 1968, pp. 488–506.

and volatile to be guided by the sober dictates of their seniors." When Elgin accepted Churchill as undersecretary [1905], he knew that he himself had no easy task. He resolved to give Churchill access to all the business, but to keep control—and to curb his temper. When it was all over, he reviewed the relationship as it had worked out:

> I think I may say I succeeded, certainly we have had no quarrel during the two and a half years, on the contrary, he has again and again thanked me for what he has learned and for our pleasant personal relations, and I have taken a keen interest in his ability and in many ways attractive personality. But all the same I know quite well that it has affected my position *outside the Office,* and the strain has often been severe.

Elgin did his best to check Churchill's exuberance—not always with the success which so well-meaning and public-spirited an effort deserved. The real point of difficulty in the relationship was Churchill's ambition. He hoped to become a full Cabinet minister as soon as possible. In his attempt to focus attention upon himself, unwittingly, perhaps, at least in part, he depreciated Elgin. He tended to maintain separate and direct contact with the men in high office. His public reputation grew at Elgin's expense. This difficulty for Elgin certainly did not escape notice at the time. . . . Three weeks before Asquith actually became prime minister, Churchill was laying his plans for obtaining Cabinet rank. In the first instance, he asked unashamedly for the reversion of the colonial office, claiming that, during the past two years, "practically all the constructive action and all the Parliamentary exposition has been mine." The first part of the claim was unjustified. He also claimed, and fairly, to have the advantage of knowing the work thoroughly. In addition, he considered himself to have established excellent personal relations in the right quarters, and to be undertaking work that was "well within the compass of my strength and knowledge." If this is a sample of Churchill's loyalty, no wonder Elgin suffered strain.

Ambition, however unpleasant its methods, was understandable. But there were two things about Churchill that Elgin found bewildering. One was the frankness of his minutes, sometimes involving an apparent indifference to concealing from the office his disagreements with his chief. Such indifference Elgin thought not merely disloyal but unbecoming and destructive of the proper conduct of government affairs. The other characteristic mystifying to Elgin was the streak of levity and irresponsibility in Churchill, which probably resulted from a compulsion always to be doing something. Churchill could concoct a cause without always bothering to distinguish between the important and the unimportant.

The first characteristic has been remarked many times . . . and needs little further elaboration. The disagreements frequently concerned small personal cases about unfortunate individuals, upon which Churchill thought that the officials were taking much too harsh a line. From the very beginning, Elgin asked Churchill to mention such matters to him directly, either verbally, or in a private letter, before minuting on the files officially. More explosive issues also were best minuted upon with great caution. In most minutes, Elgin pointed out, Churchill and he were compelled, as members of the government, to judge issues from a standpoint different from that of the office staff:

> *We* must take political considerations into account. *They* are bound not to do so.
>
> I want to put it to you that where the political element comes in, the less *we* write the better. I hope I may say that we know each other well enough now not to scruple to say what we think if we confer, or to hesitate to compromise if that becomes necessary. But I feel very strongly that nothing of that ought to appear on the Minutes, if it can be avoided.

He urged the need for a pact "only to quarrel out of school."

Churchill's apparent desire to create work was even more tiresome. Sometimes he seemed to write papers simply to amuse himself.

> Winston is a curious impulsive creature [Elgin wrote to his wife]. He came in on Friday when I was looking at a paper on which he had written a homily about the duty of receiving deputations, which anybody would have thought directed to me. I said "You have been rather hard on me here." "On you—Oh no—you always see them and they like to come to you." So he seized the paper and tore it up—"I meant that for what the Department had written."

It was always difficult to know whether or not to take Churchill seriously, but Elgin consistently gave him the benefit of the doubt. Churchill sprang to the defense of a detained African chief, Sekgoma, with one of his most teasing minutes, which seemed determined to make work and to invite trouble.

After a usurpation of twenty years' duration, Sekgoma had been removed from the Batawana chieftainship in Ngamiland, Bechuanaland. His suspension from office was in accordance with the wishes of the great majority of the tribe, among whom he had the reputation of being a bad character, whom they wished to replace by the legitimate chief Mathibi, who was now twenty-four. As Sekgoma was not taking his deprivation quietly, he was put into detention. Selborne thought that he should be deported to avoid a general disturbance. Only Churchill saw fit to question this recommendation fiercely:

> We cannot imprison him or deport him without flat violation of every solid principle of British justice. As at present advised I could not undertake even to attempt a defence of the lawless deportation of an innocent man upon an informal *lettre de cachet*. If we are going to embark on this sort of law-breaking and autocratic action, where are we going to stop? What kind of injustice is there that would not be covered by precedents of this kind? If we are going to take men who have committed no crime, and had no trial, and condemn them to life-long imprisonment and exile in the name of "State policy" why stop there? Why not poison Sekgoma by some painless drug? No argument, that will justify his deportation to the Seychelles, will not also sustain his removal to a more sultry clime. If we are to employ medieval processes, at least let us show medieval courage and thoroughness. Think of the expense that would be saved. A dose of laudanum, costing at the outside five shillings, is all that is required. There would be no cost of maintenance, no charges for transportation, no legal difficulties, no need to apply to the Portuguese, no fear of the habeas corpus. Without the smallest money or expense the peace of the Protectorate would be secured, and a "dangerous character" obnoxious to the Government, removed.
>
> If however, as I apprehend, Secretary of State would be averse to this procedure, the next best thing is to obey the law, and to act with ordinary morality, however inconvenient.

Secretary of State was very cross. He did not think it necessary to carry the argument so far as a five-shilling dose of laudanum—so Elgin's rejoinder begins. He did not mince his words. "This man is a savage—and is said to be contemplating proceedings in defiance of all law to disturb the peace." As he saw it, the measures that had only narrowly averted fighting had resulted inevitably in Sekgoma's detention. Elgin ended on a militant note; he, at any rate, was ready to take his share of the responsibility for the preservation of peace. This responsibility was, of course, to a Liberal, the primary function of African government.

This minute on Sekgoma reflects many of Churchill's characteristics. It is audacious in the extreme. Indeed, it is doubtful whether there could be found anywhere in the history of British government a more audacious minute than this by a mere undersecretary of state. Moreover it reduces the argument to absurdity. On the other hand, it shows an awareness of the necessity of safeguarding the fundamental principles of British life. It is a splendidly written piece of prose. It could scarcely have been more carefully prepared if it had been a draft for a major public speech, as in fact so many of Churchill's minutes were. It has the characteristic and favorite words: "solid," "courage," "sultry." And it has the typical flash of impish humor—hell, the more sultry clime. Yet all this effort and brilliance had gone into an ephemeral issue of no intrinsic importance, at least at that date, concerning an insignificant and unpopular usurping chief; into an issue that was properly decided on the spot. No other minister, let alone an official, would have questioned whether Sekgoma ought even to be in detention, or have seized upon the case in order to squeeze out of it issues of major principle. It is a teasing minute. The humor and the irony call its seriousness into question. It is, in this sense, irresponsible. Nobody ever contrived to get so much fun out of official business as Churchill.

It was decided to detain Sekgoma for such period as would enable the young Mathibi to establish his position completely. Elgin thought that Sekgoma could be more easily managed in a detention compound in the protectorate; setting him free would certainly result in the "calamity of a breach of the peace." He accepted Churchill's representations so far as to tell Selborne that Sekgoma's present detention was an act of state for which no actual legal authority existed, and so a special proclamation was issued, indemnifying the officers who had detained him. Elgin also agreed to veto deportation, as too troublesome, and obectionable in principle. Churchill, finally, succeeded in adding to the dispatch the observations that Sekgoma had not been formally condemned and that his power to disturb the peace might prove transitory.

One of the stories that has found its way into the folklore of political history describes how Churchill wrote a long memorandum for Elgin, ending with the words, "These are my views," and how Elgin calmly minuted upon it, "But not mine." This, and similar stories, is indeed well within the spirit of what happened. Elgin and Churchill had endless disagreements of a trivial sort. Churchill suggested shipping goods to and from East Africa on German instead of British steamship lines, because their freight rates were cheaper: Elgin denounced this as declaring war "against the flag." Elgin's hypersensitive patriotism also surfaced in a clash of opinion after he had made arrangements for 7,000 silver medals to be struck for the troops engaged in operations against the Zulus. Churchill described this as a "silver badge of shame"; Elgin retorted: "Emphatically No. This will be worn by men who did their duty in obedience to orders, and did it well."

A fantastic number of hours was spent in drafting the answers to Parliamentary questions alone. Elgin frequently deleted the more outrageous portions of Churchill's draft answers. . . . When a photograph of Kikuyu being flogged by Grogan was forwarded from Kenya, Churchill recommended publishing the photo: underneath his minute Elgin wrote: "No—I do not care to publish." Shortly after the formation of the new Transvaal government, a question was put down in the House of Commons asking whether or not the Transvaal government would reduce the size of the South African Constabulary in the Transvaal. Churchill proposed to reply that substantial reductions were certainly to be expected; Elgin deleted this, because it unfairly forestalled the opinion the new government might come to: the answer should simply say that no instructions for reduction had yet been given. "I am sorry that I entirely disagree with Mr. Churchill's minute" was a typical opening formula in Elgin's minutes. They disagreed about censuring a dead man: Churchill called for "a severe and measured reprimand" on the late Mr. Crewe Read for flogging Africans in Southern Nigeria; Elgin, however, was horrified at the idea of censuring the dead. Churchill read into an advance notice of a public meeting in Colombo to form a labor union "a serious and reasoned indictment of the Administration of Ceylon"; Elgin read the document carefully, but could not accept it as a reasoned, certainly not as a just indictment: "No action seems necessary. . . ."

Their disagreements, whether on drafting or policy, did not arise from animosity and never grew into a quarrel. To some extent, each of them sometimes liked to argue a course of action simply as a means of being sure that they were arriving at the right answer. Both of them sometimes maintained a point of view without believing in it very deeply, in order to test the strength of the other's case. Elgin never acted without Churchill's concurrence if he could see his way to obtaining it. Above all, he never forgot that Churchill in the House of Commons had "the labouring oar in the defence of our policy." The tact with which Elgin handled Churchill must clearly have been prodigious. That very intelligent man, Haldane, often told Elgin how much he admired his management of the young Churchill.

These two men were much more appreciative of each other than might be supposed. At a moment when there was a chance that Churchill might have been promoted, Elgin wrote:

> I have been dreading every post to find the rumours true and that I was to lose your help. You might think it unkind if I said I "hoped" not to hear—but however it may turn out, I shall always look back on our co-operation during this year of toil and strife with peculiar satisfaction and with real gratitude to you, not only for the courage and ability with which you have fought our case —but for the invariable consideration you have shown for me and my opinions.

The last remark is hardly ironical. Cynics may, however, wonder whether it indicates rather the way in which Elgin wished to be treated than the way in which he had been treated. Churchill was evidently pleased to have such a kind letter. He replied in a generous, if slightly patronizing way, that he had learned from Elgin's instruction and example a very great deal in the conduct of official business, which he might otherwise have remained permanently ignorant of if he had gone elsewhere. He valued highly the words of approval which his indulgent chief had bestowed. Toward the end of their association, Churchill wrote a short letter about a difference of opinion on retrenched official civil servants from the Transvaal, saying simply:

> It would never be possible for me to quarrel with you because your frank and invariable kindness always removes at once from my mind any trace of vexation which may arise from the tiresome course of business.

There is no reason to doubt the sincerity of these letters. They are not just formal exchanges. Sir Almeric Fitzroy, clerk to the privy council, asked Churchill about his relationship with Elgin, as he had commonly heard it said that their differences were acute, and as language not at all respectful to his chief was frequently attributed to Churchill:

> I was therefore agreeably surprised to find him speak of him in terms of the most cordial loyalty and admiration. They did not know each other before they became colleagues, and Winston frankly admitted that Elgin probably had prejudices not altogether in his favour; but nothing he said could exceed the confidence and consideration with which he had been treated.

For his part, Elgin undoubtedy admired Churchill's ability, found him most stimulating at all times, and often even attractive.

Churchill at the Colonial Office presents a curious combination of magisterial statesman and mischievous schoolboy. The Pitt in him jostled with the Puck in him. He was just as capable of producing a rash and unrealistic suggestion as he was of producing a reasonable and statesmanlike one. Could anything be more different than his first memorandum on the Transvaal constitution question, and his minute on the scheme for a Salvation Army settlement in Southern Rhodesia? In the case of Booth's scheme, Churchill's talents were lavished ineffectually upon magnifying out of all proportion the importance of a very vague and eccentric proposal. In the case of the Transvaal constitution, his gifts were exercised on a matter of acknowledged high policy, with considerable effect. And yet he seemed to treat the two issues as equally deserving of attention, at least in the sense of devoting equally brilliant rhetoric to them. His eagerness to support Booth's scheme suggests that he was not always very good about distinguishing between what was practical politics and what was not.

His romantic support of Booth, or of Sekgoma, also suggests that he had not mastered the art of coming to terms with the mundane, repetitive routines of day-to-day human life. He was hardly the man for the humdrum round of ministerial duties. Churchill exaggerated the importance of everything he touched. Every speck on the horizon, he assumed, would turn out to be a Cunarder, not a cockleshell. As a result of historical instincts and histrionic tendencies, he treated too many issues indiscriminately as matters of fundamental concern or historic significance. If important issues did not exist he would invent them. Not even the work of one government department could satisfy his voracious appetite for improvement. He was as fruitful in producing ideas for other departments as he was for the one to which he had been allocated. He was congenitally incapable of relaxing, even on holiday abroad. His power of concentration amounted almost to obsession.

Churchill extracted what entertainment he could from his work. A letter forwarded by the governor of British Guiana from Mr. E. A. Burgess, who offered his views on various matters, was not so readily dismissed by Churchill as by the officials. He quoted Dr. Johnson: "The applause of a simple human being is of great importance," and went on to instruct the office not to be

> too stiff and proud in answering this man's loyal and civil letter. By snubbing a would-be supporter you can nearly always make a bitter enemy. "Earth has no rage like love to hate that's turned/ Nor hell a fury like a Burgess spurned."

In perusing the estimates for the Seychelles, Churchill did not fail to notice that the income from unique postage stamps in the Seychelles was approximately the same as the annual expenditure on education and religion:

> Observe that the caprice of the philatelist yields in a normal year sufficient to defray exactly the annual cost of education and religion: and thus Christianity is sustained by variations in the watermark! Such are the unseen foundations of society.

It seems reasonable to deduce that Churchill felt some frustration in these years 1905 to 1908. He was not head of the department. He was not in the Cabinet. The issues with which he had to deal, once the Transvaal question was out of the way, were insufficiently challenging, insufficiently matters of life and death. Possibly the fact that Churchill wrote less autobiographically about this phase of his life, with the significant exception of the account of his African journey, is symptomatic.

At this time, Churchill was one of the most unpopular politicians in Britain. One of the main reasons for this was his unhappy gift for putting people's backs up by an apparently gratuitous offensiveness of manner. Even before Churchill had taken office his biographer described him as "probably the best-hated man in English politics" after Joe Chamberlain.[1] In office, no single episode did more serious or lasting harm to his reputation than his attack on Lord Milner, the hero of the British Establishment. In April, 1906, Mr. Arnold-Forster moved to reduce Churchill's salary, accusing him of being a young man in a hurry, without the excuse that age gave for haste, short-circuiting the traditional courtesies of politics, and presenting his views in an unpalatable way. He criticized Churchill for using expressions deeply wounding to Natalians, and other loyal South Africans, for "embittered and empoisoned language" on Chinese labor, and above all for insulting Milner, "a man whom so many of us esteem, honour and love."

The other main reason for his unpopularity was his apparent inconsistency, his unpredictable changes of mood and opinion, his lack of stability, both personal and political. Elgin coined the phrase "Churchill's latest *volte face*." His career between 1901 and 1911 was indeed full of contradictions, or shifts of attitude. From enthusiastic war correspondent and prisoner of the Boers to denouncer of the war and sympathizer with the Boers, from protectionist to free trader, from foremost ministerial champion of peace and disarmament to builder of the biggest ships ever built so far—all these changes were accomplished in a little over one decade. And there were a hundred other little shifts of interest and emphasis. Confronted with evidence of this kind, contemporaries said that he seemed not so much concerned with the merits of a quarrel as to be at the thick of the fight.

But the readiness with which he dropped some of his ideas cannot be explained solely by a desire to be at the center of events. Nor can they be ascribed simply to ambition, which, it is supposed, led him to swim with the tide, or, chameleonlike, to change color

1. A. MacCallum Scott, *Winston Spencer Churchill* (London, 1905), p. 241.

with the ground he stood upon, though there is doubtless some truth in each of these explanations. At a deeper level of interpretation, these changes of attitude may be seen as the result of a journalistic impulsiveness, by which he was sometimes attracted suddenly to ideas, not so much on account of their substance, as of their suitability for expression in a striking fashion. He seized on new ideas, wild or sober, without discrimination. His attachment to a particular view might, therefore, be quite superficial. It almost seemed that in these years his chief pleasure in life came from phrase-making.

Contemporaries agreed that his basic weakness was that phrases mastered him, rather than he them. He tended to be carried away by the logic of his own arguments, by the beauty of his own rhetoric. He was indeed endowed with the most rhetorical mind of any British statesman in history. Not even Gladstone thought and lived Rhetoric quite as Churchill did. His behavior was open to the interpretation that his real inclination was to conclude that a thing was right and true if it could be stated in a rhetorically effective manner. His friends agreed in 1908 that his temptation to see first the rhetorical potentialities of any policy was growing, and becoming a real intellectual and moral danger.

At this time his style was much more antithetical, polysyllabic, and prolix than it subsequently became. As a result, it was occasionally quite difficult to understand what he was talking about. In his writing, the obscurity usually resulted from verbal diarrhea, but he could also be extremely cryptic. Once he minuted merely with an exclamation mark. Such constipated restraint was rare, although he was not averse to the occasional single sentence.

Few of his colleagues would have predicted unhesitatingly in 1908 that he was destined to enjoy a glorious future. They felt that there was a big question mark written against his prospects. They were uneasy about his love of the limelight, his insensitivity to the feelings of others, to the atmosphere of occasions. They disapproved of his pugnacity and obstinacy in argument, his emotional response to situations, the element of levity and playfulness, the super-journalism of some of his phrase-making, his fluctuating sense of proportion. They noted the less than scrupulous sense of loyalty in his deference to Elgin, and the distrust he widely inspired. They thought that these tendencies might not be successfully checked, and that if they were not, he would never attain the heights.

Those men with the largest ingredient of skepticism in their forecasts of his future were the civil servants, to whom he was an *enfant terrible*. Sir Francis Hopwood, permanent head of the Colonial Office, was one of those universally admired and respected public servants whose judgment was regarded as unusually sound. His considered judgment on Churchill was as follows:

> He is most tiresome to deal with, and will I fear give trouble—as his Father did—in any position to which he may be called. The restless energy, uncontrollable desire for notoriety, and the lack of moral perception, make him an anxiety indeed!

Hopwood admitted that in all his dealings with Churchill, he fully respected Elgin's authority and judgment, but he could never understand that there was any better way of enforcing an argument than by intrigue and by pugnaciously overstating a case.

Nevertheless, Churchill's work quickly earned him a brilliant reputation. It was soon conceded that he possessed innate political flair. John Morley's assessment was penetrating. Next to Chamberlain, he wrote, Winston was (in forty years) "the most *alive* politician I have ever come across—only he has not got Chamberlain's breadth nor his sincerity of conviction. But for ceaseless energy and concentration of mind within the political and party field, they are a good match. They make other folk seem like mere amateurs, flâneurs, etc." He singled out Churchill as one of the cleverest, most original, and keenly industrious of the Liberal ministers. He diagnosed in him a "curious *flair* for all sorts of political cases as they arise, though even he now and then mistakes a frothy bubble for a great wave."

As undersecretary of state at the Colonial Office he was able to make a definite contribution to the work of the department. Not all his ideas were equally valuable, and his recommendations had always to pass the acid test of Elgin's canny common sense and varied experience. Occasionally he seemed to see the right course of action more quickly and more clearly than others. On the Parliamentary side of his duties, he was extraordinarily good at anticipating and representing the House of Commons view, even if he sometimes cleverly enlisted it upon his own side to fight a private battle. Three aspects of his achievement may be selected as standing out.

First, there is his gift for writing arresting minutes and for expounding government policy effectively in Parliament. His preoccupation with phrase-making left behind it a host of attractive aphorisms enlivening the ponderous archives of government. Some of the most trenchant and forceful writing of his life was done in these early minutes and memoranda. His skill and eloquence in the presentation and defense of ministerial policy in the House of Commons brought his talents in this direction before a much wider audience.

Second, despite his subordinate position, Churchill was able, by the sheer power of his mind and his imagination, and by the force and persistence of his rhetoric, to take a real part in the formulation of policy. He played his part in the Transvaal settlement, the major work of the Liberal government in the Edwardian empire. He provided much of the written analysis and argument upon which the Cabinet decisions were based and justified. He was himself the originator of specific points of policy, such as the establishment of the Land Settlement Board.

Third, he had a generous and sensitive, if highly paternalistic, sympathy for subject peoples, and a determination to see that justice was done to humble individuals throughout the empire. He had this sympathy to a degree that was rather rare among British administrators, and even politicians, at this time. Human juices must be injected into Olympian mandarins. By vigilant reading of routine official files he frequently uncovered what he thought were "flat" or "shocking" violations of the elementary principles of law and justice. He insisted that the principles of justice, and the safeguards of judicial procedure, should be "rigidly, punctiliously and pedantically" followed.

He insisted on questioning the Colonial Office assumption that officials were always in the right when complaints were made against government by Africans or, as was more probable, by Asians. He campaigned for an earnest effort to understand the feelings of subject peoples in being ruled by alien administrators, "to try to measure the weight of the burden they bear." The business of a public officer, he maintained, was to serve the people he ruled. The officer must not forget that he was as much their servant, however imposing his title, as any manufacturer or tradesman was the servant of his customers. It was a salutary but unpopular reminder. Churchill supported Hofmeyer's* suggestion that British civil servants in South Africa should learn Dutch, for if the people

> like to talk to him in Volapuk, he must learn Volapuk. If they have a weakness for Sanskott [*sic*], it must become his study. By humouring them, and understanding them, he will be able very often to make their wishes and their welfare coincide.

At the same time he was also a watchful champion of the interests of the colonial service, more narrowly considered. He defeated the threat to make marriage a disqualification for candidates proposing to enter the civil service in Ceylon.

In a sense, Churchill's interest in the empire was never more than circumstantial and tangential. L. S. Amery once observed that Churchill's patriotism had always been for England, not the empire or commonwealth. England was the starting point, and the ultimate object of policy, enhanced by the prestige and power of an empire of beneficent rule. Commonwealth patriotism never seriously influenced his thinking, his eloquence, or his actions.[2] There is a good deal of truth in Amery's view. It could hardly be claimed that Churchill's Colonial Office days left an indelible mark on all his future political development. His interest in the empire never absorbed him entirely at the Colonial Office, and it may indeed have been very nearly exhausted by it. At any rate, he had already begun to devote much thought to domestic problems. When he reflected upon the "fine homogeneous" majority conferred by the electoral victory, he dwelt chiefly upon its significance for domestic legislation: "I do not suppose we are likely to attain the millennium; but a few Big Acts by way of instalment ought certainly to be put on the Statute Book."

A speech at Glasgow on October 11, 1906 marks his emergence as a social reformer. Starting from the proposition that "the whole tendency of civilisation" was toward the "multiplication of the collective functions of society," he wished to see "the State embark on various novel and adventurous experiments," increasingly assuming the position of "the reserve employer of labour." He much

* The leader of the Afrikaner Bond. [ed.]

2. L. S. Amery, *My Political Life* (London, 1953), Vol. I, p. 196.

regretted that they had not got the railways in state hands. He looked forward to the "universal establishment of minimum standards of life and labour." The state must mitigate the consequences of failure in the struggle for existence and "spread a net over the abyss."

These thoughts were always at the back of his mind while he was at the Colonial Office. He began a careful study of labor problems in January, 1908, and wrote in *The Nation* on March 7 about his ideas of extending government action. Before he left the Colonial Office he had evolved the blueprint of state welfare action, which was to occupy him in practice for the following three years:

> Youth must be educated, disciplined and trained from fourteen to eighteen. The exploitation of boy labour must be absolutely stopped. . . . Labour must be de-casualised by a system of Labour Exchanges. The resultant residuum must be curatively treated as if they were hospital patients. The hours of labour must be regulated in various trades subject to seasonal or cyclical fluctuations. Means must be found by which the State can, within certain limits and for short periods, augment the demand of the ordinary market for unskilled labour so as to counter-balance the oscillations of world trade. Underneath, though not in substitution for, the immense disjointed fabric of social safeguards and insurances which has grown up by itself in England, there must be spread—at a lower level—a sort of Germanised network of state intervention and regulation.

No other Parliamentary undersecretary of state for the colonies has ever managed to evolve so important or comprehensive a program of social reform.[3] In this post, Churchill was much more influenced by the Webbs and Lloyd George, and their schemes for domestic change, than he was by any of the theorists of empire.

3. There was more than a touch of paternalism about Churchill's attitude to the social problems of the time, just as there was in his view of how the "natives" of the empire should be treated. To both problems he brought an attitude typical of the Victorian gospel of "improvement." All his social reform speeches are full of concern about the stability of society and the waste of resources.

PETER WRIGHT

Historian of the Great War

DURING THE TWENTY YEARS of his political career, Mr. Churchill has been a character in our politics so different from any other that his true features have hardly been distinguished. He is, perhaps, even different from anyone who has ever been in them, and, as a member of a class not otherwise found there, he has not been properly identified. But he is a rhetorician, and even a professional rhetorician. He has deliberately cultivated the art of verbal expression to the exclusion of his other faculties, and perhaps to their cost.

Great as the prizes are which oratory can gain in the House of Commons, it has never flourished there. The records of Parliamentary eloquence during the last two centuries are an immeasurable Sahara of dullness, unexplored even by the most curious, with here and there a fresh and wonderful oasis, like the speeches of

---

From *Portraits and Criticisms,* by Peter E. Wright.

Burke, which is certainly not haunted by the ordinary member of Parliament. For public speaking is a form of literary art, and in its combination of reason and passion one of the most difficult; far more difficult, indeed, than poetry, and there are far more good poems extant in the world than there are good speeches. But most ordinary members are not only unpracticed in this or any other art but do not really believe in the need of art at all. If they did, they would never tolerate the hideous and vulgar decorations, the loud and stagy frescoes, the ready-made and shapeless statuary of the building in which they meet.

In this philistine prejudice, however, it must be allowed they are genuinely representative, as they would not be if they insisted on having statuary and structures like those in which the citizens of Venice or Florence used to meet in an ancient and happier time. Most people, therefore, who enter Parliamentary politics are like a man determined to go fox hunting not only without ever having tried to ride a horse but disbelieving in the need of such an animal. Yet anyone mounted, even badly mounted, could lead a field that was on foot, and the first places in the kingdom have been won by very moderate powers of speech. The "bright golden flower" of eloquence is "in this soil unknown, and like esteemed, and the dull swain treads on it daily with his clouted shoon."

But, it should be added, the debates and decisions of our Parliament are none the less wise and sensible on that account. Real performers, who can draw from the lovely instrument of English speech something really worth hearing, have been few and rare. The dramatic contests of oratory supposed to take place at Westminster are the invention of lively journalists catering for a public that always requires life to be rouged, painted, and powdered before it will attend to it at all. There are no more bright colors in most debates than there are in the discussions of a board of directors.

But Mr. Churchill is abnormally æsthetic, little as he seems, with his bull neck and rough energy, to fit the conventional and perfectly false conception of such a being. The aptitude is hereditary, for it crops up everywhere in his family on both sides, and it must be very strong in him, for if he comes across a new medium, like paint, he cannot resist precipitating himself along this new road, although it does not lead to any place he wishes to reach. To this natural aptitude he has applied a tenacious, passionate study, begun early and long continued, so intense and so deliberate that even now, at the age of fifty, the influence of his models is discernible.

He has not the verbal flow and ease of his father, Lord Randolph, who took to a Parliamentary career only because his peevish temper had for a time closed to him the social circles he liked and lived in; whose style grew involuntarily out of an inveterate taste for a few masterpieces like Gibbon and Jorrocks; and who, after his resignation, returned to Newmarket and racing with far more zest than he had ever left them for Westminster and politics. But his son has steadily and patiently forged his style, not for its own sake, but as an instrument of ambition and Parliamentary success. It was consciously made to gain that opportunity for power and action which is his real object in life, unlike his father, who had none, or none so lofty.

Mr. Churchill cannot, as is well known, improvise very easily; telling as his speeches are, they are wrought, rehearsed, and often half read. To produce at all, Mr. Churchill, in his books and in his speeches, heaves like a mountain; but so do many other Parliamentary personages, and with even greater toil, yet nothing more than a literary mouse trots out. But if Mr. Churchill's throes are volcanic, so is the result—a burning flood of lava, often uneven and tumultuous, but sweeping and splendid in its general effect.

At the outbreak of the war he occupied, perhaps, the greatest position in the world. For he was first lord of the Admiralty and head of the British navy.

The chiefs of the German and French armies might well be proud: yet in the history of these armies there had been many vicissitudes, and there were many dark memories, a Jena or a Sedan, and they stood embattled on the brink of a doubtful contest. But our navy had never known defeat or even failure; it was not only unvanquished, but it went into battle with the firm and reasonable assurance that it was invincible, for never had its material strength been so great and rarely had its superiority been so overwhelming.

The first volume of Mr. Churchill's history of the war tells how the navy prepared, and assembled, and went into battle, and it is worthy of the theme. No greater praise could be given to it than this simple compliment. Many leaders of many nations have given us books about the war. But Mr. Churchill's stands first, unapproachably first, and it would be unjust and injurious to it even to compare with it the publications of the Ludendorffs, or the Painlevés, or the Czernins.

It is a vast and sumptuous panorama. Huge as it is, and crowded with figures and incidents, it remains full of life and color in every portion. Technical as many of the discussions are; often told as many passages have already been; uneventful, except for a few flashes, as were the naval operations of 1914; fluent and copious as his book is, the first large volume of which reaches only to December, 1914; yet it never sinks or even flags, so vivid, swift, and various is the large and sweeping brush with which Mr. Churchill paints the picture in.

Some portions of it are memorable. The author says the memory of Admiral Wilson is precious to him: so will the portrait of him remain to all those who have dreamed what an English sailor should be. Many of the seascapes and sea battles had been published before. Whatever their technical merits may be, they are steeped in the keen salt air of sea and battle. The whole atmosphere of high command—the excitement of struggle, the desperate uncertainty, and the sober confidence in the fighting men, the deep darkness always immediately in front, however much it lifts from day to day, as the war races and rushes along its course—these can be felt here as in perhaps no other book, for no one with such a style has ever held such a place.

Some slight reservations might be made. It is to be regretted that Mr. Churchill's models have not been writers of classical simplicity and severity rather than authors like Carlyle, whose example expands and forces Mr. Churchill's natural abundance and exuberance into still more ample and tropical luxuriance. There is perhaps rather too much controversy, and the author should have had sufficient confidence in himself to write for the large and distant public, which will be indifferent to it. The authorities and texts cited might have been conveniently grouped apart rather than in the story itself. But, whatever comments may be made, it remains a superb piece of war history such as no other country has produced.

But in the panorama thus unfolded the author himself appears, and in almost every scene he is one of the leading figures. We have thus the portrait of the artist, by himself, in many positions.

His mind is most curious, and almost abnormal. It is apparently so developed on the artistic side as to suffer almost from atrophy on every other. No criticism is made here, or could be made, of his capacity as first lord. He devoted several years of eager, ardent, absorbed study to his duties, and must have been competent to discharge them. But the world crisis he deals with included other matters than the action of the British navy; and here the contrast between his descriptive powers and his knowledge is very great. For example, a succession of bloodless diplomatic contests formed the prologue to the drama of the war. They supply the author with some splendid scenes, but only scenes. His account of them is not only superficial, based on meager information and untouched by any analysis or profundity of thought, but he is evidently content to remain uninformed and unphilosophical.

Panorama satisfies him. Whenever it is possible to test his knowledge he is not only—if a blunt and discourteous word may be used —ignorant but strangely unaware of his own blindness, and indifferent to it.

The field of knowledge is so vast that no person can possess more than a grain of it; but that possession, if full and firm, is a measure that warns him how much or how little he knows of any matter on which he must think or act. But Mr. Churchill seems devoid of this trained instinct, which very many mediocre men enjoy. He is armed only with a magnificent literary instrument and at times seems satisfied with any random set of facts and ideas out of which he can raise his lofty structure of words.

At no moment has it crossed his mind that further evidence is procurable and further analysis required. The defect is purely intellectual, of course; he is the very reverse of untruthful, and carries candor to the point of imprudence. This fault is, like his corresponding artistic power, both natural and developed. The most eminent of living Harrovians, he showed little promise at Harrow, and was quite baffled by the small sum of miscellaneous information that constitutes a school education. His early entry into public life, apparently so lucky, was really unfortunate, because he never subjugated himself to the discipline of close and exact thinking to which all his competitors have submitted themselves either in a university or a profession or a business, and which would have corrected his natural bent.

To this weakness is due his appearance of reckless presumption, a general, reiterated charge brought against him, and which appears to be corroborated by many incidents related in this book—such as his offer, in October, 1914, to take charge of the combined naval and military forces at Antwerp. But he is not really afflicted with the vanity from which real presumption springs. However truculent his manner, there is a good deal of humility of mind in him. Only difficulties do not exist for him, and everything seems easy, however technical, even the command of combined naval and military forces, because there is nothing, except words, in which he has ever acquired technical accomplishment—certainly not in practical affairs, and not even in a subject so little exacting as history. He is a professional rhetorician, by birth and by career, and his very triumphs in this field account for his failures in others.

The second volume of Mr. Churchill's book on the war is an *apologia*. He undertook, as first lord, to force the Straits. If he had succeeded at Gallipoli, he would have captured Constantinople, which has never been taken but once in its long history; destroyed Germany's oriental Ally and brought the whole hesitating East to our side; reached weapons to the unarmed, isolated, and inaccessible Russian giant, which was to perish for want of them; and thus, in the first year of the war, by a single and decisive stroke, made our ultimate victory, which was so long delayed and so long doubtful, certain and perhaps immediate. In this enterprise he failed. The whole purpose of his war book is to justify himself and to show how he was baffled by chance and fate. But, like all apologists, he has the advantage of framing himself the charge he is to meet. With this advantage it is easy for a practiced controversialist as he is to clear himself from blame. But the Gallipoli campaign was to be discussed by high military authorities before the end of the war, and as the writer had the advantage of hearing them, he will repeat their criticism.

Operations on the Gallipoli peninsula had long ago been studied by our General Staff, and all the plans existed at the War Office: it had been a subject of still closer study by the Greek military authorities. For there they could strike at the heart of their hereditary enemy. The conclusions of both staffs were the same; an operation if conducted by naval and military forces, acting by surprise, was easy and could hardly fail; under any other conditions it was hardly feasible. Our navy was in command of the sea; the Greeks were eager to join us and attack in the peninsula with their whole army. The Gallipoli campaign should have succeeded without the loss of a single English soldier.

Mr. Churchill, with his usual candor, tells us the Greeks in the early spring of 1915 were anxious to come in on our side, but that the tsar objected. It was very natural for the Greeks to have this wish, for everyone must want to undertake a war with a prospect of assured success. It was also natural for the Russians to object: they could not like to see the Greeks in Constantinople before themselves. But the tsar's objections cannot have been insuperable, or even great, for later in the autumn, when Bulgaria joined the enemy, the Allies begged the Greeks to come in, and even offered them Cyprus if they would do so. Political action should therefore have preceded and prepared the campaign, which should have been amphibious. Mr. Churchill, however, began it as an English naval attack, continued it as an enterprise mainly naval and partly military, and finished it as a combined English naval and military campaign.

Mr. Churchill's account of the early conduct of the war is thus candid enough to show us the whole system. This system had one general fault, for which perhaps no individual leader, civil, military, or naval, could be blamed, and that fault, as long as it existed, must have been what prevented the Allies winning the war. For as long as it lasted, victory seemed inaccessible, though the odds were heavily in their favor, and, as soon as it disappeared, victory was swift and easy, though the numerical odds were then heavily against them. The error, like all errors, was a mistake of emphasis. The value of the general plan was underrated, and this fault continued to haunt and thwart the Allies throughout the war, just as it did the Germans. The actual operations in the peninsula described by Mr. Churchill were based not on one but on a succession of plans. But the same criticism applicable to our enterprise in Gallipoli, as related by Mr. Churchill, can, almost without a change of a word, be leveled at Ludendorff's campaign of 1918, as related by himself.

He had a choice of plans, chose one to which there were great objections, altered it in the course of execution, and then acted without any clear design at all, but picked up, as they presented themselves to him, one expedient after another in the hope that somehow he might win through.

The victory of the Allies is commonly attributed to unity of command, and this phrase is repeated because it is to the interests of a good many people that it should be accepted as true. But such a thing never existed, as General Bliss, the American chief of staff, has pointed out in writing. Foch never had the right to command at all, but only to advise, and by 1918 things had come to such a pass that both Haig and Pétain submitted to the guidance of one mind, which they had never consented to do before they were in such an extremity of peril. Foch not only had a single conception but a conception of genius, and one so simple that when it is unfolded everyone may wonder how it was never thought of before. Having been a professor, he likes explaining and he has explained it, and called it the doctrine of a rolling ball. A battle is comparable to a ball rolling down a smooth slope; if it is never stopped, it constantly accelerates its speed as it goes, but, if it is stopped at any particular point, it at once loses the rate of speed it has already acquired, and so may never reach the bottom.

To the dismay both of English and French commanders, Foch, in his victorious attack, never bothered at all about any possible German counterattack, and secured every advance he had made by at once attacking elsewhere without any pause. If Ludendorff had thought of this, he might have won in 1918, and in May and June Foch used to stamp up and down his room, anxiously tugging his moustache and wondering whether Ludendorff "knew his business."

But it is probable that no such discovery of genius was necessary to break down the German resistance in France. If only the various commanders had looked outside their own front, or even their own arm, the outnumbered Germans could never have stood out so long. Only once before 1918 had the Allies fought according to a single idea, that of Nivelle; ill-conceived and unlucky as his plan was, it very nearly defeated the Germans. Some very considerable authorities like General Mangin have maintained that their military situation was worse in May, 1917, than at the Armistice.

Mr. Churchill's book reveals the evil of haphazard and piecemeal designs. But others, including the Germans, suffered in this way just as much as we did, and ultimate success lay with the Allies because they were the first to correct this error.

So far from being a shortcoming peculiar to ourselves, it was, on the contrary, in London, and by our leaders, civil and military, that the true road was first perceived and strenuously followed during the last period of the war. Not only did they strive for what is called "unity of command," but what might more accurately be described as fighting the Germans together in France, instead of separately, as we had so obligingly done for three years, but they were also determined to make politics and war cooperate and not conflict.

In 1915, as Mr. Churchill tells us, the tsar objected to the Greek army's participation in the Gallipoli military attack; this aid would have made it succeed without the loss perhaps of a single English life, and our statesmen had not the skill and courage to overcome the tsar's objection. But in 1918, by a single, small move, the expedition to Archangel, they stopped the flow of German troops from Russia, which in the critical days of the summer might have turned the scale against us in France. This clear and constant view of the whole, which prevailed in London from 1917 onward, as it did nowhere else, is our greatest contribution to the Allied victory.

It has been said that the war was won by "the soldiers and sailors" and not "by the politicians"; this view has gained much currency from being constantly repeated by retired colonels who, having got too old to play games of ball, spend their time denouncing politics and trying to get into them. It is an old illusion, and even our poet knew of it: he also knew men who

> Esteem no act
> But that of hand; the still and mental parts
> That do contrive how many hands shall strike,
> When fitness calls them on, and know by measure
> Of their observant toil the enemy's weight,—
> Why this has not a finger's dignity.

The War Cabinet was created by Mr. Lloyd George to direct all our various efforts according to matured and connected plans, and, mistaken as its decisions may often have been, it is to this system that we owe the glorious victories of 1918.

Foch and his school of French commanders held this truth no less clearly in the region of military operations. They were all pupils of General Bonnal, who brought Foch to the French Staff College twenty-five years ago, and whose teaching was summarized in the doctrine that strategy is conception. But, like all truths, this is almost self-evident, for in any human affair it is the policy and method of the managers that count, far more than the energy and devotion of the subordinates.

It is perhaps because our statesmen are far more men of business than those of the Continent that they found out where the direction of the war was at fault on the side of the Allies, as it evidently was, for we could not win in spite of far superior numbers. So also it was these doctrines of command that kept the mind of Foch obstinately revolving how trench warfare could be ended and the defensive deprived of the advantage it seemed to possess over the attack. He was always convinced that a method existed, and could be found, and his discovery was not fortuitous. His conviction proceeded from what he had learned and always taught, that to win the battle all that is wanted was the right idea; nothing more, but nothing less. Once found, it was so simple that Foch could direct the Allied armies from the North Sea to the Adriatic, close on 250 divisions, in one small room with the staff of a Brigadier.

If it is a truism, it is far from being obvious to everybody, as Mr. Churchill's book itself shows. Ardent as is Mr. Churchill's absorption in all warlike matters, he himself writes as if he were unaware of it. The Gallipoli operations were only a small theater of the many where the war was being played out. The wisdom of this particular enterprise can be with justice estimated only when the total forces on all these theaters, and their disposition at the time, are also considered. But these facts and figures Mr. Churchill does not tell us, nor apparently has he taken the trouble to find them out. In fact, he looks at his own enterprise just as every military and naval commander on both sides always has, either during the war or in any subsequent justification of their actions. He treats his small section of the front as the only front.

Therefore this truism, like many others, is worth repeating, and especially here. For just as military and naval men on the Continent err in one direction, and are rather bookish, so we err in the other direction, and are inclined to treat war as a matter of physical and moral qualities—in fact, as a form of sport, where intellect can be left out of account. When the Expeditionary Force landed at Rouen in August, 1914, the French crowd on the quays was astounded to see one regiment land with a pack of hounds. However little inconvenient this prejudice may be in our colonial wars, where not more than a brigade or two is engaged, it is almost disabling when sixty divisions have to be handled, as in 1917.

At least the war taught this truth to our military arm. But perhaps it has not done so to the senior service, which still looks upon its staff, a new creation, with almost unconcealed contempt. As Mr. Churchill's book shows, there was in London no staff—that is to say, mind—either for the army or the navy at the beginning of 1915. The navy did not get one until the third year of the war, and still has no staff college. Even in the fourth year of the war, when the Supreme Council of the Allies used to ask the Admiralty of the greatest navy in the world for advice, it used to receive memoranda drawn up by a paymaster that were on the level of a schoolboy's essay.

At Gallipoli the obstinate heroism of our men brought us time after time to within an inch of victory; and Mr. Churchill, with commanding eloquence, tells us how luck deprived him and them of success. But if they had got through, it would have been due to luck just as much. The expedition was badly planned, and had no right to succeed. It was, as Mr. Churchill himself called it, a gamble.

Nevertheless, Mr. Churchill can hardly be blamed. The Allied system of war was to have no system at all, and he did what everyone else did; if he was not better, he certainly was not worse. But the prize was so great, our efforts were so superhuman, the consequences so disastrous, that Mr. Churchill, great as his talents are, may never efface from himself the stigma of this failure.

Mr. Churchill's war book records a life's disappointment. For Mr. Churchill does not want to be a man of words and a rhetorician, but a man of acts and a ruler. Yet the Great War, which might have made him, as first lord, the foremost man in the world, plunged him into insignificance and, though he has recovered, no place exists exalted enough to compensate him for what he might have been. But he must console himself and reflect that hardly anyone has ever done great things and written fine books. In life a choice must be made. If he did not vindicate the superiority of English fleets to the rest of the world, he has asserted the superiority of English letters, and that may give him a higher and more enduring fame.

A. G. GARDINER

Genius Without Judgment: Churchill at Fifty

IT IS NOT TRUE that a rolling stone gathers no moss. Mr. Churchill has gathered a great deal of moss. Not that a stone, whether stationary or rolling, is a suitable symbol for this extraordinary man. He is like a rocket that intermittently dazzles the night sky, disappears, and dazzles it again; flashes now from this quarter, now from that; is always meteoric but never extinguished. The principal difference between Mr. Churchill and a cat, as Mark Twain might say, is that a cat has only nine lives. By all the laws of mortality, Mr. Churchill should have perished a score of times, sometimes in laughter, sometimes in anger, sometimes in contempt; but the funeral has always been premature, the grave

From *Portraits and Portents,* by A. G. Gardiner. New York: Harper & Row, Publishers, Inc., 1926, pp. 58–64.

always empty. You may scotch him for a moment, but you cannot kill him, and we grow weary of pronouncing his obsequies.

What is the use of insisting that he is dead when you know that tomorrow he will be so flagrantly, so impudently alive? "In war you can be killed but once," he has said, "but in politics many times." It is not always so. His father was killed by one self-inflicted wound. He died almost from the prick of a pin, but the tough fiber of the son, due to his American mother, survives as many arrows as legend plants in the body of Saint Sebastian. Like the camomile, the more he is trodden on, the more he flourishes. His failures are monumental, but the energy of his mind and the sheer impetus of his personality make his failures more brilliant than other men's successes.

At fifty, at an age when most public men are only beginning to catch the limelight, when Mr. Baldwin was unknown and Mr. Bonar Law had not held office, he looks back on thirty years of romantic adventure that would provide material for a dozen normal lives which would find a place in the *Dictionary of National Biography*; on experiences of war in more continents than Napoleon fought in; on a library of books that would not do injustice to a life spent in literature; on journalism, lecturing, painting; on a political career more full of vicissitudes than any since that of Bolingbroke; and on the tenure of more great offices in the state, not merely than any contemporary statesman, but, I believe, than any man in our political history. In spite of his ups and downs, I doubt whether anyone since Pitt has spent so large a proportion of his Parliamentary life in office. It is twenty-five years since, hot from his escape from the Boers as a prisoner of war, he entered Parliament on the "Khaki" tide, and seventeen of those years have been passed on the Treasury Bench.

He comes into the world booted and spurred to ride, and he rides at the gallop all the time. Do the citizens of Dundee cast him out of Parliament, and leave him apparently and, this time, finally dead under the load of his transgressions? He sits down, like a Caesar, to write a history of the war, as brilliant as it is brazen, and leaves soldiers and statesmen gasping at his boundless effrontery, at a nerve, a cheek, an audacity that reduces them to amazed helplessness. "I will not go back to the Admiralty," said Lord Fisher to me in the midst of the ministerial crisis of 1915. "I will not go back to the Admiralty if Churchill reappears in the Cabinet. How can I fight Tirpitz if every moment has to be spent in watching Churchill?" He is like an embodied fury in a Rugby pack. He twists and turns and wriggles and lunges, but he always emerges from the scrum with the ball racing for the goal. He obeys no one, fears no one, reveres no one. He is his own superman and is so absorbed in himself and in his own fiery purposes that he does not pay others the compliment even of being aware of them.

His isolation is unprecedented. He has personal friends—the chief being that other kindred spirit, Lord Birkenhead—and his loyalty to them is notorious; but he is an Ishmael in public life, loathed by the Tories, whom he left and has now returned to; distrusted by the Liberals, on whose backs he first mounted to power; hated by Labour, whom he scorns and insults, and who see in him the potential Mussolini of a wave of reaction. His genius is the genius of action, and he loathes "the canker of a long peace and a calm world." He sees life in terms of war, and his high and turbulent spirit is entirely happy only when politics and war are merged in one theme. The grotesque incident of the Sidney Street bombardment revealed the whole temper of a mind that has never outgrown the boyish love of soldiers; and when, as home secretary, he was confronted with a national strike, John Burns entered his room one day and found him poring over a large-scale map of the country on which he was marking the disposition of troops at strategic points. "What do you think of my military arrangements, John?" asked the young Napoleon. "I think you are mistaking a coffee-stall row for the social revolution," said Burns, leaving the room with a resounding bang of the door. There is a passage in Mrs. Asquith's (Lady Oxford's) *Autobiography* that sticks in the mind as illuminating the Churchill landscape. It is the night of the fatal fourth of August, 1914. In a room at Downing Street Mr. Asquith and three of his colleagues are awaiting the German reply to the British ultimatum on Belgium. If there is no satisfactory answer by midnight, war, with all its incalculable consequences, engulfs the land. The minutes pass in tense silence, and at last the clock strikes. "As I was passing at the foot of the staircase," writes Mrs. Asquith, "I saw Winston Churchill with a happy face striding towards the double doors of the Cabinet Room."

When someone told Harcourt that Randolph Churchill was practically an "uneducated man," Harcourt replied: "If he was educated he would be spoiled." In the academic sense, Mr. Churchill is as uneducated as his father. He was an indifferent scholar at school, and of formal learning he would still be outclassed by Macaulay's fabulous schoolboy. It is said that Randolph Churchill, on his mournful visit to South Africa after his sun had set, sought to find a career there for a lad who had to earn his living and gave no promise of a career at home. Perhaps if Winston had been educated, he, too, would have been "spoiled" in the sense Harcourt meant. He would not have been the Churchill we know, the Churchill who flings himself into life with the uncalculating vehemence and passion of the boy in the school playground. "There are times," says Mr. Wells in speaking of him, "when the evil spirit comes upon him, and then I can think of him only as an intractable little boy, a mischievous, dangerous little boy, a knee-worthy little boy. Only by thinking of him in that way can I go on liking him."

His appearance supports the impression. In spite of the bowed shoulders, the thinning hair, and the portentous gravity of bearing, there is still the sense of the intractable, unschooled boy, the terror of the playground, the despair of the master. The pouting, petulant lips give a note of childish willfulness to the face, and the smile, which borders on a grin, has a hint of boyish mischief that has not been discovered. But if he is uneducated in the school sense, and if he is rudimentary in the moral sense, his intelligence is extraordinary, his understanding powerful, his intellectual activity unrivaled, his will despotic. He has little contact with ideas or ideals, but he sees the play of life and the clash of material forces vividly and imaginatively, and leaps at his conclusions and convictions with an assurance and imperiousness that impose them on those who doubt and hesitate. One man with a conviction will overwhelm a hundred who have only opinions, and Mr. Churchill always bursts into the fray with a conviction so clear, so decisive, so burning, that opposition is stampeded.

That is the explanation of the astonishing part he was allowed to play in the war, from the Antwerp fiasco to the Russian fiasco. He triumphed by the sheer energy of his mind. He swept his colleagues by the fervor and passion of his vision. He could not be repressed; he could not be denied. If his wisdom had been equal to his force, he would have been the towering figure of the war. But, as I think

Lord Oxford once said of him, "He has genius without judgment." He sees only one aspect of a situation at a time, and the ardor of his vision exercises a maniacal and perilous spell. His inspirations, which sometimes have a touch of genius, should have been listened to, and then he should have been stood in a corner and forbidden to speak while wiser men examined them and decided. For unless Mr. Churchill is silenced, he will win in a dialectical "war of attrition." He will fight his foes to a standstill. He will wear them down by his tireless attack, by the intensity of his feeling, the versatility of his proof. For he knows his case as he knows his speeches —word and letter perfect. He leaves nothing to chance. He works at the documents like a navvy; he recites his arguments with ceaseless industry. He practices on everybody.

His life is one long speech. He does not talk: he orates. He will address you at breakfast as though you were an audience at the Free Trade Hall, and at dinner you find the performance still running. If you meet him in the intervals, he will give you more fragments of the discourse, walking up and down the room with the absorbed, self-engaged, Napoleonic portentousness that makes his high seriousness tremble on the verge of the comic. He does not want to hear your views. He does not want to disturb the beautiful clarity of his thought by tiresome reminders of the other side. What has he to do with the other side when his side is the right side? He is not arguing with you: he is telling you.

This method of self-saturation with his theme gives him an enormous power in council and on the platform. His arguments are always ready; his periods always perfectly rounded; his rhetoric has passed the test of innumerable listeners. And it is good rhetoric, occasionally, it is true, bordering on the "penny plain, twopence coloured," as in such sentences as these from his book on the war:

> Son of the Stone Age, vanquisher of nature with all her trials and monsters, he met the awful and self-inflicted agony with new reserves of fortitude.

> A world of monstrous shadows, moving in convulsive combinations, through vistas of fathomless catastrophe.

But generally his sense of language is sound and masculine, and his feeling for form hardly rivaled among contemporary speakers. And it is bare justice to him to say that, though he has few principles and few scruples, he has the courage always to be himself and to carry his political life in his hand. He possesses that honesty of speech which enabled him to say during his first candidature in the midst of the "Khaki" election: "If I were a Boer I should be fighting with them in the field." He is neither a demagogue nor a sycophant, and if he changes his party with the facility of partners at a dance, he has always been true to the only party he really believes in—that which is assembled under the hat of Mr. Winston Churchill.

Today, in the prime of life, with the dangerous "forties" navigated, with the most plentiful crop of political wild oats ever sown or ever survived, reunited to his traditional party, miraculously translated to the office from which his father fell never to rise again, he is easily the foremost figure in Parliament, with a past that would have extinguished anyone ordinarily destructible, and nevertheless with a future that is the most interesting subject of speculation in politics. He emerges today from No. 11 Downing Street, and such is his buoyancy and tenacity of grip upon the lifeboat of office that I see no reason why he should not one day emerge from No. 10. But before that happens I hope he will have given evidence that he has judgment as well as genius and that he has ceased to be "an intractable little boy, a mischievous and dangerous little boy, a knee-worthy little boy."

ROBERT RHODES JAMES

The Family Man and Writer in the 1930s

DURING THESE YEARS Churchill spent as much time as possible at Chartwell, which he had bought in 1922 when it had been long uninhabited and was, as one of his daughters has written, "wildly overgrown and untidy, and contained all the mystery of houses that had not been lived in for many years." Although Mrs. Churchill was responsible for most of the alterations and the running of the house, its personality was very much that of Churchill, and it was, as one who knew it well has remarked, "an astonishing combination of private home, Grand Hotel, and a Government Department." He kept a *pied-à-terre* in London at Morpeth Mansions, close to Westminster, but used it only occasion-

---

From *Churchill: A Study in Failure, 1900–1939,* by Robert Rhodes James. London: George Weidenfeld & Nicolson Ltd., 1970, pp. 306–16.

ally. It was at Chartwell that his real life was spent. Here, in this surprisingly peaceful part of Kent, he built walls, created lakes, roofed cottages, painted, and wrote. He devoted intense thought and applied much energy on laying out the Chartwell grounds. Every visitor—however distinguished or sedentary—was liable to summary conscription for these enterprises, which were administered with dash and spirit. His ponds were inhabited by fat and complacent goldfish, who occupied a particularly warm place in Churchill's affections. The Chartwell swans were almost equally favored. The swimming pool heated by two immense boilers with gargantuan appetites was another feature on which much care and attention, and no small expense, had been lavished. A friend has a vivid recollection of one Christmas Day, when the air was crisp and cold, and the frost lay on the ground. Chartwell was enveloped in a deep and mysterious fog. On arriving at the house, after groping his way up the drive, the guest discovered the entire Churchill family in bathing suits in the drawing room. The cause of the fog was now apparent. The bathers skipped across the frosty grass to the simmering, shrouded pool, "now bubbling like a New Zealand hot spring." Churchill entered first, and emerged gasping at the heat. The rest of the party entered the water shivering, and emerged very pink, very hurriedly. There was then a frenzied scamper back to the house.

Churchill, at home as elsewhere, imbued everything with a gusto and a freshness that was endearing and exhilarating. As Lady Asquith has written, "every ploy became 'a matter of pith and moment.'" He still retained the ardor, gaiety, and excitement of youth, and only those who knew him best also knew of the periods of deep depression, the unwelcome visitations of "The Black Dog." But Beaverbrook has not been alone in his preference for "Churchill Down" to "Churchill Up," and the emergence of the quality that Birkenhead once described as "almost feminine in its caressing charm." Light always kept breaking in. His happy family, his enthusiasms and activity, saved him from the full effects of the Churchill melancholia. He was a devoted and indulgent father. Unlike Lord Randolph, he had consolations and activities that recharged his emotional batteries, fortified him against misfortune, and gave him revivals of hope for the future.

An account by Lady Diana Cooper of a visit to Chartwell in

September, 1934, deserves to be quoted as an excellent portrait of the family at this time:

> Forty winks in the afternoon and then (unexpectedly) bathing at 7 in pouring rain, intensely cold with a grey half-light of approaching night, yet curiously enough very enjoyable in its oddness. Freda Ward, Winston, Duff, Clemmie, Randolph and a child, in fact the whole party, were splashing about with gleeful screams in this sad crepuscle. The secret is that the bath is heated, and it is Winston's delightful toy. Just now, again, twenty-four hours later, he called for Inches, the butler, and said: "Tell Allen to heave a lot more coal on. I want the thing full blast." Inches returned to say that Allen was out for the day. "Then tell Arthur I want it full blast," but it was Arthur's day out as well, so the darling old schoolboy went surreptitiously and stoked it himself for half an hour, coming in on the verge of apoplexy. Again all had to bathe in the afternoon.
>
> Then "feeding the poor little birds" is a huge joy to him. They consist of five foolish geese, five furious black swans, two ruddy sheldrakes, two white swans—Mr. Juno and Mrs. Jupiter, so called because they got the sexes wrong to begin with, two Canadian geese ("Lord and Lady Beaverbrook") and some miscellaneous ducks. The basket of bread on Winston's arm is used first to lure and coax and then as ammunition.[1]

Thus, in spite of political misfortune, and although it would be wrong to deny the existence of strains and tensions within the family circle, life at Chartwell was suffused with gaiety and happiness. As Churchill has written of this period, "I never had a dull or idle moment from morning till midnight, and with my happy family around me dwelt at peace within my habitation." [2]

During these years Churchill lived by his pen, or, as he has put it, "I lived in fact from mouth to hand." He demanded a very high standard of living, and he worked for it. With the exception of his Parliamentary salary and an unexpected family inheritance in the early 1920s, he was dependent upon writing for his income. The 1930s was in quantity if not in quality his most productive period, when he published *My Early Life, The Eastern Front, The Life*

1. Lady Diana Cooper, *The Light of Common Day,* pp. 155–56.
2. Winston Churchill, *The Gathering Storm* (Cassell, 1948), p. 62.

of Marlborough, in four volumes, and wrote most of *The History of the English-speaking Peoples.* He also wrote well over two hundred newspaper and magazine articles, and selections from these were published in *Thoughts and Adventures* (1932), *Great Contemporaries* (1937), and *Step by Step* (1939). Selections from his India speeches and those on defense and foreign affairs in the House of Commons, edited by his son and published under the title of *Arms and the Covenant* in 1938, emphasized the extent of Churchill's activity in these years. This is, by any standard, a very substantial record of work. "Writing a long and substantial book," he once remarked, "is like having a friend and companion at your side, to whom you can always turn for comfort and amusement, and whose society becomes more attractive as a new and widening field of interest is lighted in the mind."

Churchill's technique did not change very much during his life, although it became more sophisticated and professional. By this time he was able to execute his major works with some lavishness. He assembled his assistants with care, and entrusted them with particular aspects of the project in hand.[3] With the material assembled, he would dictate the narrative, frequently at inconvenient moments for his secretaries. He rewrote copiously and extensively. The work marched on from draft to draft, until the proofs, which he regarded in much the same light as most authors have to regard the penultimate typed version; he himself has testified to his pleasure in "playing with the proofs," which is an expensive form of literary satisfaction. Eddie Marsh was entrusted with the grammatical details.

In essentials, this had been the technique used in his biography of his father. In that case, Churchill had had his father's papers printed and numbered. When he wanted a document inserted he would give its number to the secretary, who would cut it out and paste it in the appropriate place. The long process of amendment and improvement would follow—and this process frequently involved the changing of the original documents to fit more neatly into the narrative, to the point where it was sometimes difficult for

3. Among the assistants during this period were Mr. John Wheldon, Mr. Maurice Ashley, and Mr. F. W. Deakin. I am most grateful to the last for advice in this section of this study.

the subsequent biographer of Lord Randolph to recognize the original.[4]

There are several aspects of Churchill's technique that require emphasis. In the first place, although he did receive assistance in his major works, he was always careful to keep the real control in his own hands. His memory was, as one assistant has recorded, "Napoleonic." Although he was always willing to receive advice and incorporate it, he could be obstinate on some points.[5] Then, he himself read very extensively on the subject, and every discussion with his assistants was a fully informed one. He did not claim that his knowledge and reading were comprehensive, but he endeavored to cover the field with great thoroughness.

It is always of interest to trace some of Churchill's most striking passages from their often crude beginnings to the final version. *Lord Randolph Churchill* opens with a magnificent description of Blenheim, which was the final version of a very long and excessively grandiose and cumbersome earlier version that is too long for quotation here. Another example may be given to demonstrate the point. He wrote to his mother on May 22, 1898: "It is the fault of all booms of sentiment that they carry men too far and lead to reactions. Militarism degenerates [in] to brutality. Loyalty promotes tyranny and sycophancy. Humanitarianism becomes maudlin and ridiculous. Patriotism shades into cant. Imperialism sinks to Jingoism. . . ."[6]

In *The River War* this theme is developed:

> All great movements, every vigorous impulse that a community may feel, become perverted and distorted as time passes, and the atmosphere of the earth seems fatal to the noble aspirations of its peoples. A wide humanitarian sympathy in a nation easily degenerates into hysteria. A military spirit tends towards brutality. Liberty leads to licence, restraint to tyranny. The pride of race is distended

4. See Winston Churchill's *Lord Randolph Churchill,* Introduction (1959), Sir Winston and the Duke of Marlborough kindly gave me permission to examine Sir Winston's drafts for the biography, in the Blenheim library.

5. One example was significant. To the dismay of his advisers, Churchill insisted upon retaining the story of King Alfred and the cakes in his *History of the English-speaking Peoples,* making the point that legends and fables are of as great importance in a nation's history as well-authenticated facts. The advisers subsequently realized the wisdom of this argument.

6. Randolph S. Churchill, *Winston S. Churchill,* Companion Volume I, p. 938.

> to blustering arrogance. The fear of God produces bigotry and superstition. There appear no exceptions to the mournful rule, and the best efforts of men, however glorious their early results, have dismal ending, like plants which shoot and bud and put forth beautiful flowers, and then grow rank and coarse and are withered by the winter.[7]

In assessing Churchill's writings, the assessment of the critic is inevitably swayed by personal likes and dislikes. It is the opinion of this critic that Churchill's literary work showed a certain decline in the 1930s. The rhetorical note is increasingly more evident than before, and the contrast between the rhetoric of *The World Crisis* and *Marlborough* is very evident if they are reread one after the other. For all its pitfalls as history, *The World Crisis* must surely stand as Churchill's masterpiece. After it, anything must appear as an anticlimax. But, even allowing for this, the weaknesses of Churchill's technique and style seem to become increasingly apparent in *Marlborough* and *The History of the English-speaking Peoples,* and in the later articles in *Great Contemporaries.* Philip Guedalla has referred to "the fatal lullaby of a majestic style"; but it is not so much this fact as the ponderousness and massiveness of his later work that limit its effectiveness. Churchill had written as a young man that "Few authors are rich men. Few human beings are insensible to the value of money. . . . Hurried style, exaggerated mannerisms and plagiarism replace the old careful toil. The author writes no more for fame but for wealth. Consequently his books become inferior. All this is very sad but very true." This description could certainly not be applied in its entirety to Churchill, but his dependence upon writing for his income was certainly an element in the decline in his very high standards, and the mannerisms became undoubtedly exaggerated. As the present Lord Birkenhead had commented: "Churchill the writer never wholly freed himself from Churchill the orator. Sometimes we feel that the rhythm is metallic and remorseless, and that the sentences spring to attention like soldiers on parade. At other moments we are conscious of his lack of historical objectivity, of the fact that he is usually justifying a policy or a cause, and that this perception of the feelings and motives of others is dim and uncertain."[8]

7. *The River War* (1951 edition), p. 35.
8. Report of the Royal Society of Literature, 1965.

Churchill's massive biography of John, Duke of Marlborough, of which the first volume was published in 1933, was his only venture into biography apart from that of his father. Like that work, it was a labor of love, of reclamation, and of family piety. The last factor was important. Churchill's sense of family loyalty was one of his most endearing traits, and he always deeply resented any slight, real or imagined, upon his family's name. It was Rosebery who had first opened the key to the biography of "Duke John" by drawing Churchill's attention to Paget's *Examen,* and the answer to Macaulay's censures of Marlborough. Churchill's account of this episode is given in the preface: "The aged and crippled statesman arose from the luncheon table, and, with great difficulty but sure knowledge, made his way along the passages of The Durdans to the exact nook in his capacious working library where 'Paget's Examen' reposed. 'There,' he said, taking down this unknown, out-of-print masterpiece, 'is the answer to Macaulay.'" (The Rosebery family version is that Rosebery, who could only move in a wheel-chair, summoned his butler and told him exactly where the book was to be found in his vast collection; the butler found it at once.)

If anything, Churchill identified himself even more fiercely with Marlborough than he had with Lord Randolph. It is indeed this intense feeling of personal identification with his subject that is so conspicuous a feature of both of his biographies. It is unfortunate that his vaguely projected biography of Napoleon came to nothing, but it is probable that in this case as well the sense of personal identification would have been predominant. In the case of Marlborough, as soon as Paget had given him the clue, he pursued Macaulay with relentless ardor, to the point that it assumed the proportions of an obsession; he was intent, as he put it, that truth would "fasten the label 'Liar' to his [Macaulay's] genteel tail-coats." Having devoted some three chapters to Macaulay's treatment of the Brest Expedition—which had been the principal contribution of Paget in 1874—he does not end there. Time and again Macaulay is summoned up —often quite irrelevantly—for further reprimands. Any historian who had accepted any part of Macaulay's thesis received similar treatment. Thus, Basil Williams, "apparently oblivious of forty years of accepted opinion and research, inertly or docilely reproduces the crude, exploded slander that 'the gallant General Talmash' fell 'as victim to Marlborough's treachery in the ill-fated

Brest Expedition.'" Historians who have in any way accepted the Jacobite Papers as genuine are slated for "an aberration of historical technique."

There is no historian so ferocious as the amateur who believes that he has got the professionals on the run. It is good lusty stuff —if that is the sort of thing you like. G. M. Trevelyan was justified in pointing out that with the exception of the Brest Expedition episode, Churchill accepted all Macaulay's facts; that Marlborough's patron was the man who kept his sister; that he took money from his mistress and invested it well; that he deserted James II when in his military service; that he subsequently corresponded with the Jacobites. As Trevelyan pointed out, "An historian who, before the days of our modern research, was deceived by these phenomena into thinking Marlborough a bad man was not necessarily dishonest."[9]

The most marked feature of *Marlborough* apart from the special pleading that characterizes it throughout, is the style. It is Churchill at his most florid. I cannot improve upon Professor J. H. Plumb's comments on this aspect of Churchill's writing:

> So long as the events or the human reactions were on a bold scale —dealing with courage, endurance, misery or defeat—he wrote with authority and with deep understanding: often his words clothed his feeling in majestic and memorable phrases. If the human or political situation became complex—a mixture of conscious or unconscious motives, of good and evil, of treachery and patriotism, existing side by side—then he tended to stumble or to evade the issues. That is why the overall pictures both of Marlborough and Lord Randolph are too simple, too direct.[10]

In *Marlborough,* the accounts of the battles—notably Blenheim and the storming of the Schellenberg—are magnificent, for the crash and pomp of the battle are faithfully reflected in the crash and pomp of Churchill's style. The same is true of the political parts, although the depiction of motives tends to be somewhat crude: "Shaftesbury was at the head of a flaming Opposition. . . . The ferocity of the Whigs knew no limit, and their turpitude lay not far behind."

9. *Times Literary Supplement,* October 19, 1933.
10. *Spectator,* July 1, 1966.

But away from battle and the high drama of politics, it does not work. Indeed, parts of *Marlborough* read like a parody of Churchill's style at its worst. The portrait of Louis XIV may be cited:

> We have no patience with the lackey pens which have sought to invest this long, hateful process with the appearances of dignity and honour. During the whole of his life Louis XIV was the curse and pest of Europe. No worse enemy of human freedom has ever appeared in the trappings of polite civilization. Insatiable appetite, cold, calculating ruthlessness, monumental conceit, presented themselves armed with fire and sword. The veneer of culture and good manners, of brilliant ceremonies and elaborate etiquette, only adds a heightening effect to the villainy of his life's story. Better the barbarian conquerors of antiquity, primordian figures of the abyss, than this high-heeled, beperiwigged dandy, strutting amid the bows and scrapes of mistresses and confessors to the torment of his age. Petty and mediocre in all except his lusts and power, the Sun King disturbed and harried mankind during more than fifty years of arrogant pomp.

So much for Louis XIV! Churchill's histories are populated with the Good and the Bad. Churchill was always greatly given to broad effects. It is not the least of the occupational hazards of politics. *Marlborough* abounds in broad effects. He writes of "public opinion" in twentieth-century terms. We read of "the mass of the nation" being "stirred to its depths" by the revocation of the Edict of Nantes, how "in the alehouses or upon the village greens ballads and songs expressed the popular sentiment against the French," and how "the sense of common cause grew across the barriers of class, race, creed and interest in the hearts of millions of men." These are exactly the kind of magnificent but wild generalizations for which the despised Macaulay received such a drubbing.

But it is the portrait of England, and England's history, that is perhaps the most intriguing and also the most revealing aspect of *Marlborough*. This portrait, to be carried forward much further in *The History of the English-speaking Peoples,* which may accurately be described as the last of the Whig histories, reflects Churchill's idealized and overromanticized concepts, and is of interest for that purpose: in particular, the glowing portrait of "the small island" carrying forward "intact and enshrined, all that peculiar structure of law and liberty, all her inheritance of learning and letters, which are today the treasure of the most powerful family in the human race." Are there not echoes here of passages in *The Story of the Malakand Field Force*?

No examination of Churchill's political career in the 1930s can ignore the significance of the tone and style of his historical writings. His sense of history was more emotional than intellectual, but it is in this period of his life that the dominance of his faith in England's historical destiny and his romanticized view of her past become particularly manifest. Much of his contempt for MacDonald, Baldwin, and Neville Chamberlain was based upon his disgust at what he deemed to be their betrayal of England's grandeur and destiny.

In this context the contrast drawn in *Marlborough* between the embattled hero and the snarling politicians at home is particularly significant. Churchill had no professional training as a historian, and had no experience, even rudimentary experience, of the complexities of historical criticism. He was not, furthermore, a man greatly interested in matters intellectual, and would demand brief memoranda from his assistants to summarize the principal points at issue rather than involve himself in the problem. His outstanding technical quality was as a narrator. His books tended to be of enormous length—in almost every case far too long, with masses of material proudly laid out, much of which could have been eliminated, and some of which had clearly not been digested by the author—but the pace is maintained to the last page.

But if *Marlborough* fails both as biography and history, its results on Churchill himself went far beyond the writing of the book. It gave him an absorbing interest at a dark moment in his political fortunes, and it also gave him a more acute realization of the problems and hazards of creating and retaining a Grand Alliance. Some of the best passages in the book deal with these complexities. In casting himself as Marlborough, grappling with the manifold problems of diplomacy, strategy, supply, terrain, and tactics, he was affording himself a kind of dress rehearsal for the problems of 1940–45. Leo Amery goes even further, and has said that "In his great ancestor, Marlborough, he discovered that fusion of political and military ideals, as well as the inspiration of family piety, for which he had all his life been groping." [11]

11. L. S. Amery, *My Political Life,* Vol. III, p. 399.

My Early Life (1930) is in so different a vein that it is difficult to believe that it came from the same mouth. Of all his books it is the most genial and, in a very real sense, warm. Churchill's memory —like that of all autobiographers—was conveniently selective. Like F. E. Smith, who dwelt so mournfully on the allegedly grinding poverty of his youth as he grew older until he firmly believed the harrowing fictions himself, Churchill subsequently exaggerated his early backwardness at school—thus providing countless wily schoolboys and troubled parents with exaggerated comfort. The narrowness by which he avoided the fate of "social wastrel" drawn for him by his father is described in detail by Randolph Churchill, and need not be emphasized here. The charm of the book lies in its warmth and wit; it contains, furthermore, some remarkable portraits of individuals, of which those of Mrs. Everest and Colonel Brabazon, commanding the 4th Hussars, may be particularly noted.

The most well-known parts of *My Early Life* are what might be called the "adventure" parts, particularly the accounts of action on the northwest frontier, in Cuba, and in South Africa, and other features of the book have tended to receive less consideration. The outstanding feature of the work is the development of Churchill's self-portrait, often wittily drawn. Some examples may suffice.

> I had a feeling once about Mathematics, that I saw it all—Depth beyond Depth was revealed to me—the Byss and the Abyss. I saw, as one might see the transit of Venus—or even the Lord Mayor's Show, a quantity passing through infinity and changing its sign from plus to minus. I saw exactly how it happened and the tergiversation was inevitable: and how the one step involved all the others. It was like politics. But it was after dinner and I let it go!
>
> Certainly the prolonged education indispensable to the progress of Society is not natural to mankind. It cuts against the grain. A boy would like to follow his father in pursuit of food or prey. He would like to be doing serviceable things so far as his utmost strength allowed. He would like to be earning wages however small to keep up the home. He would like to have some leisure of his own to use or misuse as he pleased. He would ask little more than the right to work or starve. And then perhaps in the evenings a real love of learning would come to those who were worthy—and why try to stuff it into those who are not?—and knowledge and thought would open the "magic casements" of the mind. . . .

> I am all for the Public Schools but I do not want to go there again.
>
> Twenty to twenty-five! These are the years! Don't be content with things as they are. "The earth is yours and the fulness thereof." Enter upon your inheritance, accept your responsibilities. Raise the glorious flags again, advance them upon the new enemies, who constantly gather upon the front of the human army, and have only to be assaulted to be overthrown. Don't take No for an answer. Never submit to failure. Do not be fobbed off with mere personal success or acceptance. You will make all kinds of mistakes; but as long as you are generous and true, and also fierce, you cannot hurt the world or even seriously distress her. She was made to be wooed and won by youth. She has lived and thrived only by repeated subjugations.

And there is an account of a dinner with Lord Sandhurst, at Government House, Poona:

> His Excellency, after the health of the Queen-Empress had been drunk and dinner was over, was good enough to ask my opinion upon several matters, and considering the magnificent character of his hospitality, I thought it would be unbecoming in me not to reply fully. I have forgotten the particular points of British and Indian affairs upon which he sought my counsel; all I can remember is that I responded generously. There were indeed moments when he seemed willing to impart his own views; but I thought it would be ungracious to put him to so much trouble; and he very readily subsided. He kindly sent his aide-de-camp with us to make sure we found our way back to camp all right. On the whole, after forty-eight hours of intensive study, I formed a highly favourable opinion about India. Sometimes, thought I, one sees these things more completely at first sight.

My Early Life is an authentic adventure story, full of night marches, cavalry charges, expeditions on the northwest frontier, polo matches, pitched battles against the hordes of the Khalifa or the crack shots of the Boers, with an escape from a prisoner-of-war camp and two Parliamentary elections thrown in. The touch is light, and the pace vigorous and gay. It is, deservedly, a classic of autobiography.

Churchill's books, no less than his many newspaper articles, provided him not only with essential income and a necessary outlet for his energies but the means by which he could keep his name before the public. Writing, fortunately, was a pleasure to him. "Writing a book was an adventure," as he said many years later (November 2, 1949). "To begin with it was a toy, and amusement; then it became a mistress, and then a master, and then a tyrant." He chose his subjects well, and he worked on them assiduously. Although he had his young men to research for him, the finished product very much bore the stamp of his personality; everyone who worked for him was impressed by the width of his knowledge and by the enormous care he took over his books. As a contributor to newspapers and magazines he was supremely professional, and not least over the fees he charged. If he was well paid by the standards of the time—as he was—he gave excellent value. And the money, after all, was put to admirable use.

If the thirties are to be regarded as wasted years in Churchill's political career, this opinion must be substantially offset by the opportunities given to him to study and to write. He re-created an old and valuable link between literature and public life in England. Indeed, with the possible exception of Morley,* whose best writing had been done before he entered politics, Churchill is the only British politician of the front rank in this century who has made a genuine, original, and valuable contribution to the literature of his country. And it can hardly be stressed sufficiently that Churchill's sense of history was of deep importance in his outlook on life. . . . If his interpretations were somewhat dramatic and, in a good sense, schoolboyish, it remains a very real factor in his emotional composition, and endows his work with an excitement and an immediacy which is rarely seen in the professional historian. In his views of history as in his politics, he was a romantic, with a romantic's eye on men and events. For in this, as in all else, there was no concealment and no dissimulation.

* John Morley (1838–1923), the prominent Liberal politician and man of letters. [ed.]

ISAIAH BERLIN

A Man of First Principles: Churchill in 1940

IN THE NOW REMOTE YEAR 1928, an eminent English poet and critic published a book dealing with the art of writing English prose. Writing at a time of bitter disillusion with the false splendors of the Edwardian era, and still more with the propaganda and phrase-making occasioned by the First World War, the critic praised the virtues of simplicity. If simple prose was often dry and flat, it was at least honest. If it was at times awkward, shapeless, and bleak, it did at least convey a feeling of truthfulness. Above all, it avoided the worst of all temptations—inflation, self-dramatization, the construction of flimsy stucco façades, either deceptively smooth or covered with elaborate baroque detail that concealed a dreadful inner emptiness.

From *Mr. Churchill in 1940*, by Isaiah Berlin. London: John Murray, 1949, pp. 7–39. Copyright 1949 by Isaiah Berlin. Reprinted with permission of John Murray and Houghton Mifflin Company.

The time and mood are familiar enough: it was not long after Lytton Strachey had set a new fashion by his method of exposing the cant or muddleheadedness of eminent Victorians, after Bertrand Russell had unmasked the great nineteenth-century metaphysicians as authors of a monstrous hoax played upon generations eager to be deceived, after Keynes had successfully pilloried the follies and vices of the Allied statesmen at Versailles. This was the time when rhetoric and, indeed, eloquence were held up to obloquy as camouflage for literary and moral Pecksniffs, unscrupulous charlatans who corrupted artistic taste and discredited the cause of truth and reason, and at their worst incited to evil and led a credulous world to disaster. It was in this literary climate that the critic in question, with much skill and discrimination, explained why he admired the last recorded words spoken to Judge Thayer by the poor fish peddler Vanzetti—moving, ungrammatical fragments uttered by a simple man about to die—more than he did the rolling periods of celebrated masters of fine writing widely read by the public at that time.

He selected as an example of the latter a man who in particular was regarded as the sworn enemy of all that the author prized most highly—humility, integrity, humanity, scrupulous regard for sensibility, individual freedom, personal affection—the celebrated but distrusted paladin of imperialism and the romantic conception of life, the swashbuckling militarist, the vehement orator and journalist, the most public of public personalities in a world dedicated to the cultivation of private virtues, the chancellor of the exchequer of the Conservative government then in power, Mr. Winston Churchill.

After observing that "these three conditions are necessary to Eloquence—firstly an adequate theme, then a sincere and impassioned mind, and lastly a power of sustainment, of pertinacity," the writer drove his thesis home with a quotation from the first part of Mr. Churchill's *World Crisis,* which had appeared some four years previously, and added: "Such eloquence is false because it is artificial . . . the images are stale, the metaphors violent, the whole passage exhales a false dramatic atmosphere . . . a volley of rhetorical imperatives." He went on to describe Mr. Churchill's prose as being high-sounding, redundant, falsely eloquent, declamatory, derived from undue "aggrandisation of the self" instead of "aggrandisation of the theme"; and condemned it root and branch.

This view was well received by the young men who were painfully reacting against anything that appeared to go beyond the naked skeleton of the truth, at a time when not only rhetoric but noble eloquence seemed outrageous hypocrisy. Mr. Churchill's critic spoke, and knew that he spoke, for a postwar generation; the psychological symptoms of the vast and rapid social transformation then in progress, from which the government in power so resolutely averted its gaze, were visible to the least discerning critics of literature and the arts; the mood was dissatisfied, hostile, and insecure; the sequel to so much magnificence was too bitter, and left behind it a heritage of hatred for the grand style as such. The victims and casualties of the disaster thought they had earned the right to be rid of the trappings of an age that had heartlessly betrayed them.

Nevertheless, the stern critic and his audience were profoundly mistaken. What he and they denounced as so much tinsel and hollow pasteboard was in reality solid: it was this author's natural means for the expression of his heroic, highly colored, sometimes oversimple and even naïve, but always genuine, vision of life. The critic saw only an unconvincing, sordidly transparent pastiche, but this was an illusion. The reality was something very different: an inspired, if unconscious, attempt at a revival. It went against the stream of contemporary thought and feeling only because it was a deliberate return to a formal mode of English utterance which extends from Gibbon and Dr. Johnson to Peacock and Macaulay, a composite weapon created by Mr. Churchill in order to convey his particular vision. In the bleak and deflationary twenties it was too bright, too big, too vivid, too unsubtle for the sensitive and sophisticated epigoni of the age of imperialism, who, living an inner life of absorbing complexity and delicacy, became unable and certainly unwilling to admire the light of a day that had destroyed so much of what they had trusted and loved. From this the critic and his supporters recoiled; but their analysis of their reasons was not convincing.

They had, of course, a right to their own scale of values, but it was a blunder to dismiss Mr. Churchill's prose as a false front, a hollow sham. Revivals are not false as such: the Gothic Revival, for example, represented a passionate, if nostalgic, attitude toward life, and while some examples of it may appear bizarre, it sprang from a deeper sentiment and had a good deal more to say than some of the thin and "realistic" styles that followed; the fact that the creators of the Gothic Revival found their liberation in going back into a largely imaginary past in no way discredits them or their achievement. There are those who, inhibited by the furniture of the ordinary world, come to life only when they feel themselves actors upon a stage, and, thus emancipated, speak out for the first time, and are then found to have much to say. There are those who can function freely only in uniform or armor or court dress, see only through certain kinds of spectacles, act fearlessly only in situations that in some way are formalized for them, see life as a kind of play in which they and others are assigned certain lines that they must speak. So it happens—the last war afforded plenty of instances of this—that people of a shrinking disposition perform miracles of courage when life has been dramatized for them, when they are on the battlefield; and might continue to do so if they were constantly in uniform and life were always a battlefield.

This need for a framework is not "escapism," not artificial or abnormal or a sign of maladjustment. Often it is a vision of experience in terms of the strongest single psychological ingredient in one's nature: not infrequently in the form of a simple struggle between conflicting forces or principles, between truth and falsehood, good and evil, right and wrong, between personal integrity and various forms of temptation and corruption (as in the case of the critic in question), or between what is conceived as permanent and what is ephemeral, or the material and the immaterial, or between the forces of life and the forces of death, or between the religion of art and its supposed enemies—politicians or priests or philistines. Life may be seen through many windows, none of them necessarily clear or opaque, less or more distorting than any of the others. And since we think largely in words, they necessarily take on the property of serving as an armor. The style of Dr. Johnson, which echoes so frequently in the prose of *Their Finest Hour,* particularly when the author indulges in a solemn facetiousness, was itself in its own day a weapon offensive and defensive; it requires no deep psychological subtlety to perceive why a man so vulnerable as Johnson—who belonged mentally to the previous century—had constant need of it.

Mr. Churchill's dominant category, the single, central, organizing principle of his moral and intellectual universe, is an historical imagination so strong, so comprehensive, as to encase the whole of the present and the whole of the future in a framework of a rich and multicolored past. Such an approach is dominated by a desire—and a capacity—to find fixed moral and intellectual bearings, to give shape and character, color and direction and coherence, to the stream of events.

This kind of systematic "historicism" is, of course, not confined to men of action or political theorists: Roman Catholic thinkers see life in terms of a firm and lucid historical structure, and so, of course, do Marxists, and so did the romantic historians and philosophers from whom the Marxists are directly descended. Nor do we complain of "escapism" or perversion of the facts until the categories adopted are thought to do too much violence to the "facts." To interpret, to relate, to classify, to symbolize are those natural and unavoidable human activities that we loosely and conveniently describe as thinking. We complain, if we do, only when the result is too widely at variance with the common outlook of our own society and age and tradition.

Mr. Churchill sees history—and life—as a great Renaissance pageant: when he thinks of France or Italy, Germany or the Low Countries, Russia, India, Africa, the Arab lands, he sees vivid historical images—something between Victorian illustrations in a child's book of history and the great procession painted by Benozzo Gozzoli in the Riccardi Palace. His eye is never that of the neatly classifying sociologist, the careful psychological analyst, the plodding antiquary, the patient historical scholar. His poetry has not that anatomical vision which sees the naked bone beneath the flesh, skulls, and skeletons and the omnipresence of decay and death beneath the flow of life. The units out of which his world is constructed are simpler and larger than life, the patterns vivid and repetitive like those of an epic poet, or at times like those of a dramatist who sees persons and situations as timeless symbols and embodiments of eternal, shining principles. The whole is a series of symmetrically formed and somewhat stylized compositions, either suffused with bright light or cast in darkest shadow, like a legend by Carpaccio, with scarcely any nuance, painted in primary colors, with no halftones, nothing intangible, nothing impalpable, nothing half spoken or hinted or whispered: the voice does not alter in pitch or timbre.

The archaisms of style to which Mr. Churchill's wartime speeches accustomed us are indispensable ingredients of the heightened tone, the formal chronicler's attire, for which the solemnity of the occasion called. Mr. Churchill is fully conscious of this: the style should adequately respond to the demands that history makes upon the actors from moment to moment. "The ideas set forth," he wrote in 1940 about a Foreign Office draft, "appeared to me to err in trying to be too clever, to enter into refinements of policy unsuited to the tragic simplicity and grandeur of the times and the issues at stake."

His own narrative consciously mounts and swells until it reaches the great climax of the Battle of Britain. The texture and the tension are those of a tragic opera, where the very artificiality of the medium, both in the recitative and in the arias, serves to eliminate the irrelevant dead level of normal existence and to set off in high relief the deeds and sufferings of the principal characters. The moments of comedy in such a work must necessarily conform to the style of the whole and be parodies of it; and this is Mr. Churchill's practice. When he says that he viewed this or that "with stern and tranquil gaze," or informs his officials that any "chortling" by them over the failure of a chosen scheme "will be viewed with great disfavour by me," or describes the "celestial grins" of his collaborators over the development of a well-concealed conspiracy, he does precisely this; the mock heroic tone—reminiscent of *Stalky & Co.*—does not break the operatic conventions. But conventions though they be, they are not donned and doffed by the author at will: by now they are his second nature, and have completely fused with the first; art and nature are no longer distinguishable. The very rigid pattern of his prose is the normal medium of his ideas not merely when he sets himself to compose, but in the life of the imagination that permeates his daily existence.

Mr. Churchill's language is a medium that he invented because he needed it. It has a bold, ponderous, fairly uniform, easily recognizable rhythm, which lends itself to parody (including his own) like all strongly individual styles. A language is individual when its user is endowed with sharply marked characteristics and succeeds in creating a medium for their expression. The origins, the constituents, the classical echoes that can be found in Mr. Churchill's prose are obvious enough; the product is, however, unique. Whatever the attitude that may be taken toward it, it must be recognized as a large-scale phenomenon of our time. To ignore or deny this would be blind or frivolous or dishonest. The utterance is always, and not merely on special occasions, formal (though it alters in intensity and color with the situation), always public, Ciceronian, addressed to the world, remote from the hesitancies and stresses of introspection and private life.

The quality of Mr. Churchill's latest work[1] is that of his whole life. His world is built upon the primacy of public over private relationships, upon the supreme value of action, of the battle between simple good and simple evil, between life and death; but, above all, battle. He has always fought. "Whatever you may do," he declared to the demoralized French ministers in the bleakest hour of 1940, "we shall fight on for ever and ever and ever," and under this sign his own whole life has been lived.

What has he fought for? The answer is a good deal clearer than in the case of other equally passionate but less consistent men of action. Mr. Churchill's principles and beliefs on fundamental issues have never faltered. He has often been accused by his critics of inconstancy, of veering and even erratic judgment, as when he changed his allegiance from the Conservative to the Liberal Party, to and fro. But with the exception of the issue of protection, when he supported the tariff as chancellor of the exchequer in Mr. Baldwin's Cabinet in the twenties, this charge, which at first seems so plausible, is spectacularly false. Far from changing his opinions too often, Mr. Churchill has scarcely, during a long and stormy career, altered them at all. If anyone wishes to discover his views on the large and lasting issue of our time, he need only set himself to discover what Mr. Churchill has said or written on the subject at any period of his long and exceptionally articulate public life, in particular during the years before the

1. Winston Churchill, *Gathering Storm*.

First World War: the number of instances in which his views have in later years undergone any appreciable degree of change will be found astonishingly small.

The apparently solid and dependable Mr. Baldwin adjusted his attitudes with wonderful dexterity as and when circumstances required it. Mr. Chamberlain, long regarded as a grim and immovable rock of Tory opinion, altered his policies—more serious than Mr. Baldwin, he pursued policies, not being content with mere attitudes—when the party or the situation seemed to him to require it. Mr. Churchill remained inflexibly attached to first principles.

It is the strength and coherence of his central, lifelong beliefs that have provoked greater uneasiness, more disfavor and suspicion, in the central office of the Conservative Party than his vehemence or passion for power or what was considered his wayward, unreliable brilliance. No strongly centralized political organization feels altogether happy with individuals who combine independence, a free imagination, and a formidable strength of character with stubborn faith and a single-minded, unchanging view of the public and private good. Mr. Churchill, who believes that "ambition, not so much for vulgar ends but for fame, glints in every mind," believes in and seeks to attain—as an artist his vision—personal greatness and personal glory. As much as any king conceived by a Renaissance dramatist or by a nineteenth-century historian or moralist, he thinks it a brave thing to ride in triumph through Persepolis; he knows with an unshakable certainty what he considers to be big, handsome, noble, and worthy of pursuit by someone in high station, and what, on the contrary, he abhors as being dim, gray, thin, likely to lower or destroy the play of color and movement in the universe. Tacking and bending and timid compromise may commend themselves to those sound men of sense whose hopes of preserving the world they defend are shot through with an often unconscious pessimism; but if the policy they pursue is likely to slow the tempo, to diminish the forces of life, to lower the "vital and vibrant energy" that he admires, say, in Lord Beaverbrook, Mr. Churchill is ready for attack.

Mr. Churchill is one of the diminishing number of those who genuinely believe in a specific world order: the desire to give it life and strength is the most powerful single influence upon everything that he thinks and imagines, does and is. When biographers and historians come to describe and analyze his views on Europe or America, on the British Empire or Russia, on India or Palestine, or even on social or economic policy, they will find that his opinions on all these topics are set in fixed patterns, set early in life and later only reinforced. Thus he has always believed in great states and civilizations in an almost hierarchical order, and has never, for instance, hated Germany as such: Germany is a great, historically hallowed state; the Germans are a great historic race and as such occupy a proportionate amount of space in Mr. Churchill's world picture. He denounced the Prussians in the First World War and the Nazis in the Second; the Germans scarcely at all. He has always entertained a glowing vision of France and her culture, and has unalterably advocated the necessity of Anglo-French collaboration. He has always looked on the Russians as a formless, quasi-Asiatic mass beyond the walls of European civilization. His belief in and predilection for the American democracy are the foundation of his political outlook.

His vision in foreign affairs has always been consistently romantic. The struggle of the Jews for self-determination in Palestine engaged his imagination in precisely the way in which the Italian risorgimento captured the sympathies of his Liberal forebears. Similarly, his views on social policy conform to those Liberal principles that he received at the hands of the men he most admired in the great Liberal administration of the first decade of this century—Asquith, Haldane, Grey, Morley, above all, Lloyd George before 1914—and he has seen no reason to change them, whatever the world might do; and if these views, progressive in 1910, seem less convincing today, and indeed reveal an obstinate blindness to social and economic—as opposed to political—injustice, of which Haldane or Lloyd George can scarcely be accused, that flows from Mr. Churchill's unalterable faith in the firmly conceived scheme of human relationships that he established within himself long ago, once and for all.

It is an error to regard the imagination as a mainly revolutionary force—if it destroys and alters, it also fuses hitherto isolated beliefs, insights, mental habits, into strongly unified systems. These, if they are filled with sufficient energy and force of will—and, it may be added, fantasy, which is less frightened by the facts and creates ideal models in terms of which the facts are ordered in the mind—sometimes transform the outlook of an entire people and generation.

The British statesman most richly endowed with these gifts was Disraeli, who in effect conceived that imperialist mystique, that splendid but most un-English vision which, romantic to the point of exoticism, full of metaphysical emotion, to all appearances utterly opposed to everything most soberly empirical, utilitarian, antisystematic in the British tradition, bound its spell on the mind of England for two generations.

Mr. Churchill's political imagination has something of the same magical power to transform. It is a magic that belongs equally to demagogues and great democratic leaders: Franklin Roosevelt, who as much as any man altered his country's inner image of itself and of its character and its history, possessed it in a high degree. But the differences between him and the prime minister of Britain are greater than the similarities, and to some degree epitomize the differences of continents and civilizations. The contrast is brought out vividly by the respective parts they played in the war that drew them so closely together.

The Second World War in some ways gave birth to less novelty and genius than the First. It was, of course, a greater cataclysm, fought over a wider area, and altered the social and political contours of the world at least as radically as its predecessor, perhaps more so. But the break in continuity in 1914 was far more violent. The years before 1914 look to us now, and looked even in the twenties, as the end of a long period of largely peaceful development broken suddenly and catastrophically. In Europe, at least, the years before 1914 were viewed with understandable nostalgia by those who after them knew no real peace.

The period between the wars marks a decline in the development of human culture if it is compared with that sustained and fruitful period which makes the nineteenth century seem a unique human achievement, so powerful that it persisted, even during the war that broke it, to a degree that seems astonishing to us now. The quality of literature, for example, which is surely one of the most reliable criteria of intellectual and moral vitality, was incomparably higher during the war of 1914–18 than it has been after 1939. In Western Europe alone these four years of slaughter and destruction were also years in which works of genius and talent continued to be produced by such established writers as Shaw and Wells and Kipling, Hauptmann and Gide, Chesterton and Arnold Bennett, Beerbohm and Yeats, as well as such younger writers as Proust and Joyce, Virginia Woolf and E. M. Forster, T. S. Eliot and Alexander Blok, Rilke, Stefan George, and Valéry. Nor did natural science, philosophy, and history cease to develop fruitfully. What has the recent war to offer by comparison?

Yet perhaps there is one respect in which the Second World War did outshine its predecessor: the leaders of the nations involved in it were, with the significant exception of France, men of greater stature, psychologically more interesting, than their prototypes. It would hardly be disputed that Stalin is a more fascinating figure than the tsar Nicholas II; Hitler more arresting than the kaiser: Mussolini than Victor Emmanuel; and, memorable as they were, President Wilson and Lloyd George yield in the attribute of sheer historical magnitude to Franklin Roosevelt and Winston Churchill.

"History," we are told by Aristotle, "is what Alcibiades did and suffered." This notion, despite all the efforts of the social sciences to overthrow it, remains a good deal more valid than rival hypotheses, provided that history is defined as that which historians actually do. At any rate, Mr. Churchill accepts it wholeheartedly and takes full advantage of his opportunities. And because his narrative deals largely in personalities and gives individual genius its full and sometimes more than its full due, the appearance of the great wartime protagonists in his pages gives his narrative some of the quality of an epic, whose heroes and villains acquire their stature not merely—or indeed at all—from the importance of the events in which they are involved, but from their own intrinsic human size upon the stage of human history; their characteristics, involved as they are in perpetual juxtaposition and occasional collision with one another, set each other off in vast relief.

Comparisons and contrasts are bound to arise in the mind of the reader, which sometimes take him beyond Mr. Churchill's pages. Thus Mr. Roosevelt stands out principally by his astonishing appetite for life and by his apparently complete freedom from fear of the future; as a man who welcomed the future eagerly as such, and conveyed the feeling that whatever the times might bring, all would be grist to his mill, nothing would be too formidable or crushing to be subdued and used and molded into the pattern of the new and unpredictable forms of life, into the building of which he, Mr. Roosevelt, and his allies and devoted subordinates would throw themselves with unheard-of energy and gusto. This avid anticipation of the future, the lack of nervous fear that the wave might prove too big or violent to navigate, contrasts most sharply with the uneasy longing to insulate themselves so clear in Stalin or Chamberlain. Hitler, too, in a sense, showed no fear, but his assurance sprang from a lunatic's violent and cunning vision, which distorted the facts too easily in his favor.

So passionate a faith in the future, so untroubled a confidence in one's power to mold it, when it is allied to a capacity for realistic appraisal of its true contours, implies an exceptionally sensitive awareness, conscious or half-conscious, of the tendencies of one's milieu, of the desires, hopes, fears, loves, hatreds, of the human beings who compose it, of what are impersonally described as social and individual "trends." Mr. Roosevelt had this sensibility developed to the point of genius. He acquired the symbolic significance that he retained throughout his presidency largely because he sensed the tendencies of his time and their projections into the future to a most uncommon degree. His sense, not only of the movement of American public opinion but of the general direction in which the larger human society of his time was moving, was what is called uncanny. The inner currents, the tremors and complicated convolutions of this movement, seemed to register themselves within his nervous system with a kind of seismographical accuracy. The majority of his fellow citizens recognized this—some with enthusiasm, others with gloom or bitter indignation. Peoples far beyond the frontiers of the United States rightly looked to him as the most genuine and unswerving spokesman of democracy of his time, the most contemporary, the most outward looking, the boldest, most imaginative, most large spirited, free from the obsessions of an inner life, with an unparalleled capacity for creating confidence in the power of his insight, his foresight, and his capacity genuinely to identify himself with the ideals of humble people.

This feeling of being at home not merely in the present but in the future, of knowing where he was going and by what means and why, made him, until his health was finally undermined, buoyant and gay: made him delight in the company of the most varied and opposed individuals provided that they embodied some specific aspect of the turbulent stream of life, stood actively for the forward movement in their particular world, whatever it might be. And this inner élan made up, and more than made up, for faults of intellect or character that his enemies—and his victims—never ceased to point out. He seemed genuinely unaffected by their taunts: what he could not abide was, before all, passivity, stillness, melancholy, fear of life or preoccupation with eternity or death, however great the insight or delicate the sensibility by which they were accompanied.

Mr. Churchill stands at almost the opposite pole. He too does not fear the future, and no man has ever loved life more vehemently and infused so much of it into everyone and everything that he has touched. But whereas Mr. Roosevelt, like all great innovators, had a half-conscious premonitory awareness of the coming shape of society, not wholly unlike that of an artist, Mr. Churchill, for all his extrovert air, looks within, and his strongest sense is the sense of the past.

The clear, brightly colored vision of history, in terms of which he conceives both the present and the future, is the inexhaustible source from which he draws the primary stuff out of which his universe is so solidly built, so richly and elaborately ornamented. So firm and so embracing an edifice could not be constructed by anyone liable to react and respond like a sensitive instrument to the perpetually changing moods and directions of other persons or institutions or peoples. And, indeed, Mr. Churchill's strength (and what is most frightening in him) lies precisely in this: that, unlike Mr. Roosevelt, he is not equipped with numberless sensitive antennae that communicate the smallest oscillations of the outer world in all its unstable variety. Unlike Mr. Roosevelt (and unlike Gladstone and Lloyd George for that matter) he does not reflect a contemporary social or moral world in an intense and concentrated fashion; rather, he creates one of such power and coherence that it becomes a reality and alters the external world by being imposed upon it with irresistible force. As his history of the war shows, he has an immense capacity for absorbing facts, but they emerge transformed by the categories which he powerfully imposes on the raw material into something that he can use to build his own massive, simple, impregnably fortified inner world.

Mr. Roosevelt, as a public personality, was a spontaneous, optimistic, pleasure-loving ruler who dismayed his assistants by the gay and apparently heedless abandon with which he seemed to delight in pursuing two or more totally incompatible policies, and astonished them even more by the swiftness and ease with which he managed to throw off the cares of office during the darkest and most dangerous moments. Mr. Churchill, too, loves pleasure, and he too lacks neither gaiety nor a capacity for exuberant self-expression, together with the habit of blithely cutting Gordian knots in a manner that often upset his experts; but he is not a frivolous man. His nature possesses a dimension of depth—and a corresponding sense of tragic possibilities—which Mr. Roosevelt's lighthearted genius instinctively passed by.

Mr. Roosevelt played the game of politics with virtuosity, and both his successes and his failures were carried off in splendid style; his performance seemed to flow with effortless skill. Mr. Churchill is acquainted with darkness as well as light. Like all inhabitants and even transient visitors of inner worlds, he gives evidence of seasons of agonized brooding and slow recovery. Mr. Roosevelt might have spoken of sweat and blood, but when Mr. Churchill offered his people tears, he spoke a word that might have been uttered by Lincoln or Mazzini or Cromwell but not Mr. Roosevelt, greathearted, generous, and perceptive as he was.

Not the herald of the bright and cloudless civilization of the future, Mr. Churchill is preoccupied by his own vivid world, and it is doubtful how far he has ever been aware of what actually goes on in the heads and hearts of others. He does not react, he acts; he does not mirror, he affects others and alters them to his own powerful measure. Writing of Dunkirk he says:

> Had I at this juncture faltered at all in the leading of the nation, I should have been hurled out of office. I was sure that every Minister was ready to be killed quite soon, and have all his family and possessions destroyed, rather than give in. In this they represented the House of Commons and almost all the people. It fell to me in

> these coming days and months to express their sentiments on suitable occasions. This I was able to do because they were mine also. There was a white glow, overpowering, sublime, which ran through our island from end to end.

And on the twenty-eighth of June of that year he told Lord Lothian, then ambassador in Washington, "Your mood should be bland and phlegmatic. No one is downhearted here."

These splendid sentences hardly do justice to his own part in creating the feeling that he describes. For Mr. Churchill is not a sensitive lens, which absorbs and concentrates and reflects and amplifies the sentiments of others; unlike the European dictators, he does not play on public opinion like an instrument. In 1940 he assumed an indomitable stoutness, an unsurrendering quality on the part of his people, and carried on. If he did not represent the quintessence and epitome of what some, at any rate, of his fellow citizens feared and hoped in their hour of danger, this was because he idealized them with such intensity that in the end they approached his ideal and began to see themselves as he saw them: "the buoyant and imperturbable temper of Britain which I had the honour to express"—it was indeed, but he had a lion's share in creating it. So hypnotic was the force of his words, so strong his faith, that by the sheer intensity of his eloquence he bound his spell upon them until it seemed to them that he was indeed speaking what was in their hearts and minds. Doubtless it was there, but largely dormant until he had awakened it within them.

After he had spoken to them in the summer of 1940 as no one has ever before or since, they conceived a new idea of themselves, which their own prowess and the admiration of the world have since established as a heroic image in the history of mankind, like Thermopylae or the defeat of the Spanish Armada. They went forward into battle transformed by his words. The spirit that they found within them he had created within himself from his inner resources, and poured it into his nation, and took their vivid reaction for an original impulse on their part, which he merely had the honor to clothe in suitable words. He created a heroic mood and turned the fortunes of the Battle of Britain not by catching the mood of his surroundings (which was not indeed, at any time, one of craven panic or bewilderment or apathy, but somewhat confused; stouthearted but unorganized) but by being stubbornly impervious to it, as he has been to so many of the passing shades and tones of which the life around him has been composed.

The peculiar quality of heroic pride and sense of the sublimity of the occasion arises in him not, as in Mr. Roosevelt, from delight in being alive and in control at a critical moment of history, in the very change and instability of things, in the infinite possibilities of the future whose very unpredictability offers endless possibilities of spontaneous moment-to-moment improvisation and large imaginative moves in harmony with the restless spirit of the time. On the contrary, it springs from a capacity for sustained introspective brooding, great depth, and constancy of feeling—in particular, feeling for and fidelity to the great tradition for which he assumes a personal responsibility, a tradition that he bears upon his shoulders and must deliver not only sound and undamaged but strengthened and embellished to successors worthy of accepting the sacred burden.

Bismarck is quoted somewhere as having said something to the effect that there was no such thing as political intuition: political genius consisted in the ability to hear the distant hoofbeat of the horse of history—and then by superhuman effort to leap and catch the horseman by the coattails. No man has ever listened for this fateful sound more eagerly than Winston Churchill, and in 1940 he made the heroic leap. "It is impossible," he writes of this time, "to quell the inward excitement which comes from a prolonged balancing of terrible things," and when the crisis finally bursts he is ready because after a lifetime of effort he has reached his goal.

The position of the prime minister is unique: "If he trips he must be sustained; if he makes mistakes they must be covered; if he sleeps he must not be wantonly disturbed; if he is no good he must be pole-axed"; and this because he is at that moment the guardian of the "life of Britain, her message and her glory." He trusted Roosevelt utterly, "convinced that he would give up life itself, to say nothing about office, for the cause of world freedom now in such awful peril." His prose records the tension that rises and swells to the culminating moment, the Battle of Britain—"a time when it was equally good to live or die." This bright, heroic vision of the mortal danger and the will to conquer, born in the hour when defeat seemed not merely possible but probable, is the product of a burning historical imagination, feeding not upon the data of the outer but of the inner eye: the picture has a shape and simplicity that future historians will find hard to reproduce when they seek to assess and interpret the facts soberly in the gray light of common day.

The prime minister was able to impose his imagination and his will upon his countrymen, and enjoy a Periclean reign, precisely because he appeared to them larger and nobler than life and lifted them to an abnormal height in a moment of crisis. It was a climate in which men do not usually like—nor ought to like—living; it demands a violent tension, which, if it lasts, destroys all sense of normal perspective, overdramatizes personal relationships, and falsifies normal values to an intolerable extent. But, in the event, it did turn a large number of inhabitants of the British Isles out of their normal selves and, by dramatizing their lives and making them seem to themselves and to each other clad in the fabulous garments appropriate to a great historic moment, transformed cowards into brave men, and so fulfilled the purpose of shining armor.

This is the kind of means by which dictators and demagogues transform peaceful populations into marching armies; it was Mr. Churchill's unique and unforgettable achievement that he created this necessary illusion within the framework of a free system without destroying or even twisting it; that he called forth spirits which did not stay to oppress and enslave the population after the hour of need had passed; that he saved the future by interpreting the present in terms of a vision of the past which did not distort or inhibit the historical development of the British people by attempting to make them realize some impossible and unattainable splendor in the name of an imaginary tradition or of an infallible, supernatural leader. Mr. Churchill was saved from this frightening nemesis of romanticism by a sufficiency of that libertarian feeling which, if it sometimes fell short of understanding the tragic aspects of modern despotisms, remained sharply perceptive—sometimes too tolerantly, but still perceptive—of what is false, grotesque, contemptible in the great frauds upon the people practiced by totalitarian regimes. Some of the sharpest and most characteristic epithets are reserved for the dictators: Hitler is "this evil man, this monstrous abortion of hatred and defeat." Franco is a "narrow-minded tyrant" of "evil qualities" holding down a "blood-drained people." No quarter is given to the Pétain regime, and its appeal to tradition and the eternal France is treated as a repellent travesty of national feeling. Stalin in 1940–41 is "at once a callous, a crafty, and an ill-informed giant."

This very genuine hostility to usurpers, which is stronger in him than even his passion for authority and order, springs from a quality which Mr. Churchill conspicuously shares with the late President Roosevelt—uncommon love of life, aversion for the imposition of rigid disciplines upon the teeming variety of human relations, the instinctive sense of what promotes and what retards or distorts growth and vitality. But because the life that Mr. Churchill so loves presents itself to him in a historical guise as part of the pageant of tradition, his method of constructing historical narrative, the distribution of emphasis, the assignment of relative importance to persons and events, the theory of history, the architecture of the narrative, the structure of the sentences, the words themselves, are elements in a historical revival as fresh, as original, and as idiosyncratic as the neoclassicism of the Renaissance or the Regency. To complain that this omits altogether too much by assuming that the impersonal, the dull, the undramatic is necessarily also unimportant, may well be just; but to lament that this is not contemporary, and therefore in some way less true, less responsive to modern needs, than the noncommittal, neutral glass and plastic of those objective historians who regard facts and only facts as interesting and, worse still, all facts as equally interesting—what is this but craven pedantry and blindness?

The differences between the president and the prime minister were at least in one respect something more than the obvious differences of national character, education, and even temperament. For all his sense of history, his large, untroubled, easygoing style of life, his unshakable feeling of personal security, his natural assumption of being at home in the great world far beyond the confines of his own country, Mr. Roosevelt was a typical child of the twentieth century and of the New World; while Mr. Churchill, for all his love of the present hour, his unquenchable appetite for new knowledge, his sense of the technological possibilities of our time, and the restless roaming of his fancy in considering how they might be most imaginatively applied, despite his enthusiasm for Basic English, or the siren suit that so upset his hosts in Moscow—despite all this, Mr. Churchill remains a European of the nineteenth century.

The difference is deep and accounts for a great deal in the incompatibility of outlook between him and the president of the United States, whom he admired so much and whose great office he held in awe. Something of the fundamental unlikeness between America and Europe, and perhaps between the twentieth century and the nineteenth, seemed to be crystallized in this remarkable interplay. It may perhaps be that the twentieth century is to the nineteenth as the nineteenth was to the eighteenth century. Talleyrand once made the well-known observation that those who had not lived under the *ancien régime* did not know what true *douceur de vivre* had been. And indeed, from our distant vantage point, this is clear: the earnest, romantic young men of the early part of the nineteenth century seemed systematically unable to understand or to like the attitude to life of the most civilized representatives of the prerevolutionary world, particularly in France, where the break was sharpest; the sharpness, the irony, the minute vision, the perception of and concentration upon fine differences in character, in style, the preoccupation with barely perceptible dissimilarities of hue, the extreme sensibility that makes the life of even so "progressive" and forward-looking a man as Diderot so unbridgeably different from the larger and simpler vision of the romantics, is something that the nineteenth century lacked the historical perspective to understand.

Suppose that Shelley had met and talked with Voltaire, what would he have felt? He would most probably have been profoundly shocked—shocked by the seemingly limited vision, the smallness of the field of awareness, the apparent triviality and finickiness, the almost spinsterish elaboration of Voltaire's malice, the preoccupation with tiny units, the subatomic texture of experience; he would have felt horror or pity before such wanton blindness to the large moral and spiritual issues of his own day—causes whose universal scope and significance painfully agitated the best and most awakened minds; he might have thought him wicked, but even more he would have thought him contemptible, too sharp, too small, too mean, grotesquely and unworthily obscene, prone to titter on the most sacred occasions, in the holiest places.

And Voltaire, in his turn, would very probably have been dreadfully bored, unable to see good cause for so much ethical eloquence; he would have looked with a cold and hostile eye on all this moral excitement: the magnificent Saint-Simonian vision of one world (which so stirred the left-wing young men half a century later), altering in shape and becoming integrated into a neatly organized man-made whole by the application of powerfully concentrated, scientific, technical, and spiritual resources, would to him have seemed a dreary and monotonous desert, too homogeneous, too flavorless, too unreal, apparently unconscious of those small, half-concealed but crucial distinctions and incongruities that gave individuality and savor to experience, without which there could be no civilized vision, no wit, no conversation, certainly no art deriving from a refined and fastidious culture. The moral vision of the nineteenth century would have seemed to him a dull, blurred, coarse instrument, unable to focus those pinpoints of concentrated light, those short-lived patterns of sound and color, whose infinite variety as they linger or flash past are comedy and tragedy—are the substance of personal relations and of worldly wisdom, of politics, of history, and of art.

The reason for this failure of communication was not a mere change in the point of view, but the kind of vision that divided the two centuries. The microscopic vision of the eighteenth century was succeeded by the macroscopic eye of the nineteenth. The latter saw much more widely, saw in universal or at least in European terms; it saw the contours of great mountain ranges where the eighteenth century discerned, however sharply and perceptively, only the veins and cracks and different shades of but a portion of the mountainside. The object of vision of the eighteenth century was smaller and its eye was closer to the object. The enormous moral issues of the nineteenth century were not within the field of its acutely discriminating gaze: that was the devastating difference which the great French Revolution had made, and it led to something not necessarily better or worse, uglier or more beautiful, profounder or more shallow, but to a situation which above all was different in kind.

Something not unlike this same chasm divides America from

Europe (and the twentieth century from the nineteenth). The American vision is larger and more generous; its thought transcends, despite the parochialism of its means of expression, the barriers of nationality and race and differences of outlook, in a big, sweeping, single view. It notices things rather than persons, and sees the world (those who saw it in this fashion in the nineteenth century were considered utopian eccentrics) in terms of rich, infinitely moldable raw material, waiting to be constructed and planned in order to satisfy a worldwide human craving for happiness or goodness or wisdom. And therefore to it the differences and conflicts that divide Europeans in so violent a fashion must seem petty, irrational, and sordid, not worthy of self-respecting, morally conscious individuals and nations; ready, in fact, to be swept away in favor of a simpler and grander view of the powers and tasks of modern man.

To Europeans this American attitude, the large vista possible only for those who live on mountain heights or vast and level plains affording an unbroken view, seems curiously flat, without sublety or color, at times appearing to lack the entire dimension of depth, certainly without that immediate reaction to fine distinctions with which perhaps only those who live in valleys are endowed; and so America, which knows so much, to them seems to understand too little, to miss the central point. This does not, of course, apply to every American or European—there are natural Americans among the natives of Europe and vice versa—but it seems to characterize the most typical representatives of these disparate cultures.

In some respects, Mr. Roosevelt half-consciously understood and did not wholly condemn this attitude on the part of Europeans; and even more clearly Mr. Churchill is in many respects in instinctive sympathy with the American way of life. But by and large, they do represent different outlooks, and the very high degree to which they were able to understand and admire each other's quality is a tribute to the extraordinary power of imagination and delight in the variety of life on the part of both. Each was to the other not merely an ally, the admired leader of a great people, but a symbol of a tradition and a civilization; from the unity of their differences they hoped for a regeneration of the Western world.

Mr. Roosevelt was intrigued by the Russian Sphinx; Mr. Churchill instinctively recoiled from its alien and to him unattractive attributes. Mr. Roosevelt, on the whole, thought that he could cajole Russia and even induce her to be assimilated into the great society that would embrace mankind; Mr. Churchill, on the whole, remained skeptical.

Mr. Roosevelt was imaginative, optimistic, episcopalian, self-confident, cheerful, empirical, fearless, and steeped in the idea of social progress; he believed that with enough energy and spirit anything could be achieved by man; he shrank as much as any English schoolboy from probing underneath the surface, and saw vast affinities between the peoples in the world, out of which a new, freer, and richer order could somehow be built. Mr. Churchill was imaginative and steeped in history, more serious, more intent, more concentrated, more preoccupied, and felt very deeply the eternal differences that could make such a structure difficult of attainment. He believed in institutions and the permanent characters of races and classes and types of individuals. His government was organized on clear principles; his personal private office was run in a sharply disciplined manner. His habits, though unusual, were regular. He believed in a natural, a social, almost a metaphysical order—a sacred hierarchy, which was neither possible nor desirable to upset.

Mr. Roosevelt believed in flexibility, improvisation, the fruitfulness of using persons and resources in an infinite variety of new and unexpected ways; his bureaucracy was somewhat chaotic, perhaps deliberately so. His own office was not tidily organized, he practiced a highly personal form of government. He maddened the advocates of institutional authority, but it is doubtful whether he could have achieved his ends in any other way.

These dissimilarities of outlook went deep, but both were large enough in scope and both were genuine visions, not narrowed and distorted by personal idiosyncrasies and those disparities of moral standard that so fatally divided Wilson, Lloyd George, and Clemenceau. The president and the prime minister often disagreed; their ideals and their methods were widely different; in some of the memoirs and gossip of Mr. Roosevelt's entourage much has been made of this; but the discussion, at all times, was conducted on a level of which both heads of government were conscious. They may have opposed but they never wished to wound each other;

they may have issued contrary instructions but they never bickered; when they compromised, as they so often did, they did so without a sense of bitterness or defeat, but in response to the demands of history or one another's traditions and personality.

Each appeared to the other in a romantic light high above the battles of allies or subordinates: their meetings and correspondence were occasions to which both consciously rose: they were royal cousins and felt pride in this relationship, tempered by a sharp and sometimes amused, but never ironic, perception of the other's peculiar qualities. The relationship born during the great historical upheaval, somewhat aggrandized by its solemnity, never flagged or degenerated, but retained a combination of formal dignity and exuberant high spirits that can scarcely ever before have bound the heads of states. Each was personally fascinated not so much by the other as by the idea of the other, and infected him by his own peculiar brand of high spirits.

The relationship was made genuine by something more than even the solid community of interest or personal and official respect or admiration—namely, by the peculiar degree to which they liked each other's delight in the oddities and humors of life and their own active part in it. This was a unique personal bond, which Harry Hopkins understood and encouraged to the fullest degree. Mr. Roosevelt's sense of fun was perhaps the lighter, Mr. Churchill's a trifle grimmer. But it was something that they shared with each other and with few, if any, statesmen outside the Anglo-American orbit; their staffs sometimes ignored or misunderstood it, and it gave a most singular quality to their association.

Mr. Roosevelt's public utterances differ by a whole world from the dramatic masterpieces of Mr. Churchill, but they are not incompatible with them in spirit or in substance. Mr. Roosevelt has not left us his own account of his world as he saw it; and perhaps he lived too much from day to day to be temperamentally attracted to the performance of such a task. But both were thoroughly aware of their commanding position in the history of the modern world, and Mr. Churchill's account of his stewardship is written in full consciousness of this responsibility.

It is a great occasion, and he treats it with corresponding solemnity. Like a great actor—perhaps the last of his kind—upon the stage of history, he speaks his memorable lines with a large, unhurried, and stately utterance in a blaze of light, as is appropriate to a man who knows that his work and his person will remain the object of scrutiny and judgment to many generations. His narrative is a great public performance and has the attribute of formal magnificence. The words, the splendid phrases, the sustained quality of feeling, are a unique medium that convey his vision of himself and of his world, and will inevitably, like all that he has said and done, reinforce the famous public image, which is no longer distinguishable from the inner essence and the true nature of the author: of a man larger than life, composed of bigger and simpler elements than ordinary men, a gigantic historical figure during his own lifetime, superhumanly bold, strong, and imaginative, one of the two greatest men of action his nation has produced, an orator of prodigious powers, the savior of his country, a mythical hero who belongs to legend as much as to reality, the largest human being of our time.

B. H. LIDDELL HART

Churchill in War

THE FOUR CHIEF European war leaders in World War II were Hitler, Churchill, Stalin, and Mussolini. As the governmental heads of their respective countries, they had the supreme direction of the armed forces, although only one of them had a military rank and title—Marshal Stalin. What were their qualifications for such supreme direction? How effective was their respective performance in exercising that directing power?

The fog of propaganda still lies so thickly round the figure of Stalin, and his part in the war, that it is impossible to analyze or estimate his military capacity and performance. In the case of Mussolini, it is very difficult to do so not only because he was overshadowed by Hitler but also because he rarely attempted to

---

From "Churchill in War," by B. H. Liddell Hart, *Encounter,* April 1966, pp. 14–21.

impose his views and ideas on his military advisers, or on the military executants, Italian or German. He was always keenly interested in military matters, but obviously conscious of the limitations of his technical knowledge. All that can be said with certainty is that he utterly failed to grasp the practical requirements, in military equipment, of the ambitious military policy on which he had launched the Italian people—and never faced the stern realities of the military situation.

It is only in the cases of Churchill and Hitler that a serious analysis and estimate can be made. In both cases there is now abundant evidence for investigation, even though their performance has long continued to be obscured by the haze of legend and propaganda.

Winston Churchill was a wonderful man, shining out from the gloom of an era of mediocrities in the democracies. He not only compelled admiration by his virtuosity but inspired affection despite his intense egocentricity. At times he revealed a long view, helped by his historical sense, yet was inclined to act on a short view, prompted by his tactical sense as well as blinded by the force of his feelings. Once he went into action, his fighting instinct governed his course, his emotions swamped his calculations, and reason reasserted itself too late. In brief, his dynamism was too strong for his statesmanship—and his strategy. Thus, when he got his hand on the helm in 1939, too late to avert the danger that he had foreseen, events continued to move with the same inevitability of tragedy as in the preceding period, toward further danger that he did not foresee.

Churchill the historian is to be seen at his best in the opening chapter of the first volume of his war memoirs, aptly entitled: "The Follies of the Victors." He there points out clearly how the peace treaty imposed on Germany after World War I paved the way for Hitler and another war. He indicts the economic clauses as both "malignant and silly." Next he vividly tells the story of how Britain's national government, under the joint leadership of Ramsay MacDonald and Stanley Baldwin, tragically failed to grasp the obvious threat created by Hitler's accession to power in 1933, and were fatally dilatory in developing Britain's own rearmament even when they did see the red light. His indictment is delivered with a severity that loses no force through being blended with charity. Yet it is not the whole story. There is no mention, or confession, of the fact that Britain's rearmament was handicapped from the start by the extent to which its foundations had been recklessly impaired at an earlier date.

Churchill himself was war minister and air minister combined from 1918 to 1921, the crucial period for the reconstruction of the forces. The air staff had evolved a plan under which the postwar R.A.F. was to consist of 154 squadrons, of which forty were for home defense. Under Mr. Churchill's aegis this was whittled down to a mere twenty-four squadrons, with only two for home defense, and the plan for state-aided airways covering the empire was also discarded. When he moved to a fresh office in 1921, the *Times* had this comment on the fruits of his regime at the air ministry: "He leaves the body of British flying well-nigh at that last gasp when a military funeral would be all that would be left for it."

In the War Office, too, he sadly disappointed all the progressive younger soldiers who had built their hopes on his vision and activity as foster parent of the tank early in the war. To their dismay, he allowed the older school to refashion the army on "back to 1914 lines"—thus missing the best opportunity of reconstructing it on a modern basis. Then from 1924 to 1929 he was chancellor of the exchequer, and each year the army estimates were pared down, with particular detriment to the development of Britain's diminutive but highly promising tank corps, which then led the world in ideas and design.

In 1927, the first "Experimental Mechanised Force" was formed as a result of years of argument and effort by Fuller* and myself. In the speech on the army estimates that year the project had been announced with a big flourish by the then war minister, Sir Laming Worthington-Evans. Adverse influences in the War Office, however, reduced it to a mere shadow, with the result that Fuller, who had been appointed to command it, resigned in despair. I then came out in the *Daily Telegraph* with a pungent article entitled "Is There a Mechanised Force?" This created a sensation. By writing it, I sacrificed my privileged position with the War Office, of which I had been given the free run. Nevertheless, the effect was a compensation—there were questions in Parliament; the war

* General J. F. C. Fuller, a prominent military critic. [ed.]

minister bluntly told his military advisers that they had made a fool of him; and the force was hastily formed (although the value of having Fuller to direct it had been lost). Shortly after this, Churchill, who was then chancellor of the exchequer, asked me to lunch with him and Worthington-Evans at No. 11, and there I expounded my ideas about the mechanization of the army—which had a good reception, and for a time things looked promising. Churchill had paid a visit to the exercises of the Mechanised Force and seemed much impressed. He went so far as to confront the War Office with something approaching an ultimatum for the abolition of horsed cavalry regiments, or their conversion into a mechanized form. But the forces of tradition rallied from the shock, and he yielded to their objections.

With better justification Churchill recounts his efforts from 1934 onward to spur Britain's laggard rearmament and check Hitler's ominously purposeful steps. On rearmament Churchill was always emphatic, and over Munich defiant, but on other issues he was not so clear in mind or speech about the right course as he appears now. At the time he did not seem to see the ultimate risks of permitting Japan's and Fascist Italy's initial steps in aggression and in flouting the League of Nations, while in the Spanish Civil War his own sympathy with the Francoists tended to blind him to the purpose and dangers of Hitler's and Mussolini's support of that side.

One had expected that he of all people would be quick to realize the strategic danger to us of a Fascist victory promoted and achieved by German and Italian help. Instead, his class instincts obscured his strategic vision, and led him to throw his influence against any effort on the part of Britain and France to check the German-Italian moves in Spain. It was not until April, 1938, after the war had been in progress nearly two years, and the doom of the Republicans was virtually sealed, that he reversed his line of argument and pointed out the dangers to us of a Nazi-made victory for Franco in Spain.

Even in regard to Britain's defense preparations, his influence was less effective than it could have been owing to his traditionalism and the way it confused his vision. He admits that he "accepted too readily when out of office the Admiralty view of the extent to which the submarine had been mastered," and also "did not sufficiently measure the dangers to, or the consequent deterrent upon, British warships from air attacks." Unfortunately, his confident assertions reinforced the Admiralty's obscurantism, and weighted the scales against more progressive views. He definitely aligned himself with the "battleship school," as powerfully represented by Admiral Chatfield (first sea lord, 1933–38), and tended to discount what seemed to me the almost certain threat that air power, as well as the submarine, would bring to our naval supremacy.

I have a clear recollection of his attitude on these questions in various discussions—and that recollection is confirmed by reference to a record of his pronouncements at the time. In January, 1938, he declared that "The air menace against properly armed and protected ships of war will not be of a decisive character." Eight months later he reiterated this opinion, and went on to say: "This, added to the undoubted obsolescence of the submarine as a decisive war weapon, should give a feeling of confidence and security so far as the seas and oceans are concerned, to the Western democracies."

He also discounted, though he does not mention it, the effect of air power on armies. For in 1938 his verdict was: "It may be said with some assurance that the whole course of the war in Spain has seemed to show the limitations rather than the strength of the air weapon. . . . It would seem, therefore, that so far as the fighting troops are concerned, aircraft are an additional complication rather than a decisive weapon." Many observers drew the opposite deduction from analysis of these operations—a deduction that was to be confirmed in the Polish and Western Front campaigns of 1939–40, where the German dive-bombers in combination with tanks proved the decisive factor.

As for tanks, he still thought of them in the slow-motion terms of 1918, so that he failed to understand the new blitzkrieg technique of swift and deep mechanized thrusts to cut the arteries of supply. This he admits in his account of the 1940 campaign, where he says:

> I did not comprehend the violence of the revolution effected since the last war by the incursion of a mass of fast-moving heavy armour. I knew about it, but it had not altered my inward convictions as it should have done.

That frank admission puzzled me, since he had often heard, and also read, the views of Fuller and myself about the potentialities of mechanized warfare. Perhaps the clue was provided in a significant remark made by his close friend and associate Brendan Bracken in explanation of Churchill's perplexingly ambivalent attitude toward tanks: "Bear in mind that Winston always remains the 4th Hussar."

Although he was quick to foresee, and warn his countrymen of, the potential danger from Hitlerite Germany, he showed curiously little interest in the new military technique that gave this danger its penetrative power. During discussions in which I took part, and he was present, in the last few years before the war, he dwelt far more on the quantitative aspect than on the qualitative aspect. This out-of-date outlook led him to cherish, and to foster, illusions about the power of the French army, which he described as "the most perfectly trained and faithful mobile force in Europe." That was the year before the war!

In the autumn of 1937 I was surprised to find that he no longer took the German danger as seriously as he had earlier, and in October he remarked, publicly:

> Three or four years ago I was myself a loud alarmist. . . . In spite of the risks which wait on prophecy, I declare my belief that a major war is not imminent, and I still believe that there is a good chance of no major war taking place in our lifetime.

Significantly, too, he had said in the spring: "I will not pretend that, if I had to choose between Communism and Nazism, I would choose Communism."

Once Austria was violated, however, he saw the danger to Czechoslovakia. Swallowing his distrust of Soviet Russia, he was quick to respond to her government's proposals for a Franco-British-Russian alliance to check Hitler's designs. He did all he could to combat Chamberlain's course of appeasement toward Hitler and cold-shouldering of Stalin.

Churchill was at his best and clearest in that crucial year. His instinct coincided then with the basic facts of the situation.

The following spring, after Hitler's next transgression, Neville Chamberlain abruptly reversed his course and gave the impracticable guarantee to Poland, without even securing Russia's support. Churchill endorsed it, whereas Lloyd George sagely pointed out its folly. Churchill's impulse overrode his judgment. In retrospect, he seems less certain about his choice:

> Here was decision at last, taken at the worst possible moment and on the least satisfactory ground, which must surely lead to the slaughter of tens of millions of people.

Yet at the time he, along with almost all Britain's political leaders except Lloyd George, supported this irrational guarantee in the fond belief that it would check Hitler. Never has there been a more astonishing case of collective self-delusion under the influence of righteous indignation.

The outbreak of war brought Churchill back into the government. His memoirs record his manifold activity toward accelerating military steps both inside and outside his own department. But they are also a self-revelation of his tendency "to miss the wood for the trees" in his absorption with the exciting detail points of the "war game."[1]

His pugnacity was predominant, and the reverse of prescient. From the first month of the war onward, he was agitating for action that meant violating the neutrality of the Scandinavian countries in the imagined aim of gaining an offensive advantage against Germany. This is made clear by his own account and the memoranda he includes, even though he omits some of his more inflammatory utterances at the time, which all too obviously hinted at his intention. To some extent, he saw that this was likely to provoke Hitler to take forestalling action, but he labored under the delusion that "we have more to gain than lose by a German attack upon Norway and Sweden."

Churchill regretfully records that at first the "Foreign Office

1. That tendency was increased through the way he became fascinated by striking phrases, as I had found in my own experience of him.

When the "Munich crisis" arose, and during the year that followed, he asked me to come as military adviser to private meetings of his "Focus," a small group of people who shared his views about the German danger; it included a number of subsequent members of his wartime government. At these meetings he used to call on me to deal with the strategic aspects of the situation. In the discussions that followed it often became apparent, more than in earlier years, that a point did not register in his mind unless it fitted in with his own ideas. Moreover, an apt phrase was all too apt to divert his attention from the thread of the argument while his mind revolved round the phrase.

arguments about neutrality were weighty, and I could not prevail." But his arguments were helped by Russia's invasion of Finland, and the wave of feeling it aroused in England: "I welcomed this new and favourable breeze as a means of achieving the major strategic advantage of cutting off the vital iron-ore supplies of Germany."

He was oblivious of the fatal consequences of pushing Russia and Germany closer together, and embroiling Britain in war with both—at a time when she was perilously weak everywhere, especially on the Western Front. While Hitler talked of "thinking with the blood," the leaders of the democracies unfortunately acted in accord with such emotional thinking.

Only the sudden collapse of Finland saved Britain from being at war with Russia, and thus doubly stretched and strained. Yet Churchill then reverted to the plan of action on the Atlantic coast of Norway, to gain control of that neutral area. But a small German invading force forestalled and upset the plan, capturing the chief ports at the moment when the defenders' attention was absorbed by the British naval advance into Norwegian waters. The British were caught unready to meet this retort, and their own countermoves were badly bungled. Churchill's dream castles had thus tumbled down in succession. Yet the blame fell on Chamberlain, as prime minister, and his enforced resignation opened the way for Churchill to take his place. It was the irony, or fatality, of history that Churchill should have gained his opportunity of supreme power as the result of a fiasco to which he had been the main contributor.

His habit of miscalculation, made all the worse by his misunderstanding of modern mechanized warfare, was soon shown again during the invasion of France—when his call to the armies to abandon the idea of defending water lines and rely instead on "furious assault" not only showed his failure to realize that the French army lacked the modern means of effective counterstroke, but encouraged the Allied forces to forfeit their last chance of stemming the German breakthrough. If they had concentrated every effort on holding the remaining water lines, they might have had a chance—but they forfeited this through trying to concentrate their forces, inadequately mechanized, for a counteroffensive against the German flanks in 1914 style.

In that dark time of disaster, Winston Churchill shone by his fighting spirit. But although full recognition should be given to the example he set, it would be a mistake to equate this, in a historical judgment of events, with its influence on the situation. The British have always been less dependent than other people upon inspiring leadership. Their record embraces relatively few spectacular victories, but they have a unique record in winning "soldiers' battles." The fact of being "up against it" with their backs to the wall has repeatedly proved sufficient to rally them. Thus, in their case, inspiring leadership may be regarded as an additional asset rather than a necessity. It may be a necessity when they are weary, but not when they have had a slap in the face. It was Dunkirk that braced them in June, 1940, more than any individual influence.

Moreover, Churchill's fighting spirit favored activity so profusely as to foster offensive moves inspired by fresh miscalculations. The first was the delusion about the early possibilities of winning the war by a bombing offensive. This brought, in its recoil, a danger out of all proportion to what it was able to inflict—like throwing pebbles against an opponent strong enough to throw boulders in reply. As a strategic policy it amounted to nothing better than slow suicide—from which Britain was saved only by Hitler's obsession with Communist Russia, and decision to strike at her instead of concentrating his resources on building up bomber and submarine forces sufficient to finish off Britain.

Another rash step was the attack on the French fleet at Oran—a step, taken contrary to the judgment of the admirals on the spot, which naturally drove the French in indignation toward collaboration with the Germans.

Churchill's best move in 1940, after the fall of France, was his bold decision to send reinforcements to Africa—even though it meant weakening the scanty defense of the homeland—and to take the offensive there against the Italian forces, numerically much larger but ill-equipped. That decision was justified both in principle and result. It produced a tonic success, and a distraction to the principal opponent, while opening up a new avenue for future development. But in carrying out the strategy of indirect approach and pressure, he impaired the effect by excessive dispersion of effort—by pursuing too many diverse aims, with limited resources.

His generals, who were apt to err on the side of caution, are to that extent justified in their criticism of his direction.

Audacity is a great asset in war. But to be profitable it must be calculated audacity. Bluffing on a weak hand is always perilous, as it provides both a provocation and a temptation to a stronger opponent. For while the defeat of the Italian forces in Africa was incomplete, Churchill tried to open up another fresh avenue in the Balkans. The landing of a British force in Greece naturally precipitated a German invasion of that country. Yet the force was dispatched at a time when it was clearly recognized that Hitler did not intend to move against Greece. The outcome was a second "Dunkirk," together with a reverse in Africa.

As a direct result of this rash move, Britain incurred a serious loss of prestige, and sacrificed a large part of the scanty equipment she then possessed. As an indirect result, she sacrificed the chance of completing her conquest of Libya—owing to the diversion of troops to Greece. By spurring the Germans on to establish themselves on the Greek coast, and the Aegean Islands, she also blocked the way for any subsequent Balkan move on her part when better prepared to undertake it.

Churchill's Greek venture cannot be justified by the retrospective argument that it delayed the invasion of Russia. For the Cabinet, as he himself admits, was not aware at the time that Hitler was planning such a step. Moreover, the postponement was not due to the British effort in Greece, with which Hitler had reckoned, but to his sudden fit of anger over the Yugoslav coup d'état. In any case the weather in Russia ruled out an earlier start there.

The basic situation was far worse than was commonly realized at the time—or has been recognized retrospectively, in the glow of final victory. "Where ignorance is bliss 'tis folly to be wise." On the lines that the war was then running, Britain's destination was a dead end. But reprieve came midway through the year, when Hitler turned against Communist Russia—and away from Britain. That reorientation of his concentration brought a dramatic change of outlook for Britain.

The better prospect, however, was still far from being assured. If the Russian armies were overthrown, or even crippled, Hitler would be able to concentrate on finishing off Britain. Her reprieve began to look short-lived as, month after month, the Russians reeled back under successive heavy blows.

The assurance of Britain's survival came late in the year, and in a different way. President Roosevelt had long been itching to come to the rescue—and to pursue Hitler's destruction in company with Churchill. But although he stepped further and further over the boundary of neutrality, and aided Britain more and more openly, he failed to provoke retaliatory action that would release him from "the restraints of a Congress" under which he "had writhed." Hitler was determined to avoid war with the U.S.A. if he possibly could.

Before the end of 1941, however, Roosevelt achieved his purpose in an indirect way. By comparison with Hitler's Germany, Japan was extremely susceptible to economic pressure. By putting an oil stranglehold on her, he overcame her leaders' reluctance to engage in a fight with the U.S.A. and drove them to strike back. Churchill's account makes the process vividly clear. Once Japan was at war with the U.S.A., Hiltler could not avoid supporting his ally.

The extended war opened with initial disaster in the Pacific for the Anglo-Saxon powers. Strangely enough, neither was prepared materially or mentally to meet the obvious riposte, although they had reckoned on one. The bulk of the U.S. battle fleet was sunk or disabled at Pearl Harbor, in barely an hour, while the *Prince of Wales* and *Repulse* were sunk off the Malay Peninsula three days later, thus clearing the way for the Japanese capture of Malaya and the Dutch East Indies.

These disasters cast a deeper shadow on Churchill's strategy. For his boldness in the Middle East was accompanied by a blindness about the Far East. The chief of the Imperial General Staff, General Sir John Dill, reminded him in May, 1941, that "it has been an accepted principle of our strategy that in the last resort the security of Singapore comes before that of Egypt. Yet the defenses of Singapore are still considerably below standard." Churchill replied: "I do not take that view, nor do I think the alternative is likely to present itself." In August he said: "I feel confident that Japan will lie quiet for a while," and a little later expressed his belief that the dispatch to the Far East of a "K.G.V." battleship "might indeed be a decisive deterrent."

Yet on July 26 he had taken action with Roosevelt to impose economic sanctions, which "meant that Japan was deprived at a stroke of her vital oil supplies." In earlier discussions it had always been axiomatic that such "a stranglehold" was almost bound to cause war, but at this crucial time Mr. Churchill took the risk too lightly. "I confess that in my mind the whole Japanese menace lay in a sinister twilight, compared with our other needs." That is an honest admission. But in view of the very large forces accumulated, and also frittered away, in the Middle East, it is most unconvincing when he adds, "I am sure that nothing we could have spared at this time . . . would have changed the march of fate in Malaya."

The best that can be said about these events is that America's entry into the war insured Britain against complete and final defeat more than anything else could have done. But her power and prestige suffered irreparable damage from them. They entailed the loss of her empire.

Moreover, from that time onward Churchill inevitably counted less than Roosevelt and Stalin in the conduct of the war, because of the much greater weight of resources they wielded. He became "President Roosevelt's lieutenant." But during the earlier period he counted more for good or ill than anyone else in the war—except Hitler.

The principal, and primary, issue for the Western Alliance after America's entry into the war was that of reentry into Europe, for the creation of a "Second Front" to relieve the German pressure on Russia and develop a combined offensive against Germany. This soon became, and has ever since remained, a very controversial matter.

Churchill and the British chiefs of staff were right in resisting the American desire, and the Russian clamor, for launching a cross-Channel attack in 1942. It would almost certainly have been a disastrous fiasco. That is very clear in the light of postwar knowledge of the inadequacy of the Anglo-American resources, especially in landing craft, for developing and maintaining an effective reentry in face of the number of German divisions posted in France.

Moreover, since it was psychologically important, or even essential, for the Western Allies to take some striking action that year, there was no other course so practicable and impressive as a landing in French North Africa, the northwest corner of that continent, to start the process of liberation and of loosening Hitler's grip. It threatened the rear of Rommel's army in northeast Africa and promised to make the whole Axis position there untenable.

Although the move failed to fulfill expectations of an early clearance of Africa, this failure was a blessing in disguise for the prospects of what became the Allies' next move. For the very slowness of Eisenhower's advance in November, 1942, from Algeria into Tunisia had the great compensation of drawing Hitler and Mussolini to rush large reinforcements across the Mediterranean, to hold their Tunisian bridgehead. There, six months later, they were trapped with the sea at their back, and the resulting "bag" of the whole German-Italian army in Africa cleared the way for the Allied reentry into southern Europe—which might otherwise have been easily blocked.

On the other hand, the unexpected and increasing delay in clearing the enemy out of Africa led, by degrees, to the deferment and eventually to the abandonment of a cross-Channel attack in 1943—on which the American chiefs of staff, headed by General Marshall, had set their minds and hearts. Whether such a landing in Normandy could have succeeded that year is doubtful. Montgomery, however, was among those who on this issue shared the Americans' preference for it, instead of a reentry into Europe from the south. In the light of what we know now about the narrowness of the margin by which the Normandy landing succeeded in 1944, despite the greatly superior resources then available, it seems likely that a cross-Channel attack in 1943 would have proved premature. But the balance of evidence is not definite enough to rule out the possibility of its success.

The landing in French North Africa, "Operation Torch," was mainly due to Churchill and his persuasive influence on President Roosevelt. When it had been mooted in June, 1942, the British chiefs of staff, headed by General Alan Brooke, had agreed with the Americans in regarding it as impracticable. On the evidence of Alan Brooke's own diaries he only came round to accept it in July. From then on his dominant aim was, after clearing North Africa, to concentrate the Allied effort of 1943 on the invasion of

Italy and "eliminate" her from the war. His diary entries for November 30 and December 3 have sharp complaints that Churchill's mind was "again swinging back towards a Western Front during 1943." The reason was that, besides American pressure, he and the Foreign Office feared that Stalin otherwise might make a compromise peace.

Brooke's next battle was with the American chiefs of staff. His diary for December 11 deplores that Marshall

> considers we should close down operations in the Mediterranean once we have pushed the Germans out, and then concentrate on preparing for re-entry into France. . . . I think he is wrong and the Mediterranean gives us far better facilities for wearing down German forces, both land and air, and of withdrawing strength from Russia.

The argument was renewed at the Casablanca Conference in January, 1943. Ironically, it was the failure of Brooke's Mediterranean view and the continued slow progress there that settled the matter. Not until May, 1943, was the conquest of Tunisia completed. Meanwhile, Brooke had gained his way about making Sicily the next objective. But it was almost mid-July before the landing in Sicily took place, and mid-August before the island was cleared. The further delays that had occurred, coupled with the closeness of Sicily to the mainland, helped to determine that the Allies' next step should be into Italy, as Brooke desired. It was the logic of events resulting from loss of time, more than logic of argument, that swung the Allied strategy into his channel instead of the more direct line of the English Channel.

The success of the Allied invasion of Sicily led to the overthrow of Mussolini, and its promised extension to the mainland produced Italy's capitulation. These results initially vindicated Brooke's line of strategy, although they entailed a postponement of the cross-Channel attack until 1944.

But the Germans were quicker in reacting to the emergency than were the Allies in exploiting the opportunity. The Allied advance up the mountainous Italian peninsula became sticky and slow. For the German forces, under Kesselring, speedily recovered from the shock of their Italian ally's change of sides, disarmed the Italian forces, and skilfully used the natural obstacles of the peninsula to impose repeated and prolonged checks on the Allied advance.

The claims that have been made for the value of the Italian campaign as an aid to the cross-Channel attack do not stand analysis. For the distracting effect caused by the Allies' amphibious flexibility diminished when the ubiquitous threat was translated into an actual landing. By June, 1944, they were employing in Italy a strength in troops double that of Kesselring. That was not a good investment proportionately, and justified the American argument for breaking off the offensive there after the strategic airfields in the south were gained. Moreover, its continuance did not draw German reserves away from Normandy, nor prevent them reinforcing Normandy, as the British hoped—and have claimed.

The only claim that can be made for the strategic effect of the Italian campaign, as an aid to the success of the Normandy landing, is that without its pressure the German strength on the Channel front might have been increased even more. The scale of the assault and the immediate follow-up forces there were limited by the number of landing craft available, so that the Allied forces employed in Italy could not have added to the weight of the Normandy landing during its crucial opening phase.

On the evidence of Brooke's diaries, both he and Churchill were halfhearted, as the American leaders suspected, about launching a cross-Channel attack into Normandy—and continued to seek ways of evading this commitment. As late as October, 1943, he records the receipt of a note from Churchill "wishing to swing the strategy back to the Mediterranean at the expense of the Channel" —and remarks: "I am in many ways entirely with him." The following week he records that Churchill argued the case for the Mediterranean "as opposed to" the cross-Channel attack, and himself terms the latter "very problematical."

The British strategic plan, however, received a bad knock at the Teheran Conference at the end of November, through Stalin's reinforcement of the American arguments against it. That was ominous, and ironic. For the Americans (according to Harry Hopkins's diary) had expected the Russians to team up with the British at Teheran in favor of a Balkan rather than a Normandy operation in 1944—an expectation which showed their blindness to the long-range political aims of Stalin's strategy. He naturally wished to see the British effort kept well away from Eastern Europe, and turned from Italy toward France.

So Churchill and Alan Brooke were pushed into a definite commitment, which neither of them liked. Indeed, almost on the eve of the Normandy landing, Brooke wrote in his diary that he was "torn to shreds with doubts and misgivings. . . . The cross-Channel operation is just eating into my heart"—and feared that it would prove "the most ghastly disaster of the war." Even after victory in Normandy was complete, he continued, at successive stages of the advance into Germany, to express pessimistic doubts about the prospect of early victory in that quarter.

But from the time the Normandy landing was achieved he ceased, and Churchill too, to have any important influence on the course of the war—or on its sequel. Both strategically and politically, American influence became overwhelmingly predominant, and dictated the Allies' course. Indeed, when the British prime minister began to see the ominous consequences of the "unconditional surrender" policy, which he had so lightly adopted in company with Roosevelt, he was powerless to modify it. He had in effect become, as he earlier proclaimed himself, merely the American president's "lieutenant."

In the British sphere Churchill had continued to be the great animator of the war. The collection of minutes, which fill the appendices of his volumes, provide the best opportunity of seeing the genius of the man displayed in all its abundance. No one can read them without marveling at his fertility, versatility, and vitality. He was constantly spurring or coaxing ministers, officials, and generals to greater activity and quicker progress. The characteristic use in his minutes of "Pray"—do this or that—was like a jockey showing the whip to a laggard racehorse. Daily his minutes streamed out in all directions, urging that obstacles should be overcome, that red tape should be cut, that excuses should not be accepted, that objections should be searchingly questioned, that obstruction should be brought to book.

Yet his account leaves the analytical reader with the impression that his actual influence was much less than is commonly supposed. It is astonishing to find how often he failed to get his views accepted by the chiefs of staff, even when his views were most clearly right. His account also reveals a hesitation to insist on what he considered right, and a deference to officialdom, that run contrary to the popular picture of his dominating personality. How is it to be explained? Was it due to the carryover effect of spending two years in the wilderness during World War I as a penalty for putting himself in opposition to the weight of official opinion?

Although he had himself been slow to recognize some of the decisive new trends of warfare—with unfortunate effect on the earlier course of the war—his minutes from 1940 on show him as being usually in advance of his official military advisers and executants. Indeed, both in his minutes and in his later comments he has some caustic reflections on their defective vision and time sense.

It may seem strange that he did not push them along faster, or replace them by more forward-thinking men. He himself remarks in one place:

> The reader must not forget that I never wielded autocratic powers, and always had to move with and focus political and professional opinions.

That view of his own limited powers hardly corresponds to reality, as created by his prestige and ascendancy since 1940, but it may represent the continued impress on his own mind of what he had suffered in the previous war for overriding professional opinion. If his bitter experience then had left him apprehensive, the effect was unfortunate in making him feel that he must take as a "governor" the average pace of professional opinion—for that has always been a slow march.

The point is emphasized by a minute he wrote, after the Germans' airborne coup in Crete, regretting that the previous year a proposal for creating parachute troops had been whittled down from 5,000 men to a mere 500:

> This is a sad story, and I feel myself greatly to blame for allowing myself to be overborne by the resistances which were offered.

The same happened with tanks. He bitingly remarks: "We ought to try sometimes to look ahead." At the end he says:

I print these details to show how difficult it is to get things done even with much power, realised need, and willing helpers.

But they tend to show that, owing to some inhibition, he did not truly use his power to obtain helpers who realized what was needed and were really willing. At no time in the war did Churchill insist that any of the experts in mobile armored warfare should be given a chance in high command or in the higher direction of the army. The absence of such knowledge accounted for many "grievous errors."

On the evidence of the records he prints, it would seem that he was not much helped by the guidance received from his official advisers. They repeatedly misjudged impending developments in many directions that were apparent to, and forecast by, outside observers who had no such elaborate machinery of intelligence. The evidence shakes confidence in the collective foresight of the combined staff organs in Whitehall.

A greater blindness was that which prevailed in the grand strategy of the war. Through it, the Western democracies have been in fresh and greater peril ever since the war ended. It was due to a too intense concentration on the short-term object, and failure to take a long view. As epitomized by Churchill himself, the aim was "the defeat, ruin, and slaughter of Hitler, to the exclusion of all other purposes." The "unconditional surrender" formula naturally tended to rally the German people behind Hitler, thereby prolonging their resistance—and the war. Churchill, as well as Roosevelt, seems to have been blind to the obvious fact that the complete destruction of Germany's and Japan's power of *defense* was bound to give Soviet Russia the chance to dominate Europe and Asia.

There is much significance in Lord Esher's* 1917 verdict on Churchill:

> He handles great subjects in rhythmical language, and becomes quickly enslaved by his own phrases. He deceives himself into the belief that he takes broad views, when his mind is fixed upon one comparatively small aspect of the question.

* A behind-the-scenes figure, particularly concerned with imperial defense. [ed.]

Churchill always had a deep-rooted tendency when concentrating on one problem to forget the other problems that were bound up with its solution. He lacked the power of relating one part to another, and the parts to the whole. A man may be successful as a tactician without that capacity for "comparison," and the sense of proportion from which it springs—but he will be almost certain to go astray as a strategist and still more as a grand strategist.

JOHN COLVILLE

Churchill as Prime Minister

IN MAY, 1940, the mere thought of Churchill as prime minister sent a cold chill down the spines of the staff at 10 Downing Street, where I was working as assistant private secretary to Mr. Neville Chamberlain. Churchill's impetuosity had, we thought, contributed to the Norwegian fiasco,* and General Ismay had told us in despairing tones of the confusion caused by his enthusiastic eruptions into the peaceful and orderly deliberations of the Military Co-ordination Committee and the chiefs of staff. His verbosity and

From *Action This Day,* edited by Sir John Wheeler-Bennett. London and Basingstoke: Macmillan and Company Ltd., 1968, pp. 47–138.

* The unsuccessful English campaign against the Germans in Norway, which had helped bring Chamberlain down. [ed.]

restlessness made unnecessary work, prevented real planning, and caused friction. Indeed, we felt that Chamberlain had been weak in allowing the first lord of the Admiralty to assume responsibilities far in excess of his departmental concerns, and if we had known he was conducting his own telegraphic correspondence with President Roosevelt, we should have been still more horrified by such presumption. Our feelings at 10 Downing Street were widely shared in the Cabinet offices, the Treasury, and throughout Whitehall.

The tenth of May dawned. The Germans were sweeping into Holland and Belgium and, in spite of Churchill's robust speech in Chamberlain's defense, there was no doubt whatever that the prime minister had lost the confidence of the House of Commons. We at No. 10 had hoped so much that the king would send for Halifax; but the lot had fallen on Churchill, and we viewed with distaste the arrival of his myrmidons. . . . The country had fallen into the hands of an adventurer, brilliant no doubt, and an inspiring orator, but a man whose friends and supporters were unfit to be trusted with the conduct of affairs in a state of supreme emergency. Seldom can a prime minister have taken office with "the Establishment," as it would now be called, so dubious of the choice and so prepared to find its doubts justified.

Within a fortnight all was changed. I doubt if there has ever been such a rapid transformation of opinion in Whitehall and of the tempo at which business was conducted. The new prime minister was still living at Admiralty House. There, after dinner, ministers, military chiefs, and officials would begin to assemble, using the drawing room with its dolphin furniture ("the fish room," as Churchill called it) as a promenade, while the new prime minister popped in and out, first through one door and then through another, appointing undersecretaries with Margesson,* discussing the German thrust at Sedan with the secretary of state for war, Anthony Eden, listening to the alarmist views expressed by the American ambassador, Joseph Kennedy, and soothing the antagonism already sprouting between Lord Beaverbrook and Sir Archibald Sinclair.† There was sometimes a touch of farce about

* The Conservative chief whip. [ed.]

† Beaverbrook was minister of aircraft production, and Sinclair the secretary for air. [ed.]

the performance, but the underlying realities in those May days were far from comic, nor was there the slightest buffoonery about the orders that proceeded from Admiralty House.

Churchill's own energy was ceaseless and dramatic, and his ideas flowed out to the chiefs of staff or the ministries in the form of questions and minutes, to which more often than not in those early weeks he attached his bright red label "ACTION THIS DAY." Most of the matters were of major importance relating to the battle that was raging or to aircraft production, but he always found time for the trivialities, too. Could trophies taken in the First World War be reconditioned for use? Could wax be supplied for troops to put in their ears and deaden the noise of warfare? What was to be done with the animals in the zoo in the event of bombardment? Nobody complained that he neglected the vital for the insignificant, but there were those who lamented his preoccupation with detail in matters great as well as small.

The effect of Churchill's zeal was felt immediately in Whitehall. Government departments, which under Neville Chamberlain had continued to work at much the same speed as in peacetime, awoke to the realities of war. A sense of urgency was created in the course of a very few days, and respectable civil servants were actually to be seen running along the corridors. No delays were condoned; telephone switchboards quadrupled their efficiency; the chiefs of staff and the Joint Planning Staff were in almost constant session; regular office hours ceased to exist, and weekends disappeared with them. At 10 Downing Street itself there was no respite at all. Churchill had his hour's sleep in the afternoon, whatever the situation might be, and this enabled him to work until two, three, or four o'clock in the morning and to start again on the papers in his box at eight A.M. the following day.

He had assumed the responsibility of minister of defense as well as prime minister, convinced that in war the two offices were inseparable. This double burden would have been too heavy, even for Churchill, had it not been for the almost infallible efficiency of the Cabinet offices, with their closely interconnected civilian and military sections under Sir Edward Bridges and General Sir Hastings Ismay. This tireless organization processed much of the material that emerged daily from 10 Downing Street for the civil departments and the chiefs of staff. They made themselves responsible for ensuring that all decisions were followed up and that no inquiries were left unanswered. They soothed the exasperated, and they prodded the indolent.

Churchill himself was no administrator. When he had some major problem to resolve, he turned the searchlight of his mind on it, neglecting all else in the fervor of his concentration. In December, 1940, I commented to David Margesson on the high quality of a long and subtle letter to President Roosevelt to which Churchill had devoted hours of preparation, and Margesson replied wearily that he only wished the prime minister were as great an administrator as he was a leader, orator, and writer. Again, in December, 1944, when Greece preoccupied Churchill to the exclusion of almost everything else, Sir Alexander Cadogan,* who admired and respected the prime minister as much as any man, told me Churchill was making a deplorable impression in the Cabinet because he would not read his Cabinet papers and dwelt endlessly on Greek affairs. Similarly, in April, 1945, the fate of Poland, and the unsatisfactory discussions in Washington between Eden, Stettinius, and Molotov, so obsessed Churchill that he would do no other work but talked repetitively in and out of Cabinet on these matters alone. It was on occasions such as these that the influence and diplomacy of Bridges and Ismay enabled the machine to maintain its well-oiled running capacity, and Churchill often spoke of the debt owed to Ismay for the absence in the Second World War of that friction between the Cabinet and the military leaders which had so bedeviled the administration of Lloyd George.

It would, however, be wrong to deny Churchill most of the credit for the smoothness of relations within the government, the armed forces, and Whitehall. There were grounds for complaint. The constant flow of minutes and directives often gave rise to irritation . . . The telephone inquiries to the service departments and to fighter and bomber commands were frequently harassing. One night at Chequers I was instructed, as usual, to ring up the duty captain at the Admiralty and find out if there was any news. There was none, and the duty captain promised to telephone immediately if anything of the slightest interest was reported. An hour later I was instructed to inquire again, and an injured duty captain reminded me of the promise he had given. When, at about 2 A.M.,

* Of the Foreign Office. [ed.]

I was bidden in spite of all remonstrances to try yet again, the angry officer, aroused from a few hours' sleep, let fly at me the full vocabulary of the quarterdeck in times of crisis. Churchill, hearing a flow of speech, assumed that at least an enemy cruiser had been sunk. He seized the receiver from my hand and was subjected to a series of uncomplimentary expletives, which clearly fascinated him. After listening for a minute or two, he explained with great humility that he was only the prime minister and that he had been wondering whether there was any naval news.

The exasperation, the occasional prime ministerial insistence on details that the chiefs of staff thought immaterial, the fear that many felt of Churchill (and this applied in particular to the spokesmen for the service departments); all these were outweighed by the realization of his forcefulness and competence and by the inspiration that he gave both in public and to those with whom he came into personal contact. His charm, his energy, the simplicity of his purpose, his unfailing sense of fun and his complete absence of personal vanity—so rare in successful men—were the secret weapons that outmatched any that Hitler could produce. There was another facet of his character, which gradually dawned on those who worked with him and ensured their lasting affection: he pretended to a ruthlessness that was entirely foreign to his nature, and while the thunder and lightning could be terrifying, they could not disguise the humanity and the sympathy for those in distress, which were the solid basis of his character. I never knew him to be spiteful. He once said to me, with reference to a disgraceful act which was alleged in Whitehall: "If there is one thing I abhor it is a manhunt."

If he pretended to be ruthless and this disguise was easily pierced, it was because, while Churchill could play a part, he was not an accomplished actor. He behaved in public just as he behaved in private. There were no two faces, no mask that would drop when the audience had retired. The sentiments he expressed abroad were familiar to those at home. His decisions were often unpredictable, because his mind did not operate in predetermined grooves, but a sudden whim or unexpected judgment caught his family or staff unawares no less frequently than the Cabinet or the Defence Committee. This is not to deny that he was steeped in the wiles of politics and that he might embroider his theme with a judiciously, perhaps intuitively, blended mixture of guile and persuasiveness that few could resist. A colleague, an opponent, a foreign statesman might be subjected to the full treatment; but so might humbler people whose captivation was less apparently essential.

However, if Churchill was not in the mood, he found it difficult to put on an act of affability even when circumstances positively demanded it; and insofar as he had good manners (which many would have denied) they came from fundamental kindness of heart. They were in no way cultivated, and it was unnatural for him to display a sentiment he did not genuinely feel. Thus, if he was bored by people, he showed it, not because he desired to hurt anybody's feelings but because he was too honest to dissimulate, and *les petits soins* consumed time and effort that could be more profitably employed. He drew a conscious distinction between those with whom it was agreeable to have dinner and those who for one good reason or another were part of the scene. Once his affection was given, it lasted; but his animosity was transitory, and it was not in his nature to bear a grudge.

His sympathy for people in distress was immediate, whatever he might have felt about them in the past. He blamed Baldwin for much of his country's ills, for pushing out the men of vision like F. E. Smith* and for his own long exclusion from office; but when he heard that angry crowds had thrown stones at Baldwin's car, Churchill's instantaneous reaction was to invite him to luncheon at No. 10 and spare two hours of a busy day in an endeavor to cheer him up. Several years later he said to me that, in passing judgment on Baldwin's stewardship, it was only fair to remember that "the climate of public opinion on people is overwhelming."

His verdicts on Neville Chamberlain were sometimes harsh, but once the supreme power was his, he showed the utmost consideration both for the feelings and the opinions of one who, until yesterday his chief, was now merely lord president in the new coalition government. Within three months Chamberlain was stricken with cancer; but scarcely a day passed, even at the height of the Battle of Britain, without dispatch riders taking papers and messages to his bedside at Heckfield, and, on August 15, 1940, Churchill's first thought when he returned to No. 10 from witnessing a great air battle at Fighter Command Headquarters was to tell me to tele-

* A prominent Tory politician of great dash, later Lord Birkenhead. [ed.]

phone to Chamberlain and give him the good news. I remember how overwhelmed he was that Churchill should remember him at such a time. When he died that November, Churchill paid his tribute at Church House, where the House of Commons was sitting, in a speech full of emotion and of poetry, a speech in which no insincere compliments were paid and no false credit given, but which brought lumps to the throats of the hostile no less than to those of his friends. Poor Chamberlain; indeed he "had his friends," but not all of them had stood by him so staunchly as Churchill, the man whom he had hesitated to invite as a colleague and of whom he had had deep suspicions almost to the last.

It has been said that Churchill had no interest in the common man and knew nothing of people's lives, hopes, and aspirations. This is a half-truth. It is a fact that when Churchill was preoccupied he concentrated on the matter in hand to the exclusion of all else, and the feelings or the convenience of others were of no account. . . . All his staff suffered from his lack of consideration, which could, at least in those days, be explained and excused by his urgent preoccupation with matters of far greater importance than his secretaries' need for sleep. Throughout the war years plans were changed with no thought for others, and meetings were arranged, canceled, and rearranged to suit nobody's convenience but his own. Cabinet meetings would drag on interminably, and often unnecessarily, so that in days of wartime austerity ministers and officials would find that lunch was "off" when at long famished last they reached their club or restaurant or canteen, while the prime minister had merely to take the lift upstairs to luncheon.

There was a reverse side to this coin, and a gleaming one. He was lavish with his hospitality, and there was no streak of meanness apparent. If something good came his way, he wished to share it with all at hand. He had a natural disinclination to hurt feelings, and his sympathy for those in disgrace (provided they had done nothing unpatriotic or dishonorable) was as immediate as for those in distress. The high moral tone of disapproval was something he could not abide.

He was by no means indifferent to the well-being of the people as a whole, and I quote, at random, a few examples of his consideration for the welfare of the community which I noted from time to time. On August 28, 1940, Churchill returned from Dover much affected by the bomb damage to small houses. He was determined that their owners should receive compensation (this was before the war damage measures had been contemplated) and made a note to browbeat the chancellor of the exchequer on the subject the next day. When the bombing of London began, he demanded full reports on the state of the air raid shelters and insisted on obtaining complete information as to who was responsible for what. On October 17, dissatisfied with certain rumors that had come to his ears, he held a "shelter meeting" at Downing Street and vigorously pursued inquiries into the provision of oil stoves for heating and of adequate cooking facilities. Throughout the war it was his constant desire to make people cheerful and do battle with those who seemed to favor austerity for austerity's sake. The people's diet and their entertainment were high on his list of priorities, and he took an unfailing interest in the wrongs of individuals about which he read in the press. Many a government official found himself obliged to satisfy an irate prime minister on some incident of which the only source of information to either of them was a paragraph in the *Daily Express* or the *Daily Mirror*.

In February, 1941, Leslie Burgin* complained to Churchill that the government was indifferent to certain cases of suffering. Churchill, who was largely in agreement, replied: "When one is in office one has no idea how damnable things can feel to the ordinary rank and file of the public."

On his return to office in 1951, with no war to conduct, Churchill's declared policy was to restore freedom where there was still restraint and to sweep away as quickly as possible the relics of rationing and Crippsian† austerity. The Tory program, he told me, should be "Houses and meat and not being scuppered—though perhaps not being broke is going to be the principal preoccupation." The new government was indeed heir to a grave economic crisis, and priority had to be given to surmounting it. In March, 1952, when the first budget was in course of preparation, Churchill, deeply disturbed by the effect its measures would have on old-age pensioners and widows, demanded that correctives should be found. Sentiment perhaps; because he had no experience of the hardships

* The minister of supply, a Liberal. [ed.]

† A reference to the budgets of Sir Stafford Cripps, Labour's Chancellor of the Exchequer. [ed.]

an old-age pensioner might feel; but in this case his attitude was certainly not dictated by political expediency. Early in 1953 he insisted, despite gloomy warnings from the Ministry of Food, that sugar should be derationed before the Coronation. Sentiment perhaps again; but he was determined that the queen should be crowned amidst uninhibited rejoicing and that the hundreds of thousands of foreign visitors should not come to a country still, eight years after victory, in the grip of food rationing. The Ministry of Food was, in this event, totally confounded: an ample supply of sugar proved to be available and not long afterward there was a glut.

If ever there was a Cavalier it was Churchill: let the people be merry, let there be brass bands, let the church bells ring; and if some of his colleagues were Roundheads, who took a more austere view of their responsibilities, they should nevertheless be thwarted clandestinely to whatever extent might be practicable.

It is true that Churchill had little idea how people actually lived. On the other hand, he had no Curzonian* sense of superiority, and he was anything but a snob. He merely liked his own way of life and assumed that while the reasonably well-to-do all lived as he did, the deserving poor must be cherished and enriched even though in due course this exercise would involve a leveling out, which, fortunately, he would not live to see consummated. When, at the end of 1941, I persuaded him to let me go away and become a pilot in the RAF, he approved my intention. "The RAF," he said, "is the cavalry of modern war." But he was horrified when I told him I was going off to South Africa to train, starting in the ranks as an aircraftman, 2nd class. "You mustn't," he said, "you won't be able to take your man." It had not crossed his mind that one of his junior private secretaries, earning £350 per annum, might not have his own valet.

Chivalry to the defeated ranked with honor to the brave among the sentiments he particularly cherished. When Lord Dowding† said that his men were expected to shoot at enemy pilots descending by parachute over enemy territory, Churchill expressed horror

* A reference to Marquess of Curzon, an important Tory politician until his death in 1925, and famous for his snobbery. [ed.]

† Air Marshal Dowding was in charge of Fighter Command and its defense of London until November, 1940. [ed.]

and said that an escaping pilot should be treated in all respects like a drowning sailor. In January, 1941, he was deeply worried by the fate that might be in store for Italian civilians in Abyssinia when "those savage warriors who have been burned with poison gas get among them"; and in the same month he said to me that he hated nobody and did not feel he had any enemies "except the Huns, and that is professional."

Churchill attached paramount importance to personal contacts in politics and especially in foreign affairs. The success with which, from the days when he was first lord, he established a close relationship with Roosevelt convinced him of the value of personal diplomacy. When we sailed for New York on January 1, 1952, he told me that he was going to Washington not to transact business but to reestablish relations. The briefs that had been so laboriously provided interested him far less than the impression he might succeed in making on Truman, Acheson, and the American chiefs of staff. It would, however, be wrong to assume that Churchill's friendships were political, even though their inspiration might be so. Since he was naturally affectionate, it was difficult for him not to become fond of people once he had come to know them, and his liking for Roosevelt, as subsequently for Truman and Eisenhower, was entirely sincere. . . .

Churchill could state a case and advocate a cause in a way that compelled attention and often forced the reluctant to agree. His choice of language, the unexpected use of metaphor, the resort to pathos, and the sudden turn to humor combined to sweep opponents from their entrenched positions. Occasionally it failed: he rambled or repeated himself or used arguments that carried no weight with a well-informed audience; but if he really wanted something or was deeply convinced, success was far more frequent than failure.

When he sought to persuade, his charm was irresistible, particularly on some personal matter; and there were many who entered his presence firmly resolved to decline what they knew he was going to ask and left it after giving a meek affirmative. General Ismay, awakened from slumber in October, 1951, by a summons from the new prime minister, rehearsed his negatives the whole way to Hyde Park Gate. He would accept nothing; he had earned his retirement; he was going to spend the rest of his days as a country gentleman. He knew how it would be put—whatever it was—but forewarned was forearmed. Half an hour later, bemused and unbelieving, he trod the early morning pavements as secretary of state for commonwealth relations.

The following day, on leave from the embassy in Lisbon, I was watching the Cambridgeshire at Newmarket. An official from the Jockey Club told me that I was required immediately on the telephone from 10 Downing Street. I told my wife to have no fear: I was not, in any circumstances, going to interrupt my career once again by returning to the prime minister's secretariat. "Would you be so good," said a familiar voice on the telephone, "as to come and see me this evening?—unless of course it is inconvenient." I went, a polite and grateful formula for declining word-perfect in my head; I emerged principal private secretary to the prime minister. Countless others had similar experiences, seldom, if ever, to their ultimate regret.

After dinner, when the brandy had arrived, Churchill's conversation could be sparkling and spontaneous. The power of his argument and a degree of his wit are less striking in print than in speech, because none can aspire to reproduce his manner of speaking (nor, indeed, were even the most accomplished mimics successful in imitating it); and only those who knew him can recall the suddenly engaging smile which preceded an aphorism, the skillful use of climax and anticlimax, and the riveted attention that, at his best, he could command of any audience. His after-dinner conversation was often a monologue, interspersed with comments from those who knew him well enough to risk it; but, in fact, he welcomed interruptions, however contradictory or irreverent, provided they were short, witty, and did not stem the flow or divert the theme. Sometimes, when he was tired, he used his audience as a wastepaper basket, or repeated long stories they had all heard before, but when he did this it was frequently because his thoughts were on something else, and the surface talk was an automatic exercise. I remember on one occasion he saw us yawn and he looked benignly at Commander Thompson, the "flag commander," saying: "You must admit, Tommy, that at least I do not repeat my stories as frequently as our dear friend, the president of the United States."

Often, when conversation flagged or no absorbing topic presented itself, he would declaim poetry at length. It might be Shakespeare, Pope, Swinburne, Macaulay, or his favorite poem, taken from some long-past edition of *Punch,* about the ducks in St. James's Park. The repertory, vast and by no means monotonous, was occasionally interspersed with forgotten songs from the music halls of the nineties. But this was for the family circle, which was taken to include many with no blood relationship, and although almost invariably entertaining, it was the exception rather than the rule. What was memorable, particularly during the war, were the military and political assessments, sharp as steel and flashing in their rapid eloquence, with which he would sometimes hold the table spellbound till the early hours of the morning had struck and the despairing servants had long abandoned any hope of clearing away.

Churchill often rehearsed a phrase or a line of poetry again and again in private conversation until one day it would find its place in a speech in the House of Commons. Sometimes, too, he practiced a speech on the unsuspecting or thought aloud to them a telegram or directive that he contemplated composing. I once spent a bewildering hour with him, lunching in the cottage at Chartwell. It was June 3, 1941. The situation in the Middle East was disturbing. Lord Beaverbrook was being difficult, and an important speech on the war situation was shortly due. The only other guest at lunch was the Marmalade Cat, resident at Chartwell and of all Churchill's cats his favorite. It sat on a chair at his right-hand side, and he addressed it most affectionately throughout the whole of luncheon. He cleaned its eyes, offered it mutton, and expressed deep regret that cream was not available in wartime. All the time, half under his breath, he was composing a speech, arguing with Beaverbrook and chiding Wavell on the size of his rearward services. I was conscious for the first but by no means the last time of his ability to act a part—in this particular case an exceedingly amusing one—while his thoughts were concentrated on serious realities.

The composition of a speech was not a task Churchill was prepared either to skimp or to hurry; nor, except on some convivial occasion, was he willing to speak impromptu. He might improvise briefly, but only to elaborate or clarify, and he stuck closely to the text he had prepared. He was sometimes a great orator, and there was poetry in his speeches as well as magnificent prose. He knew how to move hearts and emotions; he instinctively understood that drama must never cross the line into melodrama. Quick as was his wit and unfailing his gift of repartee, he was not a man to depart in the heat of the moment from the theme or indeed the very words that he had laboriously conceived in set-speech form. To the last he retained a sense of apprehension in addressing the House of Commons or, for that matter, any large assembly. . . .

Churchill's style was difficult to plagiarize. After serving him for many years, I found I could imitate his style but could seldom, if ever, aspire to the choice of words—the apt but unexpected turn of phrase—which was so peculiarly his. Thus, although in his second administration, with age beginning to weigh and zest to flag, there were occasions when he actually used a draft speech prepared for him on some ceremonial or social occasion; [still,] he never, to my knowledge, spoke words that were not his own in a political speech delivered as prime minister. . . .

In political philosophy Churchill was at once a radical and a traditionalist. At heart, he felt little sympathy for the Conservative Party except insofar as it embodied Lord Randolph's conception of "Tory Democracy." Even though the bearing of grudges was unnatural to him, he retained some bitterness toward "the caucus," which, first under Baldwin and then under Chamberlain, had kept him out of office throughout the 1930s; but, while remembering their deafness to his warnings about Germany, he was unwilling to take account of the more justifiable resentment and suspicion that stemmed from his factious opposition to the Government of India Bill and his attitude over the abdication. He never quite forgave the Men of Munich or, Grand Master of the Primrose League though he might be, wholeheartedly identified himself with the Conservative Party. Temperamentally, he remained a radical (just as Attlee was, by temperament, a conservative), although never anything but hostile to socialist theory.

He believed passionately that freedom at home was assured by Parliamentary government. It was vital to sustain the authority of Parliament against the executive and respect for Parliamentary institution in the hearts of the electorate. This was a precious inheritance of the English-speaking peoples, but it was not necessarily one to be imposed on others. He was never a party to the Anglo-Saxon folly of supposing that representative government is the only passport to happiness and respectability. He used to quote the statement that democracy is the worst form of government apart from any other that has ever been tried; but he felt no sacred obligation to prescribe it as the infallible remedy for every country's ills. Indeed, he regarded infallibility of any kind as a totally unacceptable dogma. It was one thing to save the Poles or the Greeks from foreign domination and oppose a system forced on them from outside; it was quite another to lecture the Spaniards, the Portuguese, or the Russians on the form of government they ought to adopt.

Churchill told me, in October, 1940, that he had learned one great lesson from his father: never to be afraid of British democracy. The British alone had managed to combine empire and liberty. He was determined that in days of national crisis the Conservatives should not allow any others to excel them in the sacrifice of party interests and party feeling. Few things needed to be changed quickly and drastically, but he shared Disraeli's belief in the gradual increase of amenities for an ever larger number of people who should enjoy benefits previously reserved for the few. The future depended not on political doctrines but first on every man having sufficient and then on the heart and soul of the individual. On visiting Harrow School in December, 1940, he told the boys that after the war the advantages of the public schools must be extended on a far broader basis, and in August [of] the following year he remarked to Lord Halifax that it was the secondary schoolboys who had saved this country. "They have," he said, "the right to rule it."

Views expressed on impulse or from sentiment can be misleading, and Churchill was not averse to dramatic statements, even in private. I do, however, remember certain considered judgments on policy and events that seem to denote the Whig rather than the Tory, the radical as opposed to the conservative. In January, 1941, he told the foreign secretary that he trusted the time would come in Egypt when the interests of the fellahin would be cherished by the British, even if some of the rich pashas and landowners had to pay taxes comparable to those paid by the wealthy in Britain. The radical sledgehammer was, he said, required in the Delta, where too many fat, insolent class and party interests had grown up under our tolerant protection. In April, 1944, he said to Attlee at Chequers that he recognized the old order was changing and that "the pomp and vanity must go: the old world will have had the honour of leading the way into the new." In the following September he told me that if at the coming general election there were a left-wing majority then "what is good enough for the English people is good enough for me." A few weeks later he said that his own program at home would be free enterprise for the individual, provided no cartels or monopolies were permitted, and the retention of high taxation on the rich until prosperity was assured for all.

In his second administration the flashes of radicalism were less frequent, but the traditionalism—the love of color, gaiety, and pageantry—remained strong. Lady Churchill told me she thought him to be the last believer in the divine right of kings: she felt reasonably sure the king was not. Certainly Churchill had the deepest veneration for the monarchy. Once when I asked him why he had taken the line he did at the time of the abdication, he replied that he could not then or ever consider disloyalty to his sovereign. Combined with respect for the institution, and a strong personal liking for the successive monarchs he served, was his conviction that political stability was founded on constitutional monarchy. "A battle is won," he used to say, "and crowds cheer the King. A battle is lost: the Government falls." He was sure that no better system could be devised. . . .

Churchill had no love for the Foreign Office, one of the very few departments of which he had never been head. He suspected it of pursuing its own policy, irrespective of what the government might wish, and he mistrusted its judgment. One evening, after he had abused the Foreign Office (which was my own department, and for which I felt both loyalty and affection) with unusual vehemence, I reminded him that during the afternoon he had been equally harsh about the Treasury. Which, I asked, did he dislike the most? After a moment's thought, he replied: "The War Office!" . . .

Being first and foremost a man of action, he took no intellectual interest in either political or social theories. In considering a problem, his test was first whether the proposed solution was right and secondly whether it was practicable. It was immaterial whether or not it fitted the tenets of a particular doctrine or philosophy. He was thus uninterested in the distinction between communism and fascism: both were vile because they denied freedom.

In 1940 he demanded the incarceration of leading British fascists, not because they were fascists, but because invasion threatened and we had before us the example of Quisling (a name which he prophesied would become, with a small *q,* a part of the language, like boycott and sandwich). Later he supported Herbert Morrison in the suppression of the *Daily Worker,* not because it was Communist, but because it incited its readers to defeatism and disloyalty. Friendship to Britain was a criterion of supreme importance. After the war he observed with distaste the venom which the left wing spat at Franco and Salazar, whose attitude to Britain was friendly, while they kept silent over the far greater cruelties and oppression exercised by regimes in Bulgaria, Rumania, and Hungary, which were noticeably more hostile to the institutions we had built and the ideals that we cherished.

Strength often marches with simplicity. In the war Churchill's burden was lightened and his task simplified by his refusal to be diverted from the single aim of victory: victory at any price, since the alternative was slavery or extinction. This suited his temperament, because although a brilliant political tactician and more fertile than most men in imagination and ideas, he was fundamentally a straightforward person who eschewed devious paths and struck out for goals that he could see. He had little of Lloyd George's cunning or the well-disguised craftiness of Stanley Baldwin. His decisions might be unpredictable, but his motives were seldom hard to fathom, and in forming his opinion of men he would have thought it an impertinence to probe too far beneath the surface.

In August, 1940, he considered the clamor for a statement of war aims ill-conceived. We had, he said, only one aim: to destroy Hitler. Let those who did not know what we were fighting for stop and see for themselves. France was now discovering why she had been fighting, and we, since we must win in order to survive, could only take the short view. In January, 1941, he made the same point to Harry Hopkins and added that when the war was over we should be content to establish a few basic principles: justice; respect for human rights and for the property of other nations; respect also for private property in general so long as its owners were honest and its scope was moderate. We could find nothing better on which to build than the Sermon on the Mount, and the closer we were able to follow it, the more likely we were to succeed in our endeavors. What more, he asked, had a statement of war aims to offer than this? He reminded Hopkins of Clemenceau's comment on President Wilson's Fourteen Points: *"Même le bon Dieu n'avait que dix."* . . .

As early as 1940, with invasion apparently imminent, I first heard him speak of the future after we had won the war. On December 12, General de Gaulle came to Chequers, as he often did, and during luncheon Churchill said he was inclined to lay stress on the fact that we were fighting the Nazis rather then Germany, even though many people had murderous thoughts toward the whole German race. De Gaulle objected that we had fought the last war against the Hohenzollerns and German militarism. We had crushed them both and then came Hitler—*"et toujours le militarisme allemand."* He thought, therefore, there was something to be said for those who blamed the Germans as a whole.

Later the same day, after de Gaulle had left, Churchill reverted to the subject and spoke at length of his ideas for the future. We had got to admit that Germany should remain in the European family: "Germany existed before the Gestapo." When we had won the war, he visualized five great European nations: Great Britain, France, Italy, Spain, and Prussia. In addition there would be four confederations: the Northern, with its capital at The Hague; the Middle European, with its capital at Warsaw or Prague; the Danubian, including Bavaria, Württemberg, Baden, Austria, and Hungary, with its capital at Vienna; and the Balkan, with Turkey at its head and Constantinople as its capital. These nine powers would meet in a council of Europe, which would have a supreme judiciary and economic council, and each would contribute men to a supranational air cohort. None might have its own air force, but each would be allowed its own militia, since democracy must be secured on a people's army and not left to the mercy of oligarchs or a secret police. Prussia alone would, for a hundred years, be denied all armaments apart from her share in the supranational air cohort.

Britain would be part of Europe, but she would also be part of the English-speaking world, which, as the reward for victory, would alone control the seas, though bound by covenant to respect the commerce and colonial rights of all peoples. Russia would fit into an eastern confederation, and the whole problem of Asia would have to be faced; but as far as Europe was concerned, a system of confederation was necessary to allow the small powers to continue to exist and to avoid balkanization. There must be no war debts, no reparations, and no demands on Prussia. Certain territories might have to be ceded, and exchanges of population would have to take place on the lines of that so successfully achieved by Greece and Turkey after the First World War. But there must be no pariahs, and Prussia, though unarmed, should be secured by the guarantee of the council of Europe. Only the Nazis, the murderers of June 30, 1934, and the Gestapo would be made to suffer for their misdeeds. A year later, on July 9, 1941, he said that after the war there should be an end to all bloodshed, though he must confess he would like to see "Mussolini, that bogus mimic of Ancient Rome, strangled like Vercingetorix." He would segregate Hitler and the Nazi leaders on some island, though he would not desecrate St. Helena.

This sketch of the future was presented at a time when Britain stood alone and most people beyond our shores thought we had little chance of survival. The blitz was at its height; the United States was still doubtful (Harry Hopkins had not yet arrived to make his report to the president); Russia was hostile; what remained of Free Europe seemed to be veering to the Axis; de Gaulle commanded but 5,000 men; Spain and Greece were the only unoccupied European countries disposed to withstand the demands of Hitler; and for us the lights in a dark world consisted solely of Wavell's victorious action at Sidi Barrani,* made possible because Churchill had denuded this island of its surviving armored strength, and "our mastery of the daylight air." As the years went by, hope began to grow, eventual victory became certain, and finally the war was won. It may be illuminating to consider how Churchill's own thoughts developed, toward Germany, Europe, and the English-speaking peoples, as the drama continued to unfold. In the course of time a new problem emerged: the Soviet Union, which in December, 1940, lay quiescent, apprehensive toward its German ally but still hostile and unforthcoming to Hitler's surviving opponent.

Churchill's attitude to Germany underwent little change. Hitler

* Retaken from the Italians in Egypt in December, 1940. [ed.]

and his gang were beyond the pale; the Gestapo was an instrument of evil with scarcely a parallel in history; but anti-German sentiment as such was unwise, ungenerous, and unrealistic. In January, 1941, he told Sir Robert Vansittart that while he thought it might be right to separate the Prussians from the South Germans, we must not let our vision be darkened by hatred or obscured by sentiment. He contemplated a reunited European family in which Germany would have a great and honorable place, even though he admitted we had "rather overdone it" in putting Germany back on her feet after Versailles.

In March the same year he said he was unmoved by bloodthirsty demands for the destruction of Germany. He would never condone atrocities against the German civil poulation. The ancient Greeks, he remembered, once spared a city not because its inhabitants were men but because of the nature of man.

Never at any stage did I hear Churchill express vindictiveness to the Axis powers, or propose anything but chivalrous treatment of them in defeat. But he did believe that bombing Germany would for a long time be our sole method of containing the enemy, since invasion of the Continent, from north or south, could not be undertaken until we had built up vast resources. As early as June, 1940, he saw that the blockade could not be effective and that overwhelming air attack on Germany would be the only powerful weapon available to us. Ten days later he was urging Beaverbrook to still greater miracles of aircraft production with the assertion that an all-out attack on the Nazi homeland was the only road open toward victory. The unthinkable alternative was stalemate, and a negotiated peace would mean "a final spring of the tiger" in a few years' time. The third possibility, our own defeat, did not enter into his calculations. . . .

His feelings toward the Soviet Union went through many vicissitudes between 1941 and 1955. On June 20, 1941, I was walking with him on the croquet lawn at Chequers when he said that he was now sure Hitler would attack Russia. Remembering the part he had played in inspiring the pro-White expedition to Archangel in 1920, and his detestation of Communism, I inquired whether this event might not put him in an awkward predicament. He replied: "If Hitler invaded hell, I would at least make a favorable reference to the devil in the House of Commons."

Two days later the expected attack was launched. I awoke Churchill with the news, and he at once directed his energies to preparing a broadcast that urged all-out support for Russia. He firmly resisted the efforts of the foreign secretary to see the text in case he should seek to tone the speech down. Now, Churchill maintained, we should forget all about the Ribbentrop–Molotov pact and about Communism: the sturdy Russian peasant fighting for his fatherland deserved every bit of help and encouragement we could provide. We must display frankness and generosity to the limit of our productive capacity. What was more, Hitler was about to make the identical mistake Napoleon had made: the German hordes would be swallowed up in the deep snows of Russia; our own hard-pressed front would be relieved; invasion no longer threatened; and, whatever General Dill, or Mr. Winant or anybody else present at Chequers that day might assert, he believed Stalin's armies would fight valiantly, and perhaps in the end victoriously, for the soil of Holy Russia.

This was the first elation. The fact that the military mission that we sent to Russia was received with scant courtesy, and at no stage taken into the confidence of the Soviet command, did something to damp that initial enthusiasm; but Churchill was confident that once he could meet Stalin face to face suspicion and misunderstanding would be dissipated like the mists of morning. . . .

When I left Churchill to join the RAF in October, 1941, he was unchanged in his determination to wipe out past quarrels with the Soviet Union, however vividly the Molotov–Ribbentrop pact of August, 1939, and Russia's naked aggression against first Poland and then Finland still persisted in our memories. I returned to his private office in December, 1943, immediately after the Teheran Conference. He was still louder in his praise of Russian courage than in his criticism of Stalin's surliness, and I believe he thought the Soviet government more sensible than in fact they were of our efforts to supply them through Murmansk and Archangel, at soul-searing loss to our convoys, and of our unreciprocated willingness to keep them informed of our military plans. Churchill was continuing to concentrate on victory rather than ideology. This was exemplified by his decision to switch British support in Yugoslavia from Mihailovich to Tito. He erred in crediting Stalin, and with a lesser degree of error Roosevelt, with the same single-minded motive.

By the spring of 1944, while the Americans still had visions of a newly inspired Soviet Union, free, benevolent and democratic, Churchill already had his doubts. At the end of February Stalin had sent an ungenerous and unhelpful reply to our proposals for a solution of the Polish problem. Churchill brooded unhappily on the fate that he began to realize the Russians were planning for Poland and on March 4 I first heard him use a sentence that became part of his theme song: "I feel like telling the Russians that personally I fight tyranny whatever uniform it wears or slogans it utters." Throughout the spring the British government's efforts to secure even an element of future freedom for Poland were met with hostility or, at the best, silent contempt. But Operation "Overlord" was approaching, and during the summer Churchill's thoughts were concentrated on the Allied campaign in northern France.

In August the Russians were approaching Warsaw. To facilitate their task the exiled Polish government in London called on General Bór Komorowski and the Polish Home Army to rise against the Germans. There then occurred one of the vilest double crosses in history: the Russians halted their advance until the Home Army, fighting in the sewers of Warsaw, had been destroyed and the supporters of the London Poles conveniently exterminated. In spite of Churchill's pleas the Russians refused the RAF permission to use their airfields to fly supplies to General Bór. Churchill discovered that Warsaw could be reached by aircraft flying from American bases in Italy. To his anger and astonishment, Roosevelt refused: we must do nothing to offend our gallant Soviet allies, and to supply the Polish Home Army, fighting against hopeless odds and desperately short of arms, would offend them.

Warsaw held out until September, and this tragic drama convinced Churchill that we now had to face an enduring Russian danger. If they could pause in their march toward Germany in order to achieve a political end and impose a Communist regime on a decidedly non-Communist country, the Western Allies must be on their guard for the future. Early in September the women of Warsaw, in their final agony, appealed to the Pope, and Churchill, stirred by the pathos of their message, drafted a telegram to Roosevelt suggesting Stalin be informed that in default of his allowing us to send assistance to Warsaw the British and American governments would take drastic action in respect of the supplies they were sending to Russia. "This world," he said to me, "is full of wolves—and bears"; and he subsequently told me that it was this treacherous episode that finally revealed to him (though apparently not to President Roosevelt and the State Department) the chasm that divided the Western from the Soviet code of honor. When Churchill returned to power in 1951, one of his first acts was to make inquiries about General Bór Komorowski, who had escaped the final massacre, and to demand assurances that provision had been made for his comfort and well-being.

Churchill accordingly went to Yalta in February, 1945, with his eyes wide open. It was too late to save the Balkans: the Russian armies had arrived. On January 23, before the expedition to the Crimea set forth, he told me that he believed he had managed to save Greece and that Stalin would respect the fact. The remaining states of Eastern Europe would be bolshevized, and there was nothing we could do to save them or, for that matter, Poland.

He returned from Yalta in somber mood. At Chequers in the evening of February 23 we listened to the music of *The Mikado* and Churchill said that it brought back his youth and the Victorian era, "eighty years which will rank in our island history with the age of the Antonines." Now, however, the shadows of victory were upon us. In 1940 the issue was clear and he could see distinctly what was to be done; but when Sir Arthur Harris* (who was present) had finished his destruction of Germany, "What will lie between the white snows of Russia and the white cliffs of Dover?" Perhaps, however, the Russians would not want to sweep on to the Atlantic; or something might stop them as the accident of Genghis Khan's death had stopped the horsed archers of the Mongols. Be that as it might, there was an unspoken fear in many people's hearts. After this war we should be weak; we should have no money, and our strength would have been drained away. We should lie between the two great powers of the U.S.A. and the U.S.S.R. If he lived, he would concentrate on one thing—the air.

* The commander in chief of bomber command. [ed.]

Harris interjected that it would have to be rockets since "the bomber is a passing phase and, like the battleship, it has nearly passed." . . .

Nothing the Americans did—the futile landing in the south of France, Warsaw, Yalta, or Churchill's deep distress at Eisenhower's failure to take Berlin and Prague when they lay within his grasp—for one moment damped his faith in the essential virtue of the United States. Ancestral feeling and a genuine love of America marched with policy both during and after the war. Unlike most Englishmen, he knew the history of the United States, and American poems were well represented in his repertory. "The Great Republic" was always in his thoughts, and, from the moment he became prime minister in 1940, he was convinced that America would and must come into the war. His confidence in victory, even in the darkest days, was at least partly based on his certainty that Roosevelt would not desert us.

There were periods of exasperation, and the deliberate leakage of his most secret messages to the Washington columnist, Drew Pearson, was enough to try anybody's temper. There were times when he found the State Department, the U.S. chiefs of staff, and the president himself almost unbearably obtuse and impervious to argument. Very occasionally his faith in American altruism was shaken, as when in November, 1944, he learned from an ashamed Ambassador Winant that the U.S. government was threatening to change its attitude on lease-lend unless it was guaranteed certain civil aviation advantages; and when in April, 1945, the Americans demanded that we should consult the Soviet government before sending any more arms to the Greeks, Churchill wrote: "This is the usual way in which the State Department, without taking the least responsibility for the outcome, makes comments of an entirely unhelpful character in a spirit of complete detachment."

All this was as nothing to the admiration and gratitude that were predominant in his thought. The future was America's, but Britain had an important part to play. In February, 1945, Churchill said to President Benes of Czechoslovakia that a small lion was walking between a huge Russian bear and a great American elephant, but that perhaps it would turn out to be the lion that knew the way. I believe Churchill hoped that one day the close understanding of the English-speaking peoples, which was always the consideration of primary importance for him, would develop into something yet more significant. Some years after the war he gave me a lecture on protoplasm. It was, he said, sexless. Then it divided into two sexes, which in due course united again in a different form to their common benefit and gratification. This should also be the story of England and America. Whether this particular venture into science originated, as was normally the case, with something Lord Cherwell had explained to him, I do not know; but certainly in 1952 Cherwell told me, quoting Churchill, that if Roosevelt had lived and Churchill had been returned to office in 1945 the United States and the United Kingdom would have progressed far along the road to common citizenship. It was, at the last, something he achieved uniquely for himself: I think he would have chosen it for all his countrymen.

How did this unwavering faith in the unity of the English-speaking peoples synchronize with his hopes of a United Europe? He never for one moment during or after the war contemplated Britain submerging her sovereignty in that of a United States of Europe or losing her national identity. He wanted to see Europe one family and during the war he reverted again and again to the subject; but, in his vision of the future, Britain was only linked to Europe. Her true destiny was the moral leadership of the English-speaking peoples to which she had a historic right endorsed by her single-handed championship of freedom. He spoke to me in 1940 of the European Federation that was to come, "with their Diets of Worms," and shuddered at the prospect of the intricate economic and currency problems. In January, 1941, at Ditchley, he went so far as to say that there must be a United States of Europe and that he believed it should be built by the English: if the Russians built it there would be communism and squalor: if the Germans built it there would be tyranny and brute force. On the other hand, I know he felt that while Britain might be the builder and Britain might live in the house, she would always preserve her liberty of choice and would be the natural, undisputed link with the Americas and the commonwealth.

Years passed, and Churchill, by then leader of the Opposition, agreed to sponsor the European movement. In this he was encouraged and to a considerable extent carried along by his son-in-law, Duncan Sandys. He was, I am sure, in search of a striking policy and there were few that offered themselves. He followed consistently the line he had taken in the war, but his thoughts were closer to those of de Gaulle than of Spaak, Monnet, and Schuman. When, once again prime minister, it fell to him to encourage the formation of the European Defense Community, his main preoccupations were Western Defense, the fear that America, sickened by French prevarication, might resort to a threatened form of withdrawal known as "Perimeter Defense," and a by no means contradictory desire to initiate top-level discussions with the Soviet Union.

The European Defense Community was worthy of support because it was a method of bringing the Germans and the French together; but it was, as he said to Acheson and a group of leading Americans in January, 1953, "a sludgy amalgam" and infinitely less effective than a grand alliance of national armies. One thing must be taken for granted: there would be no British contingent in the E.D.C., although we should keep our divisions in Germany as long as the Americans did the same. I have no doubt at all that he would have been equally averse to our signing the Treaty of Rome. Association with Europe was to be encouraged; but "Westward look, the land is bright" was the immutable inspiration of his faith for the future and the cornerstone of his policy. Lord Crewe told me that Asquith once said to him: "Lloyd George has no principles and Winston has no convictions." However that may have been in 1910, the Churchill I knew had at least one unshakable conviction. . . .

After dinner one evening in August, 1940, Churchill declared to Desmond Morton* and me, as he waved away the brandy and demanded iced soda water: "My object is to preserve the maximum initiative energy. Every night I try myself by court-martial to see if I have done anything effective during the day. I don't mean just pawing the ground—anyone can go through the motions—but something really effective." His energy was indeed startling for a man of sixty-five, not only mentally but physically. He liked to see things for himself, and this involved inspecting troops, dockyards,

* An intimate friend of Churchill's since 1917, particularly concerned with military questions. [ed.]

coastal defenses, and bombed towns. When he reached his destination, he would set off at a pace that left men years younger panting to keep up. One of his favorite evening interludes was to stride across the Foreign Office courtyard to inspect the building operations at the Central War Room, to penetrate underground passages, clamber over girders and temporary walls that obstructed his passage, and to offer the workmen advice about a traverse or the method of bricklaying. On one such occasion he leaped off the top of a high girder into a pool of liquid cement. His feet were embedded. "That," I said, "is your Waterloo." "Blenheim," he corrected; "but how dare you! I am not a Frenchman." He would climb hills near Chequers for target practice with rifle and revolver, since he always envisaged the possibility of having to defend his life against invading parachutists. He took no regular exercise and constantly defied all the rules, dietary and otherwise, that any doctor would have prescribed, but by October, 1941, after two gruelling years of endless work and never a day's holiday, he was gay, resilient, and apparently tireless.

By the time I rejoined his staff, two more anxious years had passed with scarcely a moment's respite, his heart had given a flutter, and he was recovering from a serious attack of pneumonia. It was December, 1943, and the war was to last another eighteen months. I flew out to Carthage with Mrs. Churchill expecting, as she did, to find him desperately ill and perhaps dying. Instead, he was sitting up in bed, smoking a cigar and in the best of humors. Within a few days he was up and about, and on Christmas Eve five commanders in chief arrived to discuss Operation "Shingle," Churchill's personal brainwave for a landing at Anzio, on which he had been brooding during his enforced confinement. There was a touch of Gallipoli about the Anzio landing: it was Churchill's own conception; he left no stone unturned to obtain the necessary equipment (in this case landing craft) from all ends of the earth; it might, if successful, have shortened the war; and it was in the event a failure. As he said to me after the landing, "I intended to throw ashore a hell-cat and all I got was an old stranded whale." . . .

The approach of Operation "Overlord" redoubled Churchill's energies and multiplied the excitement on which he throve. What fun, he said, to land with the troops on D Day and perhaps get there ahead of Monty! It required the king, not Lord Moran,* to stop him. Much as he disliked Operation "Dragoon," the landing in the south of France on which the Americans had insisted, he put to sea to witness it. He was becoming increasingly prone to lung complaints and illnesses of short duration, and, although he seldom spoke of his health except to his doctor, he told me in January, 1944, that his heart had been giving him trouble. But he remained undaunted and showed no signs of worry or dejection. On August 29, 1944, he arrived back from Italy with a temperature of 103° and an agitated Moran. By September 1 his temperature was normal, and he was in tearing form. . . . It was the same at Quebec ten days later; a temperature on the outward journey, but once established in the Citadel a keen, cheerful, and assiduous Churchill, who told me he feared the president was "now very frail."

There was no doubt that Roosevelt was sinking into a physical decline. Churchill's own zest was diminished only at intervals and his ability to shake off both worry and occasional lethargy showed little tendency to weaken. His exhaustion was sometimes evident, notably in December, 1944, while the Greek crisis approached its climax and his suspicion of Soviet intentions in Eastern Europe intensified; but the Churchill who flew to Athens on Christmas Day had thrown off all signs of fatigue. Nor were his expeditions in 1945, including that to watch the 21st Army Group crossing the Rhine, undertaken by a man of declining force. Circumstances had changed: at Yalta and Potsdam we had powerful allies whose policy and interests frequently failed to coincide with our own; but to me Churchill at seventy seemed as apt a performer, as powerful an orator, and as much in command at home as he had been in the momentous summer days of 1940. If one looks at it with an open mind, I think one will find that the choice of 1948 as the year in which Churchill's physical powers began to deteriorate would be a more historically convincing exercise; and even then the decline was a slow one. . . .

There are, I suppose, few if any normal human beings who are never depressed, and, though Churchill was the exception to many rules, this was not one of them. But if there were times when he seemed moody and introspective, gaiety and ebullience were far

* His doctor. [ed.]

more often the order of the day, and the sun was seldom long behind the clouds. I remember an occasion toward the end of 1944, when Churchill lay in bed at No. 10 Annex, trying to throw off a cold and sunk in indignant gloom because Attlee had written to protest about the length of his monologues in the Cabinet and to complain that he was wasting his colleagues' time. Outraged by the letter, which Attlee had discreetly typed himself, Churchill sought a denial of the distasteful thesis first from Lord Beaverbrook and then from Brendan Bracken. Both said they thought Attlee was quite right. He had then turned to Mrs. Churchill for consolation and support, only to be met with the reply that she admired Mr. Attlee for having the courage to put into writing what everybody else was thinking. Churchill spent the afternoon in a state of ill-tempered depression. His friends, even his wife, had deserted him at a time when he desperately needed support. It was a Saturday, and, because of his cold, he had put off going to Chequers. Suddenly, at about 4 P.M., he threw back the bedclothes, gave me a beaming smile, and said, "Let us think no more of Hitlee or of Attler: let us go and see a film." And for the rest of the weekend the sun shone.

As for his dreams, which Churchill seemed to remember with clarity, he seldom referred to any that distressed him, but he frequently retailed those that struck him as particularly ludicrous. On one occasion in August, 1953, he told me he had had a nightmare. He had found himself making a speech in, of all places, the House of Lords, and it was an appalling flop. Afterward the first Lord Rothermere had come up to him and said: "It didn't even *sound* nice."

To Churchill, courage was the greatest virtue. He revered it in others, and he himself was brave both physically and morally. If he thought a course of action right, he would proceed with it fearless of the consequences and sometimes, too, regardless of political expediency. He might worry about a speech, but not about his own safety. One morning in October, 1940, we told him that an unexploded landmine was in St. James's Park and that, unless it could be defused, No. 10 was in grave danger. We might have to evacuate. He merely looked up from his papers at the Cabinet Room table and expressed concern for the ducks and the pelicans.

At about the same period I walked with him during a noisy air raid from 10 Downing Street to the Annex in Storey's Gate. As we emerged from the India Office arch into King Charles Street, we heard the loud whistles of two descending bombs. I dived back under the arch for shelter, and the bombs exploded in Whitehall. Churchill, meanwhile, was striding along the middle of King Charles Street, his chin stuck out and propelling himself rapidly with his gold-headed walking stick.

The political scene when Churchill returned to office in October, 1951, still bore some resemblance to that he had left six years previously. Many of the faces were the same, and the problems of peace, more complicated than those of war, were still to a considerable extent the flotsam and jetsam left by the receding tide of conflict. The Tories, like the Labour Party thirteen years later, inherited a financial crisis and the growing realization that it might prove to be endemic. Individual poverty was on the way out, but national economic stability required an entirely different capacity for endurance and provided a much less easily identifiable goal than victory over Hitler. Churchill was well aware of this, and the complexity of the issues sometimes appalled him. He accordingly set himself a number of tasks that he could isolate, since it was his nature to go bald-headed for what he could understand and to leave the rest to the experts.

In retrospect it seems that the years of his second administration, 1951–55, flowed smoothly past: nothing went seriously wrong, austerity vanished from the land, the Korean War ended, the queen was crowned amid universal rejoicing, controls were loosened, and freedom of enterprise was admitted to be respectable. Perhaps fortune smiled on Churchill in his last years of office to make amends for so many frowns in earlier times; but perhaps, too, the presence at the summit of a gigantic figure, still eager for the rancor and asperity of party politics, but loved and revered even by his opponents, did something to ensure calm and avert unrest.

His eightieth birthday on November 30, 1954, was celebrated on a national scale. In the eyes of the world and, I think, in his own, it represented an apotheosis rather than a sunset. He had mellowed since 1945. In October, 1951, the office keeper at 10 Downing Street laid before the prime minister's seat at the Cabinet table a sheaf of "ACTION THIS DAY" labels, which had been carefully preserved against the day of Churchill's return. They remained there for three and a half years; and they were never used. Perhaps this was symbolic of the change that had taken place. The sense of urgency had not entirely vanished, but it was no longer Churchill's constant companion. Slower to anger, content to feed his golden carp and to play bezique, more amenable to argument and readier to listen to advice, he was none the less the undisputed master of the House of Commons and of the Cabinet. He was distressingly deaf, less resilient than of old, quite often lazy; but, when he chose, he could still rise to the heights of oratory, could charm a disenchanted colleague, turn aside the most awkward question with a reply which made the House of Commons laugh, and, though less frequently than of old, sparkle with conversational wit. The skill with which he could play on words remained: "What! Give him a peerage? Well, perhaps, provided it's a disappearage."

When he asked me to rejoin him, he said it would probably be only for a year. He did not intend to remain long in office, but wished to initiate the recovery of the country under a Conservative administration. He was glad to leave to R. A. Butler, the chancellor of the exchequer, most of the intricate problems of finance and commerce; nor did he show more than a passing interest in such matters, except at budget times, when he was more interested in the effects that fiscal charges might have on the widows and old-age pensioners than in the possibilities of reducing surtax and death duties for which many of his supporters were pressing.

His objectives were to recreate a special, personal connection with the president of the United States; to revive the influence of the United Kingdom in the world; to denationalize steel and transport; to abolish rationing and all relics of Crippsian austerity; and to establish, as he believed he could, a relationship of trust and goodwill between his government and organized labor. As time went on, a further most laudable ambition possessed him: to put an end to the Cold War by convincing the Soviet leaders that while we were not afraid of them, and were fully prepared to meet any threat they mounted, we were also waiting to extend the hand of friendship if they showed the least inclination to grasp it.

Before considering his pursuit of these objectives, and the measure of his success or failure, it is as well to describe two events, one of which made a strong impact on his thought and the other on his capacity.

One morning in February, 1954, I walked into his bedroom at No. 10 and found him with the *Manchester Guardian* open on his bed table. Alone among the newspapers, all of which he read carefully every morning, it published an account of a speech in Chicago by Mr. Sterling Cole, which contained a detailed description of the explosion in the Pacific of the first hydrogen bomb. Churchill had vigorously supported the decision of the Attlee government that Britain should make her own atomic bombs; but he resented the fact that, while in 1940 we had pooled with the United States our nuclear knowledge and discoveries, and while he had secured a favorable agreement with Roosevelt at Hyde Park after the second Quebec Conference, the Labour government had traded our rights under that agreement for concessions in the eventual use of atomic power for civil purposes. He had got the story slightly wrong and persisted in keeping it so; but he could never forget that when he told Senator McMahon of the Hyde Park Agreement, the senator volunteered that had he known of its existence he would never have sponsored the act which bore his name and which prevented the United States from sharing its atomic secrets with any foreign power, including Great Britain.

Here, however, was something entirely new. He read aloud to me the account of the Chicago speech and said, with a mixture of triumph and indignation, that he had just rung up in turn the foreign secretary, the secretary of the Cabinet, and all three chiefs of staff. None of them had had the slightest idea of what had happened, and yet he believed we were now almost as far from the atom bomb as the atom bomb itself had been from the bow and arrow. This tremendous event would alter the history of mankind, because it would make wars of the old-fashioned kind impossible for this and future generations. Its immediate effect must be to alter our own strategic thinking in Egypt and elsewhere, and perhaps to make easier a *rapprochement* with the Soviet Union. It was lucky, he concluded, that at least one person in Whitehall read the newspapers.

The second event, previous in time, that made an impact on Churchill personally was the stroke that he suffered on the evening of June 23, 1953. It was not his first. He had been stricken while staying with Beaverbrook at Cap d'Ail in 1948, and in February, 1952, Moran had come to tell me that Churchill had had an arterial spasm, which might well be the precursor of an immediate stroke. At any rate, Moran was sure that unless pressures were relaxed results might be disastrous. In May I noted that Churchill's periods of "lowness" were increasing, and age was beginning to show. In June he seemed depressed and bewildered and said to me, "The zest is diminished." By November, 1952, he was finding it hard work to compose a speech and complained that ideas no longer flowed. Paradoxically, when the blow fell in the following June, the threat of paralysis and the obvious expectation that he would now resign had a certain tonic effect. Here was a challenge to survival, political no less than physical, and he summoned to his aid the formidable resources of his natural courage, resolute obstinacy, and powerful constitution.

On the day after his stroke, Moran tried to dissuade him from attending the Cabinet and, so it appears from his book, he believed he had succeeded. As soon as Moran's back was turned, Churchill got up, dressed, and presided at the Cabinet. Rab Butler told me a week later that nobody had noticed anything wrong, although Churchill had been unusually reticent and had allowed each item on the agenda to be taken without intervention on his part: an introductory wave of the hand to the minister concerned and that was all. Escorting him into the Cabinet Room, I had felt sure the telltale droop of his mouth on the left side and his slurred speech would betray the secret, but in the event no member of the Cabinet had noticed anything awry. That afternon Churchill and I drove to Chartwell, and he asked me to tell nobody at all what had happened. The following morning Moran came into the library where I was working, closed the door, and said that he did not expect the prime minister to live over the weekend.

Here was a pretty pass. I had Churchill's instructions to tell nobody, and his undisputed successor, Anthony Eden, was in Boston undergoing a serious abdominal operation. I felt I had no choice. I telephoned to Sir Alan Lascelles, asking him to warn the queen that she might have to find a new prime minister on Monday morning, and I wrote personal letters, which I sent by dispatch rider to Churchill's closest friends: Bracken, Beaverbrook, Camrose, and Alexander. I also got in touch with Churchill's senior Cabinet colleagues: R. A. Butler, for whom in the preceding months Churchill had been developing a growing esteem; and Salisbury.

We had been due to sail for Bermuda in H.M.S. *Vanguard* the following Tuesday for a meeting with Eisenhower, and it was necessary to cancel the arrangements without explaining the whole truth.

Meanwhile, Churchill, who at first went rapidly downhill, losing the entire use of his left arm and leg, began to improve. His recuperative powers, both mental and physical, invariably outstripped all expectation; but on this occasion it was more than surprising that after a week he should have made such startling progress, even if his ability to concentrate appeared slight and he preferred Trollope's political novels to Cabinet papers. Bracken and Beaverbrook, more assiduous in their attentions and demonstrative of their affection than they had been for years, urged him not to resign but to continue in office as, in Bracken's words, "a lazy prime minister." Churchill himself, at quite an early stage, set a target: if he could acquit himself with distinction at the Conservative Party Conference at Margate in October, he would remain; if his performance was below par he would make way for Eden.

By July 19 I observed that Churchill's powers of concentration had greatly improved; that he was working on his box* and approving answers to Parliamentary questions; that he sparkled at dinner; and that afterward he went carefully and meticulously through an important speech in the House that Butler had brought to show him. By August 8 he had moved to Chequers and was fit enough to preside authoritatively over a meeting to discuss the Soviet reply to a Three-Power note. On this occasion he proposed action that was entirely contrary to that advocated by the Foreign Office, and Selwyn Lloyd, though defeated in the argument, told me he found it refreshing to receive simple and clear instructions, which were such poles apart from "the mystique of the Foreign Office." At the end of the luncheon that followed, Churchill, drinking brandy for the first time since June 23, informed those present that all his life he had found his main contribution was by self-expression rather than by self-denial. On August 18 he again took his seat at the Cabinet and set his mind to reconstructing his government, and by October 9, after a brief holiday at Cap d'Ail (during which he was still undecided whether to go or stay) he was ready for the test at Margate. It was a striking success, and when it was over Churchill

* Of official papers. [ed.]

told me he would remain prime minister until the queen returned from Australia in the spring of 1954.

When that moment arrived, circumstances had changed, in Churchill's mind if not in Eden's. The facts about the hydrogen bomb necessitated new thoughts on strategy, for which Churchill considered himself more fitted by experience than any of his colleagues; Anglo-American relations were still not intimate enough for his full satisfaction; the foreign secretary and the prime minister were at loggerheads over the withdrawal of British troops from the Suez Canal zone; and, above all, Churchill believed with increasing conviction that an understanding with the new rulers of Russia and the end of the Cold War could and should be achieved by him alone as his final contribution to the welfare of his country.

Churchill's last year of office was bedeviled by the ups and downs in his health, for he was fighting with grim determination and often with success to stem the decline of his powers and the ebb of interest and energy which flowed from it. He continually changed his mind about the date of his resignation, to the natural exasperation of his successor; but it is convenient to look backward from the day of his eventual resignation on April 5, 1955, in order to see to what extent he attained his objectives.

Steel and transport had been largely denationalized, and private enterprise was again to the fore; three hundred thousand houses a year had been built by Harold Macmillan, a promised figure that the Opposition had begun by laughing to scorn; rationing and austerity were forgotten nightmares; in July, 1954, Eden had skilfully negotiated at Geneva a settlement of the war in Indochina, and in September of the same year the London Conference had established the basis of Western European Union; a final solution of the Persian oil dispute had been reached to the satisfaction of all concerned; Walter Monckton, as minister of labor, had established trust and friendship with the trades union leaders, and Churchill included them among his guests at Downing Street whenever he gave a party; industrial peace reigned at home (though it was ironic that Churchill's final departure should synchronize with a newspaper strike); Templer* had restored security and order in Malaya; the commonwealth, apart from the Mau Mau

* Field Marshal Sir Gerald Templer, who was now governing and directing military operations in Malaya. [ed.]

excesses in Kenya, appeared contented and still devoted to the mother country; and in spite of the victory (and Thoughts) of Mao Tse-tung, and recent experiences in Korea, nobody considered China anything but a distant long-term menace.

Historians may claim it was in these years we missed our chance of entering and leading Europe. In so doing, they would disregard the strongly held convictions of the House of Commons, the electorate, and the commonwealth. If Churchill spoke of the proposed European army as "a sludgy amalgam," he certainly thought any conception of European Federation unrealistic and probably undesirable in the foreseeable future. He agreed with Eisenhower to bring all possible pressure on France to ratify the European Defense Community Treaty, but only because he had temporarily failed to persuade the United States that Germany must be invited to join NATO. He feared that if the Americans carried out their threat to fall back on "Perimeter Defense" in the event of the E.D.C. Treaty failing, France might become Communist-dominated and finally go the way of Czechoslovakia. His colleagues, and the Opposition leaders, were equally insensible to the possibility of a European solution.

Churchill was certainly a man of vision, sometimes an Old Testament prophet, and he might therefore have been expected to see into the mists of the future on this issue. In fact, his gaze was fixed in another direction, and he sought in his second administration, as he had in his first, to concentrate on partnership with the U.S.A.

His reception by Truman in Washington, for which he set sail as soon as he could after forming his government, was frank and friendly, but it fell short of the almost miraculous recreation of the earlier connection for which he was hoping. He addressed, as of old, a session of Congress, and his words in the Capitol, at the embassy, and to the Washington Press Club were greeted with rapturous applause. But in the meetings at the White House a reserve, almost a suspicion, could be detected: patriotic officials clustered round Truman to protect him from the insidious magic of a dangerously legendary wizard. At home Churchill concentrated attention on the American ambassadors, first Walter Gifford and then Winthrop Aldrich, both of whom had the entrée to No. 10 without reference to the Foreign Office; and he courted Eisenhower, the prospective Republican candidate, with an eagerness facilitated by their wartime relationship.

There were encouraging signs. On May 15, 1952, Eisenhower dined at No. 10 on the eve of his departure from S.H.A.P.E. to become the Republican candidate. There were thirty-two to dinner, including all the wartime military leaders, and as Ike left he said that if he were elected he would pay only one visit outside the U.S.A., and that would be to the U.K. in order to advertise the special relationship. In August Churchill persuaded Truman to join him in sending a message signed by them both to the Persian prime minister, Mossadeq. It was the first time since 1945 that the Americans had agreed to joint action against a third power, at any rate openly.

Thus, Churchill, although always privately declaring himself a Democrat in American politics, thought he had cause to be equally optimistic whichever party won the November presidential election. He confided to me that, if it was Ike, he had every hope of a joint approach to Stalin, proceeding perhaps to a Congress at Vienna, where the Potsdam Conference would be reopened and concluded.

Eisenhower was elected, and it was with high hopes that we sailed for America after Christmas, 1952. Churchill had arranged to see the incoming administration in New York and then pay a courtesy visit to Truman in Washington. On January 3, after dinner in the Verandah Grill of the *Queen Mary,* Churchill asked me to imagine myself to be the American press and fire at him the kind of questions he was likely to be asked on arrival in New York. I fired about thirty, and his answer to the last of them was, "If Britain and America refuse to be disunited, no ill can come."

This was his supreme article of faith, but he found Eisenhower's colleagues less eager than he had hoped. He stayed with Bernard Baruch, at whose apartment he had long talks with Eisenhower, Dulles, and Dewey. Baruch himself set the tone the first night when he said that European unity in some striking form was essential if America was not to tire of her efforts, and only Churchill could bring it about. England had three remaining assets: her queen ("the world's sweetheart"), Winston Churchill, and her glorious historical past. The following day, January 6, 1953, Churchill sent me to the Commodore Hotel with some papers to show Eisenhower, who spoke to me at length, presumably for onward transmission, about the dangers of collusion. He was in favor of it clandestinely, but not overtly, since it was important for the United States not to offend other nations. On January 7 Dulles and Dewey sought to dissuade Churchill from returning to Washington with Butler in February for economic discussions. Dulles explained that the American public thought Churchill could cast a spell on all American statesmen and that if he were directly associated with the economic talks the fears of the people and of Congress would be aroused to such an extent that the success of the talks would be jeopardized. Churchill was furious and spoke so harshly both to Dulles and to Dewey that Christopher Soames and I, seeing them off when they left, felt obliged to explain rather lamely that a sharp debate was Churchill's idea of a pleasant evening. The fact was that Churchill now realized, to his bitter disappointment, that he was welcomed and revered in America much more as Winston Churchill than as the prime minister of the United Kingdom.

He was not discouraged for long, but as his project for ending the Cold War increasingly absorbed his thoughts, and the world applauded his great speech of May 11, 1953, on this theme, he was more and more distressed by the cold, negative response not only of the Foreign Office but of the White House and the State Department. In October he revived his plan to sail to the Azores in *Vanguard* to meet the president, but Eisenhower was far from keen. Churchill wished to press the matter, but was stopped by a chance remark of mine when I asked, "What subjects are you going to discuss when you get there?" It suddenly dawned on him that everything he might say to the president about Russia would necessarily be met with a negative response, and that on other topics, such as Egypt, he himself would have nothing to offer but criticisms and complaints of the American attitude. He said that to bring the president a thousand miles just for that seemed discourteous and unfair.

At the Bermuda Conference in December, 1953, things looked up a bit. Eisenhower declined to accept Churchill's view that since Stalin's death there was "a new look" about Russia, but personal relations were unclouded and both Churchill and Eden were successful in bringing influence to bear on American defense policy in Europe. After one particular meeting *in camera* Eden told me that Churchill had done brilliantly and he had really "turned the minds of the Americans." The fact, however, that the French had been invited to the conference, even though Laniel and Bidault played little part in its deliberations and the main importance lay in the Anglo-American discussions out of conference hours, proved that the Americans were determined not to admit openly the unique family relationship in which Churchill so ardently believed.

In June, 1954, Churchill returned to Washington. It was thought that on almost every topic—Indochina, atomic policy, Europe, Egypt—there was greater Anglo-American friction than for years. Churchill was thus overjoyed when on June 2, the very day of his arrival, Eisenhower agreed to talks with the Russians. Good progress was also made on the vexed topic of Egypt. Churchill was elated by success and in a state of excited good humor. On June 26 the Russian project was expanded, by the president himself, to take the form of a meeting in London to include the French and West Germans, and to be attended at the opening by the president in person. On the 27th, after Dulles had spoken privately to the president, the prospects of a large conference grew dimmer, but Churchill was assured that if he chose to meet the Russians, the American government would not object.

Churchill and Eisenhower then proceeded to issue a joint declaration of principles, which was a pale imitation of the Atlantic Charter and lacked all the fire and eloquence with which the Churchill of earlier years could have inspired it. It scarcely aroused a flicker of interest in the world, but at least Churchill left America for the last time as prime minister content with the progress he had made and fully reassured as to his influence with the administration. In fact, he had achieved little: the United States never succeeded in resisting the personality of Winston Churchill; he could and did bewitch them; but by the time he left office in 1955 he was no nearer to attaining the happy state of the protoplasm, with its two parts reunited "to their common benefit and gratification," than he had been in 1951. Indeed, eighteen months after his resignation Anglo-American relations were to reach their least fine hour.

He was, in the event, no more successful in attaining his other great objective, a détente with the Soviet Union. But it was not for want of trying, even though the Russians themselves knew little about it. In July and August, 1953, Churchill spoke much on this subject. Talks, he said, might lead to a relaxation of the Cold War, and a respite during which science could use its marvels so to improve the lot of man that the leisured classes of his youth might give way to the leisured masses of tomorrow. "We must go no further on the paths to war," he said, "unless we are sure there is no other path to peace." The Foreign Office and the State Department disagreed, and Churchill told me he thought their policy, unchecked, would consign us to years of hatred and hostility. He was depressed to hear that Salisbury, who returned from Washington in July, had found Eisenhower violently russophobe, even more so than Dulles, and that Salisbury believed the president to be personally responsible for the useless pinpricks and harassing tactics that the Americans were using against Russia in Europe and the Far East.

Churchill was looking into the mists of the future in search of a permanent cure for the antagonism between the East and West. He was therefore less impressed by the immediate obstacles than were those impelled by duty to consider the problems of the day. It is only fair to recall what these were. The negotiations to create a European Defense Community, so as to establish a genuine European deterrent to aggression, had been fraught with every kind of difficulty, and had finally foundered on the rock of French senatorial opposition. The leading Western powers were therefore seeking to make alternative arrangements which would bring Germany into NATO and would substitute a Treaty of Mutual Assistance for the original Brussels Treaty, which had been aimed not at aggression from the East but at the ex-enemy powers, Germany and Italy. The Soviet government was naturally making every effort to prevent the successful negotiation of a new treaty, and it seemed to many that the Russians would seize the opportunity of an approach by the British to sow suspicion in French and German minds. Even as things turned out, the results of the London Conference in the autumn of 1954 were ratified by only a very narrow margin. Churchill's wider conception appeared to Eden and the Foreign Office as almost certain to jeopardize the immediate objective, and it was this fear, rather than mere obstinacy or russophobia, that raised serious doubts in their minds.

Impatient of opposition at home and in Washington, Churchill determined to press on with his own policy. At the end of September he spoke earnestly of the need for Eden and himself to meet Malenkov and Molotov face to face. He can scarcely be blamed for not realizing how transitory this particular Soviet regime was to be. At Bermuda, in December, he advocated a policy of strength toward Russia combined with gestures of friendship, personal contacts, and trade negotiations. Only by proving to our peoples that we should neglect no chance of easement could we persuade them to accept the sacrifices necessary to maintain strong armed forces. He brushed aside the Foreign Office advice that a visit might lead to appeasement (by him of all people!) and would discourage our European allies who would be only too glad of an excuse to relax the defense efforts to which we were goading them. The Foreign Office and the State Department were at one in maintaining that the slightly more reasonable attitude detected in the Kremlin was due not to Stalin's death but to the success of our own policy of constant pressure and increased strength. Churchill was unmoved by their arguments, reinforced though they were by Eisenhower personally and by the entire French delegation at the Bermuda Conference.

It was against this background that Eisenhower's sudden change of front in Washington at the end of June, 1954, gave Churchill new hope and new zest. He would, he said, redouble his efforts to avert war and procure a "ten years' easement during which our riches and ingenuity could be diverted to ends more fruitful than the production of catastrophic weapons." He would go to Russia and demand the freedom of Austria as an earnest of better relations.

We set sail for home on the *Queen Elizabeth*. On July 2 Churchill dictated to me, in spite of protests that I knew no shorthand, a long telegram to Molotov proposing talks with the Soviet leaders, in which the United States government would not participate but could be counted on to do their best with its own public opinion. Churchill asked me to show the telegram to Eden and then to have it dispatched. Eden told me he disapproved of the whole thing. He had been adding up the pros and cons and was sure the latter predominated. Moreover, it was in his view a practical certainty that nothing would come of the meeting and the high hopes of the public would be shattered. He much disliked the idea of the telegram being dispatched without submission to the Cabinet. Why could Churchill not wait till we were home and then let Eden deliver the message to Molotov, whom he would be seeing at Geneva? Would I tell him that if he insisted he must do as he wished, but it would be against Eden's strong advice? Churchill told me that he would make the matter one of confidence with the Cabinet. They would have to choose between him and his intentions. If they opposed the visit it would provide him with the occasion to go. He finally agreed to send the telegram to the Cabinet provided he could say that Eden accepted it in principle. Eden, in despair, agreed.

Back in London Churchill faced an uneasy Cabinet. Salisbury* decided to resign. "Cecils are always ill or resigning," said Churchill cheerfully. But Salisbury was not alone in his discontent, and Harold Macmillan sought an interview with Lady Churchill to tell her that the Cabinet was in danger of breaking asunder on the issue. Churchill admitted to me that he had quite deliberately made up his mind to dispatch the telegram without consulting the Cabinet. The stakes were so high and, as he saw it, the possible benefits so crucial to our survival that he was prepared to adopt any methods to procure a meeting with the Russians. This is the only instance I remember of his contemplating an important action without first submitting the proposal to the Cabinet for approval.

After a meeting on Friday, July 23, the Cabinet dispersed for the weekend with the threat of Salisbury and Crookshank resigning, and the still more alarming possibility that Churchill, the bit between his teeth and behaving like a prophet new-inspired, might resign, announce his reasons for so doing, and split both the Conservative Party and the country. The telegram still awaited dispatch. The crisis was resolved by the Russians themselves taking an initiative, which demanded a meeting not of Churchill and Malenkov but of thirty-two powers to discuss a European security plan. "Foreign Secretaries of the World unite; you have nothing to lose but your jobs," was Churchill's comment. It was, however, clear that his own initiative must be at least postponed.

He had failed in his last great objective, although he went on

* Robert Gascoyne-Cecil, Marquis of Salisbury, Lord President in the Cabinet. Members of his family [Cecils] had been active in politics for generations. [ed.]

hoping for a meeting of the Big Three, and as late as March, 1955, he saw a glint of hope in a proposal from Washington for a meeting between Eisenhower, President Coty, and Dr. Adenauer in Paris on the tenth anniversary of VE Day to ratify the London-Paris Defense Agreements, which had replaced the defunct E.D.C. proposals. But this was not the same as a meeting with the Russians, and Churchill felt that he could battle on no further against such hopeless odds.

His eightieth birthday had passed, and during the winter months of 1954–55 he repeated to me again and again, "I have lost interest; I am tired of it all." He stayed on longer than some hoped and many thought possible. Reluctance to relinquish the reins joined forces with a genuine belief that he could still achieve something worthwhile on the international stage to haul him back from the final step into retirement. He could still compose and deliver a great speech, but he was aging month by month and it was tedious for him to read official papers or to give his mind to anything he did not find diverting. More and more time was given to bezique and ever less to public business. The preparation of one answer to a Parliamentary question might consume a whole morning; facts would be demanded from government departments and arouse no interest when they arrived. It was becoming an effort even to sign a letter and a positive condescension to read Foreign Office telegrams. Yet on some days the old gleam would be there, wit and good humor would bubble and sparkle, wisdom would roll out in telling sentences, and occasionally the touch of genius could still be seen in a decision, a letter, or a phrase.

But he was no longer the man to tame the Russians or to moderate the Americans. Physical blows had indeed fallen, and now in 1955 fortitude was his main surviving asset. It was time to go, on a wave of popular acclaim and affection that was felt far beyond the shores of Great Britain. If he had not achieved all the goals for which he had striven, he could still claim an unusually large score.

WOODROW WYATT

In Parliament After the War

NINETEEN FORTY-FIVE to nineteen fifty-five were the last ten years of Sir Winston's active Parliamentary life. It was in that great decade of his later maturity that he achieved, in conditions of unbridled party warfare, a domination over the House of Commons that is not likely to be seen again in our lifetime.

In this period, during which I watched him almost daily when the Commons was sitting, Sir Winston Churchill did not of an afternoon walk into the House. He appeared in it suddenly from behind the Speaker's chair. He did not seem to have legs like other human beings: his face and body looked all of a piece like some fabulous Humpty Dumpty. The moment this miraculous

---

From *Winston Churchill Distinguished for Talent,* by Woodrow Wyatt. London: The Hutchinson Publishing Group Ltd., 1958, pp. 194–215.

creature was noticed coming into sight the atmosphere changed tangibly. Visitors, if they were at the back of the Strangers' Gallery, stood up or, if they were at the side, thrust their heads over the railings to make sure of at least one glimpse of this phenomenon. Members became sharper and more aware. Murmurs of "Here comes the old man" passed along the benches. The huge, almost babylike face was carefully examined for signs of entertainment, excitement, or tranquillity to come.

There was no concealment on that face: on the broad white canvas an emotion was set for a moment, wiped off, then instantly replaced by another that might make the spectator wonder how its predecessor ever got there. There was the scowl, directed at everybody. There was the baleful, nearly malevolent, look sometimes concentrated on an individual member to whom Sir Winston had taken a temporary dislike. There was the child's sulk when, perhaps, he thought the Speaker, or the Opposition, had been unfair to him. There was the twinkling eye—a signal to the House that a Churchillian joke appreciated by its author was on the way. There was the large, full-sized smile, which seemed to divide Humpty Dumpty somewhere at the middle when he felt he had made an opponent uncomfortable. There was the air of mock penitence. There was the convulsed, or laughing, face when the world, the Opposition, or a Parliamentary situation that had turned to the ridiculous, struck him as grotesquely wonderful. There were the looks magnanimous, contemptuous, indifferent, very bored, mischievous, somber, despairing, arrogant. All were emphatic, unmistakable, rich, and firmly lined. Only one look was missing—the look apologetic.

He might not utter a word, yet as long as he sat on the bench, the great head moving round, the face animated or so lifeless that it had the quality of a bust worn by time, the changed temper of the atmosphere was sustained. Every gesture, every move of hand to ear, had significance. When he got up to go, something of the vitality of the House went with him. It settled down to a quieter jog, like a reception after the guest of honor has gone.

This Humpty Dumpty had a magic that touched all, even those who sincerely, or affectedly, declared that they were indifferent to, or detested, him. From his opponents he evoked successively violent hatred, dislike, derision, friendliness, and love.

From his supporters he called out the two last emotions and added to them bewilderment, frustration, misery, and enthusiasm. Like the shape in which it lived, the personality was round and full, embracing everything a human being can encompass. It could not act in the assembly of the House of Commons without provoking ripples: "I have lived nearly all my life in the House of Commons and I believe it to be the enduring guarantee of British liberties and democratic practices."

Parliament always came first with Churchill. He gave more of himself to it than to anything else. His achievements as an author, an administrator, and a statesman, vast though they are, do not reach the level of his genius as a Parliamentarian. Parliament was his stage, and Parliament responded to him.

Queen Victoria still reigned when Sir Winston first took his seat. He had been jerked into national prominence by his adventures in South Africa. He was familiar with battle and physically brave. But even he was intimidated by the House of Commons' serene and unswerving timelessness. There he could not speak without memorizing every word beforehand. That is an inconvenience in an institution where the course and mood of debate can alter so quickly that a previously prepared speech may become as irrelevant as the nine o'clock from Paddington to Birmingham is to the man who wants to go to Brighton. The way Churchill approached his maiden speech was a sample of the future. He worked at it with a thoroughness infused by an energy above mere industry. In his seventies, if he was to speak in the House, he applied himself as hard as when he was twenty-six. In the worst moments of the war he continued to put the preparation of a Parliamentary speech in front of all his other duties. In *The Hinge of Fate* he writes of the speech he made on January 27, 1942, when the war had brought the biggest single accumulation of disasters: "I did not grudge the twelve or fourteen hours of concentrated thought which ten thousand words of original composition on a vast, many sided subject demanded. . . ."

This unremitting work was at the heart of his success as a speaker. He was not a natural speaker. In his set speeches every word had been gone over several times before. But he knew what he was going to say so well that he did not read, but acted, his phrases: yet it was more than acting because he was the author and believed in his script. He might deliberately provoke an interruption, and the answer to it was often already written in his notes. In later Parliamentary life he was able to speak briefly, but uncomfortably, without preparation; retorts and answers to questions from long practice and custom came more quickly to his mind: in the Parliamentary sense at least his brain moved faster in old age than it did when he was young. But for years he floundered if he had to leave the script. As F. E. Smith (Lord Birkenhead) once remarked, he "devoted the best years of his life to the preparation of his impromptu speeches."

So it was with his maiden speech. He arrived to speak in a debate on the South African war with a number of different speeches ready to deliver. One of them, he hoped, might be suitable. As the moment that he would be called grew closer, he despairingly tried to think of some opening sentence that would smooth the way into his speech and appear to have some connection with the speech then being delivered by the young Lloyd George whom he had to follow. Lloyd George had put on the order paper an amendment moderately critical of the government, but it was not certain whether he would move it. Aid came to Churchill in his unhappiness, now nearly defeated by his own terror, from an old Parliamentarian, a Mr. Bowles, sitting nearby. Only someone who has had to make a speech in the House and is certain at the last moment that he cannot do it can fully understand the extent of Mr. Bowles's charity. Mr. Bowles whispered, as brilliant phrases dropped unheard around the young Churchill: "You might say 'instead of making his violent speech without moving his moderate amendment, he had better have moved his moderate amendment without making his violent speech.'" Churchill repeated the words as he stood for the first time in the House of Commons. The Commons is always pleased, if it can, to help a new speaker through the agony of his first speech. There was a glad laugh, and Churchill put the most appropriate of his prepared speeches into gear and drove away.

His speech, while not outstandingly brilliant, was not as colorless as most maiden speeches. The Conservative government, and he was then a Conservative, was for the ruthless prosecution of the war and for damnation to all Boers. "If I were a Boer," he said, "I hope I should be fighting in the field." He went on to demand that it should be made "easy and honourable for the Boers to surrender." The whole of his speech, which generously recognized the claims and feelings of the Boers, contradicted the trend of government and majority thinking. That may not seem much to the non-Parliamentarian, but for an ambitious young man, aware of the consequences, to go against his own government so early needed courage.

If application was the ground on which his Parliamentary career was built, courage was its foundation. Courage is the element that lifts a member out of the ordinary. Many are brash, but few are brave. Courage is not contrariness, which is often akin to pleasure at shocking or being in a tiny minority. It is the deliberate refusal of a man who has the ability to be politically successful to shirk saying things he feels to be true even though no one would comment on his failure to say them. It is something more than sincerity, although that is included. A man can be sincere in everything he says and yet take care not to say anything that will disconcert his potential supporters.

No Parliamentarian can be of the first rank without courage, and Churchill has always had it. In the thirties he could at any time have joined the government if he had been more willing to compromise with his views on the dangers of Nazism. He could have softened his criticisms of the government's feebleness in front of Hitler, he could have been less frank without in any way being untruthful, but he thought it was his duty to Parliament to speak as he did and that unless he used powerful language his warnings would have no effect at all. Office was worth less to him than truth; and that, since human beings are as frail in politics as elsewhere, is remarkable.

Simply to have the capacity to endure hours of preparatory drudgery and a courage large enough to impress the House is not sufficient to establish a dominating role in Parliament. Members of the House of Commons individually are fallible in their estimates of each other. Collectively, they rarely make a mistake. The combined judgment of the House of Commons on a man's character and abilities contains a high element of accuracy. No assembly can be more forgiving, more charitable, more shrewd, or fairer. It searches out all a man's qualities and weaknesses as they show up in good fortune and in bad, in the interplay of debates, and in the association of many years with his colleagues. It was the proof of Winston Churchill's stature as a Parliamentarian that he passed through all the tests, and because of the huge volume of accumulated respect he earned in the House he could get away with breaches of the rules and traditions that would never have been allowed to others.

The British temperament is peculiarly suited to Parliamentary government, and it has fashioned a chamber of exactly the right shape in which to exercise it. Churchill has understood that completely, as the memorandum he wrote as prime minister on the rebuilding of the blitzed House of Commons chamber shows:

> Its shape should be oblong and not semicircular. Here is a very potent factor in our political life. The semicircular assembly which appeals to political theorists, enables every individual or every group to move round the centre, adopting various shades of pink according as the weather changes. . . . It is easy for an individual to move through those insensible gradations from Left to Right, but the act of crossing the Floor is one which requires serious consideration. I am well informed on this matter, for I have accomplished that difficult process, not only once, but twice. . . . Logic, which has created in so many countries semicircular assemblies with buildings that give to every member not only a seat to sit in, but often a desk to write at, with a lid to bang, has proved fatal to Parliamentary government as we know it here in its home and in the land of its birth. . . .
>
> It should not be big enough to contain all its members at once without overcrowding, and there should be no question of every member having a separate seat reserved for him. The reason for this has long been a puzzle to uninstructed outsiders. . . . Yet it is not so difficult to understand if you look at it from a practical point of view. If the House is big enough to contain all its Members nine-tenths of its debates will be conducted in the depressing atmosphere of an almost empty or half-empty chamber. The essence of good House of Commons speaking is the conversational style, the facility for quick informal interruptions and interchanges. Harangues from a rostrum would be a bad substitute for the conversational style in which so much business is done. But the conversational style requires a fairly small space, and there should be on great occasions a sense of crowd and urgency. There should be a sense of the importance of much that is said, and a sense that great matters are being decided, there and then, by the House.

In making formality informal and informality formal Churchill excelled. When he spoke, each member of the House felt that he was taking part in something important. He could not avoid being flattered by the immense pains that had been taken to impress him. Sometimes, because the speeches had been prepared in the expectation of the House being in a different mood to the one it assumed in the event, they misfired. His speeches on India and Burma in the postwar Parliament were quite disconnected from the main movement of ideas in the House—making him seem like a materialized ghost from a dead age posturing in front of perplexed and unhappy supporters. Once in the 1945 Parliament the Labour Party deliberately disconcerted him by a conspiracy to remain completely silent throughout the whole of his speech. The voice grew quicker and sharper, the hand and the chin were thrust forward to provoke the anticipated interruption —which was to be smitten down at once by the previously polished retort—but no interruption came. Instead of angry shouts, there was an atmosphere of stolid complacency. It was difficult even for the great composer and conductor to make the symphony sound well with some of the loudest instruments silent when their harsh background was most needed.

Occasionally Churchill has had periods of indifference or even arrogance toward the House, which it has resented. Surprisingly these cleavages have at times gone deep. Sir Stafford Cripps told me of a time during the war when, in his view, such a divergence had occurred, and he said so to Churchill.

"Two things I put above everything in my life," said the prime minister, "God and the House of Commons."

"Well," said Sir Stafford, "I hope you treat God better than you do the House of Commons."

But these were only temporary patches of misunderstanding. Usually the touch was sure, and with time it so matured that it is hard to believe that there has ever been anything better in Parliamentary artistry than the handling of the House of Commons by Churchill in his seventies.

Yet, underneath it all, there lay a hint of arrogance, of contempt for those who disagreed. There was something in the criticism that Churchill did not often take the opinion of the House into consideration when executing policy. He paid the

House of Commons elaborate respect but little attention. His aim was usually either to control the House for his purposes or to use it as a vehicle for appealing to the nation and the world.

Churchill always gave great care not only to his phrases, in which much use was made of the unexpected adjective and noun, but to the construction of his speeches. Since the speeches were elaborately fashioned in advance he could not make adjustments to suit the vagaries of the House as such debaters as Aneurin Bevan can. Consequently, he had to impose himself on the mood of the House. This could be done only if his anticipation of the likely reactions of the House was not too wide of the mark. During the early months of the 1945 Parliament he had a number of successes by provoking the interruptions he wanted from the great Labour majority—about half of whom were new to the House and easily tricked. Hearing him for the first time during the debate on the Address in 1945, I marveled at the cunning way he trapped us. In the general election campaign he had made Harold Laski, then chairman of the Labour Party, into a national bogeyman. He had tried to convince the country that the Cabinet of a Labour government would for the first time in British history be responsible to some Politbureau-like outside body—Mr. Laski and the national executive of the Labour Party—and not to Parliament. After the election Laski, still ebullient, made a speech announcing that British policy in Greece was to be altered.

In the House Churchill dealt, in a style to become familiar, with the excited rows of government supporters, still resentful of his broadcast suggestion that socialism in Britain would eventually lead to a police state. The more we grew indignant the better he enjoyed himself.

> MR. CHURCHILL: What precisely is Mr. Laski's authority for all the statements he is making about our foreign policy? How far do his statements involve the agreement or responsibility of the Secretary of State for Foreign Affairs? We know that Mr. Laski is the Chairman of the Labour Party Executive Committee.
>
> LABOUR MEMBERS (*derisively*): Gestapo.
>
> MR. CHURCHILL (*blandly*): Everybody has a right to describe their own party machine as they choose.
>
> This is a very important body. I have been told—I am willing to be contradicted and to learn—that it has the power to summon

> Ministers before it. Let us find out whether it is true or not. Evidently it has got great power, and it has, even more evidently, a keen inclination to assert it.
>
> I see that Mr. Laski said in Paris a few days ago that our policy in Greece was to be completely changed. What is the meaning of this? I thought we were agreed upon our policy towards Greece especially after Sir Walter Citrine's and the Trade Unions' report.

Here a babel of fury and shouts broke out from the Labour benches, particularly from the substantial section that during the next few years was vehemently to criticize Ernest Bevin. Churchill was ready for the interruption because he had intended it. With great solemnity he stood squarely at the dispatch box, gazing almost sympathetically at the benches opposite: "I would say to hon. Members not to speak disrespectfully of this report," and here he sharpened the emphasis with heavy point on each word and with the utmost significance on the last three: "or they may be brought up before that body."

The effect of this comical surprise was devastating on the crowded Labour benches, which were transfixed with astonishment.

If his speeches could not avoid the use of many figures and technicalities, there were always breaks in them designed to restore the attention of the House to a high pitch should it have grown a little bored. In March, 1953, he was obliged to make a complicated speech on defense policy. To relieve the gloom of the manpower statistics, there were at intervals of about ten minutes such passages as this:

> I must now warn the House that I am going to make an unusual departure. I am going to make a Latin quotation. It is one which I hope will not offend the detachment of the old school tie and will not baffle or be taken as a slight upon the new spelling brigade. Perhaps I ought to say the "new spelling squad," because it is an easier word. The quotation is *Arma virumque cano* which, for the benefit of our Winchester friends, I may translate as "Arms and the men I sing." That generally describes my theme.

A speech on the international situation in December, 1950, was designed to annoy the Opposition by the inclusion of a demand that during the difficulties caused by the Korean War the Labour government should drop the nationalization of steel. At times he had lost the sympathy of the House, as he probably knew he would. To regain it there was a passage that suddenly broke the partisan nature of his speech and lifted it to another level:

> When nations or individuals get strong they are often truculent and bullying, but when they are weak they become better mannered. But this is the reverse of what is healthy and wise. I have always been astonished, having seen the end of these two wars, how difficult it is to make people understand the Roman wisdom, "Spare the conquered and confront the proud." I think I will go so far as to say it in the original: *Parcere subjectis et debellare superbos.* The modern practice has too often been, "Punish the defeated and grovel to the strong."

In April, 1951, he was dealing with a complicated argument about the appointment of an American supreme commander in the North Atlantic and the proposed appointment of a supreme Allied commander in the Mediterranean. He was arguing through a maze, which was becoming a trifle tedious, that the government had made the wrong decision in allowing an American North Atlantic supreme commander through ministers failing to keep a sufficiently firm grip on the negotiations:

> This very serious mistake arises from the fault of planning from the bottom instead of planning from the top. When the top are incompetent to plan or give guidance, the process naturally begins from the bottom. We suffer from the fallacy, *deus ex machina,* which, for the benefit of any Wykehamists[1] who may be present, is "A god out of the machine." There are layers of committees and super committees, and the business is passed upwards stage by stage to a decision. When all the process has been gone through the machine speaks, but what one gets at the end is not truth or wisdom or common sense: it is a White Paper. All that comes out of the machine is unreal and meaningless formulae expressed in official jargon and accompanied by fatuous grimaces.

Each speech was a composition. After the war in some respects they were even better than the wartime performances. Then he made orations, pointed very directly at the country and the world, in an atmosphere of party unanimity. They did not ignore the

1. Sir Winston was always amused by the fact that Winchester, the public school with the highest academic record of all, has provided a number of distinguished Labour leaders such as Sir Stafford Cripps, Hugh Gaitskell, R. H. S. Crossman, and Douglas Jay.

House but they did not have to give it first place as the speeches since 1945, delivered among the unrepressed and bubbling informalities of party discord, had to. In his last speaking years all his Parliamentary experience and wiliness were blended with his great gifts of meticulously contrived expression.

When Churchill was to follow a major spokesman from the other side, if it was a controversial debate, he frequently began with a skillfully wrought reference to him. In these references there was sufficient humor slightly to neutralize the anger of the Opposition but enough venom to indicate that the performance would include a number of violent blows.

In May, 1947, the Labour government, during the course of the National Service Bill through the House, had been forced by a number of Labour dissidents to announce a reduction in the period of military service prescribed in the bill from eighteen months to twelve months. The Conservatives, having once indicated their willingness to support the government in their demand for the longer period, were indignant at this reversal. Mr. A. V. Alexander, the minister of defense, after previously justifying the absolute necessity for the longer term of service, was now obliged to give the reasons why the shorter period would do. He was uncomfortable in introducing the amendment to the bill on the committee stage. When he had finished, Churchill began:

> I have been looking around for something upon which to congratulate the right hon. Gentleman. After some difficulty, I have found at least one point on which I can offer him my compliments, and that is the control of his facial expression, which enabled him to deliver the ridiculous and deplorable harangue to which we have listened, and yet keep an unsmiling face. Indeed, there were moments when I was not quite sure whether he was not taking his revenge on the forces which compelled him to his present course of action, by showing them how ridiculous their case was, and how absurd their position would be when it was presented to the House of Commons.

A similar beginning to a Churchill speech, infused by an impish mischievousness which often broke out, came after the general election of October, 1951. The Bevanite split in the defeated Labour Party was still raw, and there was a slight tendency in the Labour leadership to try to win over the malcontents. Mr. Attlee had just finished criticizing the new government's King's Speech on behalf of the Opposition.

> The right hon. Gentleman will excuse me if I say that he does not seem quite to have got clear of the General Election. A great deal of his speech was made up of very effective points and quips which gave a great deal of satisfaction to those behind him. We all understand his position: "I am their leader, I must follow them."

Herbert Morrison frequently provided the machinery by which Churchill levered himself into a speech or into forewarning the Opposition that he was out to hurt. Early in the 1945 Parliament, when the dislike he had formed of Morrison in the War Cabinet was still on him, he said:

> I hope he is not going to lecture us today on bringing party matters and party feeling into discussions of large public issues. There is no man I can think of from whom such rebukes and admonitions come less well. I would not go so far as to describe him in the words used by the Minister of Health [Mr. Bevan] a year ago, when he was in an independent position, as a third-class Tammany boss. I believe that was the expression his colleague used about him, which I resented very much at the time. I thought it was very much to be deprecated using disparaging expressions about important institutions of friendly countries.

He was still using Morrison nearly six years later as a vehicle for getting himself under way:

> The right hon. Member for Lewisham, South [Mr. Morrison] is a curious mixture of geniality and venom. The geniality, I may say, after a great many years of experience, is natural to himself. The venom has to be adopted in order to keep on side with the forces below the Gangway. [Where Labour Members critical of their party leadership usually sit.] Some parts of his speech were unexpectedly moderate, but, obviously, he had thought it necessary to prepare the way, as I often see hon. Gentlemen doing, in putting himself on good terms below the Gangway by saying a number of things in which I know he does not believe and of which I am sure he is ashamed.
>
> The right hon. Gentleman accused me of being cowardly in asking my right hon. Friend to open the debate. Does he believe that I am really afraid of opening a debate? Why would I be afraid? I can assure the right hon. Gentleman that the spectacle of a number of middle-aged gentlemen who are my political oppo-

> nents being in a state of uproar and fury is really quite exhilarating to me. I have not had fifty years' actual service in this House without having got used to the rough and tumble of debate.

Churchill always enjoyed a noisy House. As he said later the same year:

> Hon. Members opposite will give me credit for not being afraid of interruptions or noise. It even would be much easier to be shouted down continually or booed down, because I have not the slightest doubt that I could obtain publicity for any remarks I wish to make, even if they are not audible in the House.

The speaker who is the center of a disturbance has, if he remains cool, an advantage over his interrupters. He can wait until they subside and no further business can be done, if he keeps standing, until order returns. It is he who has the floor. He need not give way to any individual member who wants to interrupt him but he can make his own choice of a remark out of the confusion to which to make an effective reply.

In his last Parliamentary period Churchill was brilliant at quickly selecting the right target. One of his most frequent interrupters was tiny Sidney Silverman, who sat in a corner seat in the front row below the Gangway with his short legs hardly touching the ground. During a debate on the long delays in bringing German generals to trial for war crimes Churchill was commending Mr. Harold Macmillan, who had opened, for what he called "his very restrained and carefully phrased speech."

> MR. SIDNEY SILVERMAN (*shouting*): I wonder what the right hon. Gentleman would say if he abandoned restraint.
>
> MR. CHURCHILL: The hon. Gentleman is always intervening. On this occasion he did not even hop off his perch.

The House collapsed into laughter.

During a debate about Allied Command appointments Mr. Shinwell interrupted him to observe: "All I say to him now is that the discussions about the Mediterranean and the discussions about the whole command have been taking place simultaneously." To which Mr. Churchill promptly replied: "They may have been taking place simultaneously but one ended before the other. That sometimes happens in horse racing."

When interruptions are dealt with in this way, it is the speaker who scores heavily, by encouraging his own side as well as by neutralizing his opponents. By staying unmoved in the face of hostility, a speaker can get an ascendancy over the House, if he has a strong personality and the ability to regain the thread of his speech unbroken. Churchill was not only unafraid of such scenes but welcomed them. He rose to the excitement, and if he was a little somber at the start he was gay by the end. Sometimes he would stimulate an uproar to divert attention from the fact that he did not know the answer to some pointed question put to him by the Opposition—if he was for once making a bad case.

A lively passage in the House was to Churchill an indication of vitality. He several times remarked in the House that politicians should not be too mealy-mouthed in what they say, and he never hesitated to live according to his dictum. It was of Aneurin Bevan that he said early in the 1945 Parliament that he threatened to be as great a burden in peace as he had been "a squalid nuisance in time of war." His invective against Stafford Cripps was more polished but equally severe. In condemning him for taking the leading role in the Indian mission of the three Cabinet ministers, which prepared the way to the independence of India, he said:

> No one more than he has taken responsibility in this matter, because neither of his colleagues could compare with him in that acuteness and energy of mind with which he devotes himself to so many topics injurious to the strength and welfare of the State.

Perhaps his most remarkable abuse was directed at Ramsay MacDonald when MacDonald was prime minister of the 1929 Labour government, which stayed in office by permission of the Liberals. Frequently they let him down, and the government would either be defeated or have to withdraw some proposal or bill. Each time, however, that MacDonald was humiliated, he behaved as though nothing had happened and as if it did not matter. Churchill, who despised him, said:

> I spoke the other day, after he had been defeated in an important division, about his wonderful skill in falling without hurting himself. He falls, but up he comes again smiling, a little dishevelled but still smiling. . . .
>
> I remember when I was a child being taken to the celebrated Barnum's Circus which contained an exhibition of freaks and

> monstrosities, but the exhibit on the programme which I most desired to see was the one described as "The Boneless Wonder." My parents judged that the spectacle would be too revolting and demoralizing for my youthful eyes, and I have waited 50 years to see the Boneless Wonder sitting on the Treasury Bench.

Nor did he in the least resent what was said to him. Once in 1947 I happened to follow Churchill after he had made a speech deploring the grant of independence to Burma. I vigorously attacked him. Afterward I met him outside the chamber and he kindly said that I had made a very good debating speech. I said, as I was a very young member, I hoped that he did not think I had been too rude to him. He answered: "I ask for no quarter and I bear no malice."

He could be mean and almost petty, but never for long. Up came the generous side of his nature suddenly to dispel the animosity that he himself had created. This virtue was in such abundance that it touched magnanimity without giving any impression of offensive patronage. In an assembly whose business is almost entirely based on the clashes of human beings this is one of the main qualities which, added to his others, made him a great Parliamentarian. Of the same quality was the dogged loyalty that he held for his friends or for any member of his government who was in trouble. Occasionally this personal loyalty might appear to conflict with the public interest; but that was such a human failing that it enhanced and did not diminish his Parliamentary stature. A typical incident was when Duff Cooper, who as chancellor of the duchy of Lancaster during the war had been in the Far East, was being blamed for the disasters in that theater. The prime minister in the House of Commons flatly declared: "When I am invited under threats of unpopularity to myself, or the Government, to victimize the Chancellor of the Duchy and throw him to the wolves, I say to those who make this amiable suggestion—I can only say to them—'I much regret that I am unable to gratify your wishes'—or words to that effect."

This comprehensive human being lacked no emotion nor avoided arousing every range of feeling in the rest of the House. I have seen him with tears on his cheeks and they were never simulated. He in turn could make the tears move on one's own. To those who knew Stafford Cripps well and who followed the course of his last fluctuating illness, the poignancy of Churchill's tribute in the House of Commons was deeply affecting. After describing generously and accurately his merits, he suddenly, in referring to Lady Cripps, lit the pathos of the final situation: "Our hearts go out to the noble woman, his devoted wife, who through these long months of agony, *mocked by false dawns,* has been his greatest comfort on earth."

He brought the Parliamentary art nearly to perfection in every sphere. In my ten years in the House at the same time as Churchill it seemed to me that he could be defeated decisively in only two ways. One way to get under his armor was to suggest that he was either speaking against or failing to uphold some British interest. If he felt slightly guilty or unhappy about the matter, this rarely failed, even if he could make a good show of rationalizing his conduct over the particular issue by justifying it in a wider context. The other way was to take advantage of the slowness with which his mind sometimes alerted itself to a new point or complication in debate or at question time: curiously, this became more difficult and not easier with time, demonstrating that despite his age he had not lost mental vigor or grip on affairs.

Churchill is the only man of our epoch to be declared an ancient monument in his own lifetime. All his Parliamentary life he screwed the maximum advantage from any position. He was very sensible in his later years of the political usefulness of the public's veneration while he enjoyed it. To be old has its drawbacks—why not try to counteract them with any benefits that age may incidentally bring? was his thought. If he could persuade the House of Commons that it was in some way un-Parliamentary, unpatriotic, or unworthy to trip him up or to attack him, that was the fault of the House of Commons and of the public—not his. He did not ask for special treatment, nor did he think it wrong of anyone to refuse to give it him. But if he could confound his enemy by canalizing on him public and Parliamentary indignation that a great statesman and national hero should be flouted in his last years, he did not hesitate. The notice that decorated him, to the effect that care must be taken not to damage or treat roughly this national institution, was a political asset to him, but it was totally unnecessary as a means of protection.

As a Parliamentarian, he never scrupled to use any weapon

that came to hand. He might shrink from belaboring his opponents with some stick that attracted him by its power of injury because it would be unwise to use it but never because it would be unfair. If a debate was going hard against him, and he was in office, he did not, for example, have qualms about suddenly producing some forgotten document designed to discredit his opponents, although its production hardly accorded with Parliamentary ethics. When denounced or exposed, he would admit his fault with a happy smile and shrug his shoulders. He would swiftly move from consideration of great matters on the highest plane to some very disagreeable party maneuver and accompany the change by a look that said, "Well, we are all politicians, aren't we? Do not let us be over-nice."

To challenge Churchill in the House was enjoyable. If it was at question time, he would sometimes (after his hearing began to go) look at you with a slightly amused air, wielding his hearing aid, unusually shaped like a lollipop, as an additional Parliamentary artifice. If a point went home, there would be a sudden frown or perhaps quick indignation. If he thought defeat might be coming and he did not feel in the mood to try to avoid it at once, he would not listen, or seem not to listen, to what was being said. Then he would slowly get up and make a reply that had almost nothing to do with the subject in hand—but as it was probably prepared in advance he would by making the House laugh appear to have won where he had really lost. If he was in a good humor and the question was not unfriendly, he might smile amiably as he rose slowly to answer, and the accumulated charm of decades poured out into the chamber.

Attacking Churchill in a speech, and not by question and answer, it was essential that there should be nothing halfhearted in the onslaught. To activate him, there had to be a series of hard knocks delivered without the slighest compunction. After he had been banged at for ten minutes or so the colossus began to stir—if there was substance in the thumps. At some point anger might be forced up in him. Then you had got him. He might be stung into making some impromptu observation, which, if he had had time to think, he would have left unsaid or phrased differently. His defenses were down, and for a brief glorious second he could be destroyed: to rise again as fresh and formidable as ever a moment later.

This wonderful ornament to Parliament, and to British democracy, contained in his Parliamentary days all the contradictory virtues and defects that make the full man. Where he was dishonest, he was at the same time honest. Where he was unscrupulous, he was still fair. Where he was vindictive, he was nevertheless generous. Robust and extrovert, he was capable of introspective thought. Keenly awake, he could slump into lethargy. The only other person I ever met to compare with him is someone whom he would feel to be utterly alien to him—Gandhi. Gandhi was a great man because he was not afraid of the elements in his own character. When a politician denies the defects in him, he dams up a force inside him that will burst and destroy him or pervert him to second-rate usefulness. He must recognize to himself what he is and allow the bad and the good to move inside him. By knowing the bad and watching it he can canalize it constructively.

Churchill and Gandhi have had the ability to get energy and fullness from their faults. In them, what might have been vice turned to a mischievousness, adding charm and lovability. Both were amazingly arrogant in their youth, and both mellowed into justified, but not overweening, assurance. A mercurial quickness in change of mood and attitude was common to both. Because they made no attempt to obliterate or conceal their defects, both managed to derive from them strength and an identity with vast numbers of their fellow human beings.

After all the brain power, the industry, the hard-won oratorical gifts, the acute political judgment, the patriotism, the tremendous driving power are taken into account, superb greatness is only achieved if at the end a man still comes through to himself, remains himself, and is himself.

It was Churchill's achievement as a Parliamentarian to portray and combine his manysidedness in a cohesive whole without losing the virtue from any one element. For anyone who has ever sat in Parliament at the same time as Churchill, it will be a privilege that they will recall with pride as long as they live. He stamped himself and his being on the House of Commons, of which he was an active member for nearly sixty years. Until the end of this century speakers and politicians in the House who rise to prominence will find themselves compared—as a guide to their stature—with Churchill. Although he often disregarded the opinions of Parliament in his zenith, he always loved it—which is quite another matter. He cherished its ceremonial and enlarged its customs. No intelligent newcomer, ambitious for a great Parliamentary career, will set out on it without studying the way in which Churchill approached the varied facets of Parliamentary life—particularly in the ten years after the war. For decades to come, politicians will learn from the manner in which Sir Winston presented himself and his thoughts.

PART TWO

ARNO J. MAYER

The Power Politician and Counterrevolutionary

IN HIS SCHOLARLY CAPACITY a historian should not deliver eulogies; nor should he perpetuate or embellish legends. When reviewing an extraordinary life like Churchill's, he has an obligation to examine this life critically in the context of its time. Historians hold that just as the greatness of a leader cannot be properly appreciated without a close look at the era on which he left his mark, so the forces agitating any given era cannot be understood without a careful evaluation of the great men who bent these forces to their will. In brief, great men and their times illuminate each other.

Let us begin by raising, but not answering, a question with which Churchill himself is likely to have wrestled: was his own

From *The Critical Spirit,* edited by Kurt H. Wolff and Barrington Moore, Jr., Boston: Beacon Press, 1967, pp. 328–42.

leadership essential to the survival of Britain, the Western world, and Soviet Russia in 1940–41? Historians will forever speculate about this unanswerable question, so much more so because Churchill's life history prior to the invasion of France and the Low Countries did not commend or qualify him for his epochal historical assignment. He was anything but a modern man: he was guided by archaic ideas; his personality and conduct were remnants of a bygone age; and he was consumed by nostalgia for a vanished elitist society and a faded imperial grandeur.

Indeed, he and de Gaulle have much in common. Both reconciled themselves to modernity in only one major sphere: in the technology of war. They were equally sensitive to the accelerated movement, time, and space of twentieth-century military battles. Whereas Churchill pushed the modernization and growth of naval, tank, and air power, de Gaulle pioneered in tank warfare and in the *force de frappe*. Both had a purely instrumental interest in industrial modernization, social reform, political stability, and administrative efficiency. Churchill and de Gaulle left others to plan and implement these improvements provided they dutifully placed themselves and their achievements under their command for the pursuit of the national interest, as they saw it.

In May, 1940, Churchill became the man of the hour—not unlike de Gaulle in 1958—because at home Britain's deadlocked political situation invited, if not demanded, the ascendancy of a resolute autocrat; while in international politics his vague and inconsistently held concepts of power and balance of power momentarily became relevant.

Let us consider, first, Churchill the man and the politician; second, Churchill the counterrevolutionary; third, Churchill's foreign policy and effectiveness in the 1930s; and last, his ambivalent diplomatic role during and after the Second World War.

Throughout his public school days Churchill was consistently at the bottom of his class, while at the same time doing miserably in sports. Moreover, he was unpopular with his classmates. Worse still, in that sober pre-Freudian era, he refused to worry or brood about his unpopularity—quite the contrary. He relished the solitude in which he took his walks and read his books. Yet, his academic achievements and motivations were so low that he passed his entrance examination to the Sandhurst Military Academy only on his third try; and even then he barely qualified for the obsolete cavalry, "which accepted lower standards for men who had independent means."[1] But once he was in, and with the sudden explosion of his passion and interest in warfare, Churchill applied his stupendous intellectual gifts and energies to his studies.

No doubt the fascination for the study of military affairs, which stayed with him all through his life, suited Churchill's romantic and heroic view of political leadership. He was not cut out for harmonious teamwork; he never discovered the meaning of personal loyalty; and he cruelly severed relations even with long-time associates the moment they threatened to embarrass him or his career. He had an artist's or a robber-baron's temperament, in that he was volatile, selfish, unreliable, and ambitious. For relaxation he sought out the company of men of similar dispositions. He laughed, sang, drank, and recited poetry with self-made men rather than with titled aristocrats who thrived on patronage, provided these self-made men aspired to be part of the established power elite and demonstrated their reverence for, and familiarity with, Europe's, particularly Britain's, cultural heritage. In his personal relations, except with members of his family, Churchill tended to be crude and boorish. At the same time, he belonged to that rare species, that is, the cultivated men of action: as an *engagé* intellectual, he admired the historical style of Gibbon and Macaulay; as a practicing politician, he carried the English language and rhetoric to new heights; and he incessantly recharged his vital intellect and psyche by seeking repose and self-expression at his writing desk and at his painting easel.

In brief, Churchill was a Renaissance man of exceptional gifts, driven by one overriding passion: and this passion—to which all else was subordinated, harnessed, and attuned—was politics. Paradoxically, however, he was not a good politician. To be sure, he would have excelled in an era of deferential politics. But precisely because of his archaic temperament, outlook, conduct, and style, he was unsuited for this modern age of mass, party, and pressure politics. He had an elitist's contempt and distrust for the mass electorate and a patrician's disdain for routinized party accommo-

1. Virginia Cowles, *Winston Churchill: The Era and the Man* (London, 1953), p. 37.

dation and discipline. That he was a great orator is beyond question. However, under conditions of mass literacy, universal suffrage, and party competition, oratory is only one of many ingredients for political effectiveness. Except for a very brief spell, throughout his political career he was never really popular with the British electorate; nor did he ever enjoy solid party loyalty and confidence in Commons. Moreover, he was not an outstanding Parliamentarian, though on the floor of the House few prime ministers ever surpassed him in repartee during the question period.

This, then, was the man and the politician. What about his political vision, projects, and policy? Both friendly and critical students of Churchill persist in stressing his repeated party shifts as evidence of an erratic and inconsistent but ultimately successful striving for leadership. Accordingly, in 1899, Churchill began his political career as a member of the Conservative Party. In less than six years he defected to the Liberal Party, where he soon joined the radical faction. But within four years he moved back into the moderate wing of his newly adopted political home. During and immediately following the Great War he was a Lloyd George Liberal and cheerfully contributed to the fatal schism in the parent Liberal Party. Finally, in the mid-1920s he returned to the Conservative fold, having toyed with the idea of starting his own center party both before and after this return. And within this Conservative Party he repeatedly was torn between the Tory, the center, and the progressive wings.

These shifts in party affiliations cannot be explained away. But how important were they? As I suggested, Churchill was not cut out to be a regular party man. He was a virtuoso, with a flaming sense of destiny. At the same time, to understand Churchill it will not do simply to attribute his changing party affiliations and postures to his inordinate political ambitions and pretensions. Such strivings are the stuff of which so many political leaders, and not only Churchill, are made.

Perhaps Churchill's political behavior emerges in a more consistent light once it is viewed in the broad context of the fundamental political encounter of his time. His career was coextensive with the confrontation of revolution and counterrevolution in Europe, including Britain, during the first half of this century and with the related clash of nationalism and imperialism in the non-Western world.

Churchill was an equally resolute opponent of socialism and of anti-imperialist nationalism. Whatever his party affiliation may have been at any given moment, his purpose remained constant: to maintain Britain's political, social, and economic system at home while upholding her imperial glory in the international arena. But even his strategy and tactics were not that erratic. Except for a few years, 1904–10, when he experimentally championed timely reforms as the best antidote to revolutionary change, his policies stayed within a narrow spectrum ranging from congealed conservatism to outright reaction. That his flirtation with radical reformism should have been so short-lived is not surprising, given his tradition-bound and orthodox values and behavior patterns as well as his fascination with warfare. Precisely because he never reconciled himself to the revolution of rising expectations in either Lancashire or Bengal, he was by far more interested and effective in the realm of foreign and military policy than in domestic affairs.

Let us look briefly at Churchill's political career in this context of the confrontation of revolution and counterrevolution. In 1899 (June) he fought his first election on the Conservative ticket in Oldham, a typical Lancashire working-class district. Ignoring Disraeli's and his father's injunction not to neglect social issues, he campaigned with slogans extolling the virtues of the High Church, of imperial unity, of the existing social system, and of Conservative rule. His thorough defeat at the polls came to him not only as a personal rebuff but also as a revelation of the ineffectiveness of conventional political appeals among the lower urban classes.

Almost by rebound he rushed off to South Africa to cover the Boer War as a special correspondent for the *Morning Post,* Britain's leading jingoist daily. On the strength of his stories and of his courageous bearing in captivity, he soon returned to England to stand once again as a Conservative candidate in Oldham. In this first khaki election of the twentieth century a groundswell of superpatriotism carried the Conservative Party, including Churchill, to victory.

During his inaugural term in Commons, Churchill distinguished himself by the skillful rhetoric with which he expounded the wilting Conservative credo of the Victorian sunset. He advocated isolationism from Europe, military retrenchment, imperialism, free trade, and fiscal orthodoxy. Moreover, while the Boer War was in its guerrilla phase, Churchill rationalized the high military, moral, and diplomatic costs of counterinsurgency—such as concentration camps, the burning of farms of suspect guerrillas, and the censure of the entire civilized world.

Soon he began his move first to the back bench and then across the floor to the Liberal side of the House. Admittedly, in some measure, impatience with his own advancement in the Conservative Party motivated this defection. Nonetheless, he charged the Conservative high command with abandoning the time-honored policies of government economy and free trade. Still insensitive to the rising social unrest and unconcerned about the mounting Anglo-German trade and naval rivalry, he could not join those Conservatives and Liberal imperialists who meant to solve these problems through costly imperial ventures, navalism, and protectionism. In any event, ideas of fiscal and economic orthodoxy prompted Churchill to switch to the Liberal Party, which, under the pressure of its own radicals, was about to stage a frontal assault on the establishment.

It was not until after he fell under the spell of Lloyd George and Sidney Webb that he discovered labor and social problems; advocated spending less on guns in order to be able to afford more butter; and insisted that only daring social reforms could contain the fledgling Labour Party on the left. As an aristocrat, a soldier, and a renegade Tory, he found it convenient to legitimize his shift to creeping welfarism with allusions to his father's abortive campaign for Tory democracy in the 1880s. Once he succeeded Lloyd George at the Board of Trade in 1908—his first Cabinet post—he was in a position to act on his strident criticism of sweated industries and unemployment by setting up trade boards and labor exchanges.

By 1910, his reformist zeal began to cool. Whereas he still favored small and gradual tax reforms to finance welfare measures, he was not prepared to undermine the foundations of existing class relations and political institutions. Specifically, he balked when Lloyd George set out to emasculate the powers and prerogatives of the House of Lords, that glorious citadel and symbol of Britain's traditional, stratified, and deferential society.

But he could not switch back to the Conservative Party for fear of further compounding distrust of himself in Westminster as well as in the clubs. Besides, Asquith made him home secretary, thereby charging him with the maintenance of law and order in a society shaken by labor disputes. His engrained conservatism and his flair for military action informed the repressive measures with which Churchill handled the coal strike in Wales in November, 1910, the bogus anarchist scare on Sidney Street in January, 1911,* and the railway strike in August of that same year.

Presently Asquith moved Churchill to the Admiralty because his home secretary was under attack by radicals and Labourites for reveling in precipitate police and military repression, and also because a man with martial talents and disposition was needed in that post.

Actually, the Panther incident at Agadir, which in July, 1911, exposed Germany's hostile and offensive intentions, helped Churchill to disentangle himself from the internal social and labor struggles, struggles in which he was being ground up by the fast-growing polarization between the Right and the Left. Overnight he forgot about reform, retrenchment, and appeasement. From the Admiralty he pressed for a bigger navy, regardless of cost and fiscal burden. If he still backed home rule for Ireland, he did so both to win radical votes for his high naval estimates and to promote civil peace in the face of external dangers.

In any case, in July–August, 1914, at the age of thirty-nine, he was the most ardent interventionist in the Liberal Cabinet. He did not wait for the violation of Belgian neutrality to provide a moral purpose for war; his arguments for declaring war were couched in terms of balance of power, security, prestige, and the sanctity of England's commitment to France.

I need not elaborate on his brash but abortive pledge to hold Antwerp against the advancing Germans; on his share of the responsibility for the Gallipoli fiasco; and on his resignation from

* A famous episode: Churchill personally helped direct the siege of six burglars—some thought they were anarchists—who earlier murdered three policemen. Churchill's participation in the incident caught the popular imagination. [ed.]

the Admiralty under Conservative pressure. Instead, let me emphasize that the war and the Bolshevik Revolution combined to push both the Conservative and the Liberal parties further to the Right while radicalizing Labour, the Irish nationalists, and the Indian Congress Party. In the second khaki election of the century, the one coming on the heels of victory in 1918, Churchill once again condoned and benefited from the upsurge of jingoist superpatriotism. With Lloyd George he intoned the Tory clamor for hanging the kaiser, for exorbitant reparations, and for colonial booty. The new House was overwhelmingly dominated by those hard-faced men who had benefited so much from the war. Since the Liberal Party was in shambles, Labour became His Majesty's Loyal Opposition. The wartime coalition continued, with Prime Minister Lloyd George and his "coupon" Liberals beholden to the Tories.

Lloyd George repeatedly, though unsuccessfully, tried to disengage himself from these Tory shackles in order to secure a moderate peace, domestic reforms, and an accommodation with the Irish and Indian nationalists. Churchill not only failed to support his chief in this endeavor; he actually sabotaged him. In his capacity as secretary of state for war and air he became the government's most fiery advocate of direct and large-scale military intervention in Russia for the purpose of overthrowing rather than merely containing the Bolshevik Revolution. He was the first in high office to charge publicly that Russian Bolshevism was worse than German militarism, and as of 1919, not unlike after 1945, he urged that Germany be made into the principal continental bulwark against Communism. Not surprisingly, the Tories exploited Churchill's summons for a full-scale anti-Bolshevik crusade to press their own opposition to the recognition of the Soviet government and to withdrawal from Russia. In turn, this opposition to peaceful coexistence with the revolutionary regime abroad was an integral part of a preemptive offensive against both Lloyd George reformism and the Labour Party at home.

In the election of 1922, Churchill again ran as a Lloyd George Liberal. However, he was defeated; the Lloyd George faction was reduced to 57 seats; and Labour rose to 142. Churchill now sought to return to the Conservative fold, without, however, breaking altogether with liberalism. His stern treatment of strikers and anarchists before the war, his decisive advocacy of belligerency in July, 1914, and his unremitting enthusiasm for intervention in Russia had done much to restore his credit with the Conservatives. Presently he decided that by agitating and magnifying the specter of Bolshevism he could complete his reconciliation with the Conservatives while at the same time frightening Liberals to rally behind him.[2]

Accordingly, he set out to red-bait the Labour Party. In January, 1924, he declared that

> the enthronement in office of a Socialist Government would be a serious national misfortune such as has usually befallen great states only on the morrow of their defeat in war . . . all . . . prospects [of a foreign policy consonant with the national interest and of social reform] will be destroyed by the accession to office of a minority party innately pledged to the fundamental subversion of the existing social and economic civilization and organized for that purpose and that purpose alone. Strife and tumult, deepening and darkening, will be the only consequence of minority socialist rule.[3]

This was the first of a stream of broadsides warning that a Labour government would subvert Britain's political and social institutions. In 1924 he fought two elections on an outright antisocialist platform. Even though he lost both races to a Labour rival, Churchill hereafter stood forth as Britain's leading counterrevolutionary.

In the fall of that year he returned to Commons as a Conservative in good standing. Partly because he feared Churchill's machinations if left outside the government, Prime Minister Baldwin made him chancellor of the exchequer. As a member of the Baldwin administration, he not only introduced a budget that aggravated Britain's trade depression and unemployment; he also played a key role in the suppression of the general strike of 1926 —which was called in support of the coal miners—denouncing it as a sinister revolutionary plot. But even before this strike was over, he was off on a trip, which, among other places, took him to Rome, where he conferred with Mussolini about Italy's new society. Before returning home he gave the Italian press the following statement:

2. *Ibid.*, pp. 249 and 252.
3. Cited in *ibid.*, p. 252.

I could not help being charmed as so many other people have been by Signor Mussolini's gentle and simple bearing and by his calm detached poise in spite of so many burdens and dangers [he began]. If I had been an Italian I am sure that I should have been whole-heartedly with you from start to finish in your triumphant struggle against the bestial appetites and passions of Leninism. But in England we have not had to fight this danger in the same deadly form. We have our own way of doing things. But that we shall succeed in grappling with Communism and choking the life out of it—of that I am absolutely sure.

I will, however, say a word on an international aspect of Fascism. Externally, your movement has rendered a service to the whole world. The great fear which has always beset every democratic leader or working-class leader has been that of being undermined or overbid by someone more extreme than he. It seems that continued progression to the Left, a sort of inevitable landslide into the abyss, was the characteristic of all revolutions. Italy has shown that there is a way of fighting the subversive forces which can rally the mass of the people, properly led, to value and wish to defend the honour and stability of civilized society. She has provided the necessary antidote to the Russian poison. Hereafter, no great nation will be unprovided with an ultimate means of protection against cancerous growths, and every responsible labour leader in the country ought to feel his feet more firmly planted in resisting levelling and reckless doctrines. . . .[4]

Of course, in the early 1930s he also held Labour and radical influences responsible for the government's appeasement of Indian nationalism. In late 1930 he proclaimed that "Gandhism and all it stands for will, sooner or later, have to be grappled with and finally crushed. It is no use trying to satisfy a tiger by feeding it on cat's meat." [5] Shortly thereafter he was alarmed and nauseated by the sight of

Mr. Gandhi, a seditious middle-Temple lawyer, now posing as a fakir of a type well-known in the East, striding half-naked up the steps of the vice-regal palace while he is still organizing and conducting a defiant campaign of civil disobedience, to parley on equal terms with the representative of the king-emperor.[6]

4. *Times* (London), January 21, 1927; cited in Cowles, pp. 271–72.
5. Cited in Cowles, p. 280.
6. Cited in Cowles, p. 280.

Needless to say, the Government of India Bill of 1935 never produced any of the dire consequences predicted by Churchill.

The point I wish to make is that in the 1930s the man who couched his warnings about the approaching international crisis in terms of power politics and military strength was England's foremost ideological warrior. On social and imperial questions he was not just a meek, bland Conservative; he was an aggressive, diehard Tory. Here, then, was Churchill, leading the battle against Bolshevism at home while, at the same time, trying to rally political support for a foreign policy designed to contain, if not overthrow, Europe's foremost anti-Bolshevik dictators and regimes.

Since many Tories and Conservatives sympathized with the counterrevolutionary regimes on the Continent, Churchill was not likely to gather support in that quarter. As for the Labourites and radicals, they were not about to trust this Tory who was such a recent convert to bipartisanship in the face of foreign danger. To be sure, even after the Labour Party recognized that international danger—and Labour did so as of 1933—it remained opposed to rearmament.

Still, the Left continued to have good reasons to suspect Churchill. He never retracted his praise of Mussolini. Moreover, as late as September 17, 1937, he still declared that, while disliking the Nazi system, he nevertheless hoped that should Britain ever be defeated she would "find a champion as indomitable [as Hitler] to restore our courage and lead us back to our place among the nations."[7] Apparently he still preferred Nazism to socialism, since at this late date he once again charged that socialism could make its way only "in some semi-barbarian Asiatic country or in a nation ruined by defeat in war."[8] Then, in 1945, when on the morrow of victory—not of defeat—Labour was on the verge of gaining a majority, Churchill stuck to his guns, except that he now prophesied that socialism would mean a "Nazi state" and "a Gestapo."[9]

Apart from never exposing the destructive political and ideo-

7. Winston S. Churchill, *Step by Step, 1936–1939* (London, 1939), p. 170.
8. *Ibid.*, p. 148.
9. See Ronald B. McCallum, *The British General Election of 1945* (London and Oxford, 1947), p. 142.

logical tap-roots and objectives of Fascism and National Socialism, Churchill equivocated on some of the major international crises of the 1930s. Right down to the outbreak of war he favored the appeasement of Mussolini in the hope of tying Italy to Britain and France. He completely evaded the Abyssinian question. In supporting the national government's do-nothing response to Italian aggression in Africa, he went so far as to declare that no one could "keep up the pretense that Abyssinia was a fit, worthy, and equal member of a league of civilized nations."[10]

Churchill was equally evasive with regard to the Spanish Civil War. He again backed the government's nonintervention policy, even though he knew that this policy benefited Franco. In his view, the Spanish welter was none of Britain's and France's business: these countries should simply "send charitable aid under the Red Cross to both sides, and for the rest, keep out of it and arm."[11] In other words, while he claimed not to want to make a choice between a Fascist and a Communist Spain, the net effect of nonintervention was to favor the cause of counterrevolution on the Iberian peninsula. And, incidentally, it is rather strange that, as a champion of the balance of power and of Britain's security needs, Churchill barely hinted at the danger to Gibraltar and the western Mediterranean should Franco and Hitler join forces.

It should be stressed that whereas this appeasement of Mussolini and Franco was popular with the Conservatives, including the diehard Tories, it was scathingly criticized by the Labourites and radicals. Churchill himself conceded that Britain's Spanish policy was not dictated by military unpreparedness but by internal political division over the question of intervention,[12] as was also the case in France. But, except for this casual admission, throughout most of the 1930s Churchill deliberately created the impression that England's military unpreparedness, particularly in the air, was at the root of appeasement.

His position on Russia was also far from straightforward. To be sure, especially following the purges, there was room for doubt about the Red Army's military capability. Just the same, as early

10. Winston S. Churchill, *While England Slept: A Survey of World Affairs, 1932–1938* (New York, 1938), p. 233 (October 24, 1935).
11. Churchill, *Step by Step,* pp. 53 and 57 (August 10 and 21, 1936).
12. *Ibid.,* p. 228 (April 5, 1938).

as September, 1936, Churchill acknowledged that these purges were "less a manifestation of world propaganda than an act of self-preservation by a community which fears and has reason to fear, the sharp German sword."[13] But it was not until a few months before Munich that Churchill unequivocally called for diplomatic and military cooperation with the Soviet Union in order to resist Germany. Will it ever be known whether this delay was due to his low assessment of Russia's military capabilities rather than to his long-standing and bitter hatred of the Soviet regime? Meanwhile, he continued to play the Italian card while also invoking the "powerful military republic of Turkey."[14]

Obviously, Churchill was caught in a double bind. His own kind were reluctant to listen to him: they had hidden sympathies for the Axis dictators and were fearful that popular fronts as well as the Soviet Union would benefit from a successful anti-Nazi crusade. At the time of Munich, barely forty Conservatives shared Churchill's sense of danger and urgency.

On the other hand, Labourites and radicals were hostile to the Axis regimes precisely because of their counterrevolutionary objectives and methods. And yet, how could they rally behind Britain's foremost counterrevolutionary for this battle, particularly since Churchill appeased Mussolini and Franco and dragged his feet on cooperation with Soviet Russia?

Not that Churchill failed to work at overcoming Labour and radical reticence. Since Labour claimed to oppose increasing armaments because the Tories could not be trusted to use them for democratic and progressive purposes, he advanced the formula "arms and the Covenant." Ever since Woodrow Wilson's days, the British Left and not Churchill had been loyal to the League of Nations. He now favored collective security within the framework of the covenant in order to "secure a measure of unity at home among all classes and all parties, which is indispensable to the efficiency of our foreign policy as well as to the progress of our defense preparations."[15] And, indeed, as of the fall of 1938 this wooing of the Left began to pay dividends.

I am suggesting, then, that the lack of popular, party, and Par-

13. *Ibid.*, p. 62 (September 4, 1936).
14. *Ibid.*, pp. 309–10 (December 15, 1938).
15. Churchill, *While England Slept*, p. 373 (December 21, 1937).

liamentary support for Churchill's foreign policy prescriptions cannot be traced to any significant extent to rancor over his party infidelities; to immunity to his spurious prophesies of doom; or to misgivings about his personal eccentricities and his lust for power. Nor will it do to pin the responsibility for appeasement on the pacifism of the public at large; on the failure of the Foreign Office and Chamberlain to recognize the expansionist drive of the Nazi regime; or on the low level of military preparedness.

Instead, it would seem that Churchill remained isolated because most Conservatives hesitated to endorse a foreign policy that had progressive if not revolutionary overtones; because Labour distrusted a counterrevolutionary's advocacy of a progressive cause; because Churchill's equivocal attitudes toward Fascist Italy, Franco's Spain, and Soviet Russia reinforced this Labour distrust; and because right up until Munich Churchill's summons for a return to pure power politics was intermittently infused with ideological concerns.

This same intermingling of power and ideology reemerged during and after the Second World War. Accordingly, in October, 1944, it was Churchill, the hardheaded power politician—and not Roosevelt, the naïve idealist—who first recognized Russia's predominance in Rumania and Bulgaria, and her vital interests in Yugoslavia and Hungary, in exchange for British predominance in Greece. On the other hand, there was a strong ideological motivation behind Churchill's advocacy of an assault on the allegedly soft underbelly of Europe; behind his reluctant support of the leftist partisans in Yugoslavia; behind his battle against the guerrillas in Greece; behind his hostile suspicion of the Italian and French partisans; and behind his defiant braggadocio that he had not been appointed by His Majesty the King to preside over the liquidation of the British Empire.

Similarly, his Fulton speech of March 5, 1946, which signaled the formal start of the Cold War, had an unmistakable ideological flavor. Churchill not only indicted Soviet Russia for lowering an "iron curtain . . . from Stettin in the Baltic to Trieste in the Adriatic," but also asserted that the Soviets were out for "the infinite expansion of their power and doctrines." And yet, at the time, as a student of power, he must have known that Russia was altogether exhausted; that there was no serious danger of the Red

Army advancing into Central Europe; and that to the extent that there was a Communist danger in the Western world it was an outgrowth of internal conditions, particularly in Italy and France.

Perhaps Churchill welcomed the Cold War because, not unlike the Red Scare after 1918, it could be used to dish the Labour Party, which threatened permanently to disfigure his beloved traditional England. In any case, Churchill should be remembered as a champion of the balance of power as well as of counterrevolution. I have a hunch he himself would not mind this epitaph.

CLEMENT ATTLEE

Churchill on Balance

CHURCHILL, I consider, was the greatest leader in war this country has ever known. Not the greatest warrior. As a strategist, he was not in the same class as Cromwell, and if he had ever commanded armies in the field I doubt if he would ever have been a Marlborough. But a war leader must be much more than a warrior, and do much more than make war. Above all he must stand like a beacon for his country's will to win. And give it constant voice, and translate it into action.

I rate him supreme as Britain's leader in war because he was able to solve the problem that democratic countries in total war find crucial and may find fatal: relations between the civil and military leaders. Lloyd George had an instinct that told him when

---

From *Churchill: An Observer Appreciation,* by Clement Attlee. London: The Observer, 1965, pp. 14–35.

the generals were doing anything wrong, but he did not have the military knowledge to tell the generals what was right. Churchill did. He did not overrule the generals. But he always had chapter and verse with which to meet their protests and to lead them to a positive course of his own.

Much more often, however, he compelled their respect as an ex-soldier who had fought with weapons in his hand, who had conceived high strategy and knew the inside of military problems at all levels. And if sometimes he did what they wanted instead of what he wanted to do himself, everybody always knew who was the boss. He knew his stuff. And the generals knew it.

In the whole of the First World War there had been only one brilliant strategical idea—and that was Winston's: the Dardanelles. It was the one attempt to get away from the mutual slogging match in the mud and blood of Western Europe, and make an imaginative strategic flanking movement that might cripple the enemy with one blow. I thought he was right at the time. The Germans were very sensitive to an attack on them in the Near East. If the direction of the war had not been in the hands of such a vacillating man as Kitchener, and if the campaign had not been entrusted to incompetent men whom Kitchener had appointed, Winston's scheme would have worked.

History said for two decades that he was wrong simply because the Tories of his day would not believe anything good of him. But in the Second World War it was the same imaginative outflanking movement, the left hook or the right, that set the stamp of Britain's overall strategy. This was the stamp of Winston himself.

In my view, he was a greater leader in war than Chatham because he personally made more impact on the men who fought. He had the capacity for being a symbol, a figure that meant something to the individual fighting man. As a public figure he was much more attractive, and therefore more influential, than the younger Pitt, and he set the impress of a single mind—essential when a fight is on—much more effectively on his colleagues and subordinates.

Winston's concrete contribution to the war effort, namely the setting up of the intragovernmental machine that dealt with the war, was most important. Winston, on becoming prime minister, also became minister of defense. Within the Cabinet he formed a Defence Committee which, of course, he dominated in his twin capacity as prime minister and minister of defense. The committee had a nucleus of permanent members: myself as deputy chairman, the service ministers, and the three chiefs of staff. Other ministers attended as required.

The prime minister also frequently conferred with the three chiefs of staff on detailed matter. In addition, from time to time, larger meetings were called for a specific purpose, for example, to deal with the submarine menace. Here all kinds of people, scientists as well as military, brought their contributions to the common pool to help solve the problem of the Battle of the Atlantic.

Given Winston's knowledge of military men, his own military experience and flair, his personal dynamism, and the sweeping powers that any prime minister in wartime can have if he chooses to use them, the deadly problem of civilians-versus-generals in wartime was solved. Everybody involved should get some credit for this. But Winston's role has only to be described for its overriding importance to be clear.

If somebody asked me what exactly Winston did to win the war, I would say, "Talk about it." In the Cabinet he talked about practically nothing else. After about 1942, when he and the chief of staff concentrated on the running of the war, and left John Anderson and myself to deal with domestic affairs, if Winston couldn't talk about the war he would rather not talk at all. The only part of home affairs he was interested in were those which bore upon the war effort. He took no interest in the famous White Paper on Post-War Britain. Indeed, we had some difficulty in persuading him to read it.

Now and again he would pick up some document on home affairs in the Cabinet, take up one of the memoranda on top, or pounce on one of the minutes written halfway through it, and ask some question in the tone of a man who had read the whole thing through several times, and discovered the critical weakness in it, and was now going to hold a grand inquest.

"What about *this!*" he would say, glowering around the room. Sometimes we would have to point out to him that the passage he quoted was followed by its refutation and was not a recommendation. If he was in the mood, quite unabashed, he would try another. Or again, he might ignore our observation, and hold forth for ten or fifteen minutes about something that no longer existed.

We used to let him get it off his chest, and not interrupt—indeed, it was extremely difficult to interrupt him because not only had he no intention of stopping, but frequently he had no intention of listening. His monologues sometimes went on for very long periods indeed.

Much has been written about the way he would send out memoranda on small points of detail, which gave generals out in the field the impression, until they came to know better, that he had grasped every detail of what they were doing—and not doing. "What are we doing about the tents for signalers on Salisbury Plain?" is the kind of flash that would go out, much to the consternation of the unfortunate recipient. It frequently created a lot of confusion, because once Winston had decided to find out what was happening about those tents the whole war effort was held up until somebody had told him.

Very often the only thing that Winston knew about an operation was the point of detail he had covered in his memorandum. Some of the generals out in the field thought that Winston was like Big Brother in Orwell's book, looking down on them from the wall the whole time. Now and again somebody would tumble to it that this was a trick, and, realizing that Winston could not possibly know about every operation in detail, take advantage of the fact. Here Winston's colossal luck or guardian angel often intervened. For this operation would sometimes turn out to be one of the many that Winston knew from A to Z. There would be hell to pay.

What Winston really did, in my view, was to keep us all on our toes. He did very little work in the Cabinet. Churchill's Cabinets, frankly, were not good for business, but they were great fun. He kept us on our toes partly by just being Winston, and partly because he was always throwing out ideas. Some of them were not very good, and some of them were downright dangerous. But they kept coming, and they kept one going, and a lot of them were excellent.

In my view, the best were those that came out of his gift of immediate compassion for people who were suffering. I remember him coming back from a quick visit to a south country town just after it had been fearfully bombed. Winston had been much struck by the sight of a little home and shop, all exposed by the walls being blown down. He described it, with tears in his eyes. "We've got to do something about that damage *now,*" he said. Within twenty-four hours officials were working on a scheme that speedily developed into the War Damage Commission.

My relations with him in Cabinet always seemed to me to be very good. He talked to me extremely frankly—more frankly, I suspect, than he talked to some of his Conservative colleagues. He did not have much use for those who had supported Neville Chamberlain. He never took it out on them, he was too good-natured and, anyway, he had too high a regard for political loyalty. What he did do, however, was to get most of these Chamberlainites at as great a distance from himself as he could, and he did it very nicely. Halifax went to the United States; Sam Hoare to Spain; Malcolm MacDonald to Canada; Harlech to South Africa; and Swinton to West Africa.

Winston and I sometimes, but not often, had a blazing row. I remember one on India, but he was quite all right next morning and indeed accepted my view. He was always smoking a cigar in the Cabinet room, and now and again he would give me one. Whether it was because at that moment I had said something he particularly approved of, or because he could no longer stand the smell of my pipe, I have never discovered. I never thought of asking him.

The only thing that Winston had against me was that I was a socialist. He used to complain about this quite bitterly at times, but I told him there was nothing he could do about it. Whenever we got on to the subject of planning for postwar Britain, Winston was ill at ease. He always groused about my being a socialist. Whenever a Cabinet committee put up a paper to him on anything not military or naval, he was inclined to suspect a socialist plot. Even wartime schemes for controls and rationing used to irritate him. We could never get him to understand that these were as essential to a conservative country at war as to a socialist one.

He became increasingly suspicious about the possibility of the socialists putting something over on him. He thought the socialists were cleverer than the Tories, anyway, and this naturally only increased his apprehensions. So whenever he got wind that a report or a memorandum on something outside his ken was coming up, he would get somebody to spy out the land so that he could prepare an onslaught on our "machinations." Winston used to describe this artlessly, as "getting a second, highly qualified and objective opinion on the issue." In fact, what he wanted was a hatchet job.

The first man he singled out as his hatchet man was Lord Cherwell, whom we called "Old Man River." Half the time, poor old Cherwell would not know half the facts that the Cabinet subcommittee had been working on. He and Winston would then put their heads together, without anybody else around, of course, and concoct some reason for not doing anything, based mainly on Winston's prejudices and supported by Old Man River's ignorance. Those Conservatives who knew the facts of the matter were usually united with us in thinking that the thing ought to be done. This only made Winston the more recalcitrant.

I got a little tired of this. One day I said to Winston: "If you value Cherwell's opinion, why not put him on the appropriate committee? This will save a lot of time." Winston thought this was a capital idea. So Cherwell came on to the committee. To do him justice, as soon as he was given full access to the facts, Cherwell saw things very much as we did, and he was honest enough to report back in this sense to Winston. Winston was obviously annoyed. He gave up Cherwell as hopeless for his purpose and looked around for another hatchet man. This time it was Beaverbrook, who, though keen enough, was not very effective. And by the time he had learned enough to be a saboteur, the war was over and we had won the election.

If Winston's greatest virtue was his compassion, his greatest weakness was his impatience. He never understood that a certain time was always bound to elapse between when you ask for something to be done and when it can be effected. He worked people terribly hard, and was inconsiderate. On the whole, he did not vent his impatience on people in bursts of temper or in bullying. But, as Alanbrooke has reported in his Diaries, he kept people working impossible hours in order that he should not have to contain himself, or defer anything that he had become enthusiastic about.

Another thing about him that I did not care for was that he was not generous in praising his subordinates. He was especially inconsiderate, I thought, to those whom he did not regard as his own discoveries and protégés. John Anderson and Ernest Bevin, for instance, should have been given the honor for a great many things that have been credited to Churchill. And Winston was to blame for this.

It wasn't that he was mean; he just did not seem to think that it mattered that other people had worked hard, and that the idea that had produced the success had come from somebody else.

I think this was an effect of Winston's egotism. So far as the running of the country was concerned, he always thought of himself as the only person who really mattered. He had what you might call the "heroic" conception of government. Everything must be done by, and through, the big national leader. The hero of the finest hour. Seeing and hearing from anybody else did not matter in the least, he thought, and this led to confusion. So far as government was concerned, Winston was not a natural democrat. He was an autocrat.

He was also a poor judge of men, and he made some curious appointments. He was always likely to take a good man from a job he was doing well and give him something to do for which he was quite unsuitable.

One time he had the bright idea of making Sir John Anderson viceroy of India. I was appalled at the prospect, so was Field-Marshal Smuts. John Anderson would have made a magnificent viceroy, but at that time he knew more about the war as it affected the civilian population of Britain than any man alive. It would have been a mistake to send him to India. We stopped that one.

Winston made some good appointments, too. Many a statesman would make better appointments sometimes if he was braver about them. Winston never had a tremor in selecting a man for a job—though he hated sacking people—and considerations of party would not stop him. I remember the appointment of Temple in 1942 as archbishop of Canterbury. Somebody asked Winston why he had made a socialist archbishop of Canterbury. "Because," he said, "he was the only half-crown article in a sixpenny-halfpenny bazaar."

I've said before that Churchill was not a great Parliamentarian, mainly, of course, because he was too impatient to master the procedures. He was not even a great House of Commons debater in the way that Lloyd George and Birkenhead were. His speeches were magnificent rhetorical performances, but they were too stately, too pompous, too elaborate to be ideal House of Commons stuff. It was the occasions that gave the speeches their historic quality.

I heard so many of these speeches in preparation that perhaps I am not the best judge of them. He would walk up and down the room, throwing out remarks. "I'll go to them and tell them," he would say, and out would come some brilliant phrases to be worked later into a speech. In my view his best speeches were those which described historical moments—a victory, such as Alamein, or a defeat, such as Dunkirk. Those speeches are unique.

So far as Churchill the historian is concerned, I have always admired his prose much more than his content. It seems to me that somebody would get a curious idea of what has been going on in this country for the last 2,000 years if they had to get it all from Winston. He leaves too much of the important stuff out.

Churchill was great not only as a leader but also as a human being. For the range of his qualities as a man one would have to go back to the Renaissance. That is the period which is his spiritual niche. His range of interests and curiosities was so vast that they seemed more those of a child than a grown man. Indeed, the idea of a child comes to mind when one considers many things about him. His naughtiness for example, and his short-term sulkiness, which were soon followed by complete oblivion of who or what it was that had upset him.

If there was one thing that marked him off from the comparable figures in history, it was his characteristic way of standing back and looking at himself—and his country—as he believed history would. He was always, in effect, asking himself, "How will I look if I do this or that?" And "What must Britain do now so that the verdict of history will be favorable?" All he cared about, in Britain's history, of course, were the moments when

Britain was great. He was always looking around for "finest hours," and if one was not immediately available, his impulse was to manufacture one.

His greatest virtue, his compassion, has never properly been appreciated. It was his compassion, coupled to his energy, that made him so "dynamic." Cruelty and injustice revolted him. His will to fight them took him in many directions, not all of them wise, and not all of them to my liking; but I never questioned that profound fund of humanity, benevolence, love, call it what you like, in his character which made his hatred of cruelty the steering gear of his great life.

I remember the tears pouring down his cheeks one day before the war in the House of Commons, when he was telling me what was being done to the Jews in Germany—not to individual Jewish friends of his, but to the Jews as a group. Criticism of him for thinking too much in terms of nations and masses and not enough in terms of individual human beings is frequently misplaced.

I do not believe that he became a lieutenant of Lloyd George and a pioneer of the welfare state through political opportunism. He was an opportunist, certainly. But he cared about his fellow men. You only had to bring home to him an instance of cruelty and injustice, and he would respond to it. When his feelings were moved, he acted. Few men I have met in public life were less prone than Churchill to paying mere lip service to a humanitarian cause.

He was so eclectic in his attitude to party that sometimes I used to wonder what he would be like in the labor movement. I could imagine the zest with which he would churn out phrases about "Capitalists grinding the faces of the poor." So far as language went, he would have put Marx and Lenin in the shade. However, he would never have become a socialist even if he had joined the Labour Party. A socialist must regard it as essential to bring about certain forms and institutions, and eliminate others—though I do not believe that a socialist should have a final view of what society should be. I am enough of a Hegelian to believe that all being is becoming.

Winston, however, took society as he found it. He wanted to alter it only by removing cruelty and injustice and promoting generosity and understanding. Men like me would not tolerate a feudal society, even if everybody seemed reasonably content in it—for us, there would be too much degradation of human nature on the bottom rungs. But Winston would not have minded being in a feudal society.

His views on society are very difficult to sum up. He was rather like a layer cake. One layer was certainly seventeenth century. The eighteenth century in him is obvious. There was the nineteenth century, and a large slice, of course, of the twentieth century: and another, curious, layer which may possibly have been the twenty-first.

The way Winston flung himself into whatever cause he was supporting at the moment was unique. It made most impression, of course, on the side he had just deserted. People used to wonder how he could do it. I think it was because he was too honest to pretend to feel shame when he did not. He changed horses for the same reason that a huntsman does: to keep up with the hounds, not to chase a different quarry. And energy came into it. Even if he had wanted to go easy on arriving in the new camp, and have a breather, so to speak, before starting to bash his late friends, his zest in putting everything he had into what he was doing would not have let him.

Winston was a most generous enemy, perhaps the most magnanimous of his generation. He had great pity for the loser, and he was the last man to hit somebody when he was down. Getting him down he regarded as the greatest of fun, but having done it, he wanted to pick him up again.

In the First World War, even before it was over, he was one of the first to talk sympathetically about the Germans, not only as a group of individuals, but as a nation. It was the same in the Second World War.

He always made a distinction between the people and its leaders. And it is worth while noting that when he took a very tough line against the Bolsheviks in the First World War, he had nothing against the Russian people.

He enjoyed his revenge, however. He enjoyed the double revenge that his rise to greatness exacted from the Conservative Party. They had broken his father—and had tried to break the son. Winston and his father were revenged. But Churchill's revenges, I think, never came from a vein of sadism. They came from a profound feeling for poetic justice.

His egotism, of course, was monumental. "Of course I am an egotist," he said to me in the Cabinet Room one day. "Where do you get if you aren't?" Chatham said in his great hour, "I know I can save this country, and I know that nobody else can." That was Winston, too. But not only did he believe in his own destiny: he believed in the destiny of Britain. His courage in the darkest hours was partly due to having the nerves of a rhinoceros, but partly due to a conviction that Britain could not lose.

He has spoken of himself as merely the lion's roar, and undoubtedly he would not have been able to roar so well if the spirit had not been there in the country. But he called it out. When some men describe their love of their country, I find it rather embarrassing. But when Churchill spoke of Britain, he always struck a chord in me.

He was rather insular about Britain, of course. He talked a good deal about the commonwealth, and nobody understood its importance better than he did. But Britain—England—really was his limit so far as feeling went. This may be why his judgment on commonwealth affairs was often bad—notably on India.

Churchill's views on India were very much conditioned by his first-hand experience of that country. When he was a young man in India, the empire was at its most self-conscious, and, being at the height of its strength, was liberal (though paternal), not reactionary and repressive. For Winston, the British Empire, free trade, the expansion of opportunity, world order, the progress of man, and war on cruelty and injustice, all went together, with his vision of England, so to speak, crowning everything. He never really grew up to the view that, for instance, Indians did not see things like this, and that by the time he had got to middle age the facts of life had changed, that the role of Britain in the Empire had been altered altogether.

The first time I saw Winston was at the time of the Sidney Street siege in 1911. He was in one part of the street, directing operations, and I was some distance away among the onlookers. Earlier, when, since my father was a Gladstonian Liberal, I had become a Conservative, I admired him. A young Tory myself, I praised Winston as the kind of chap who was saying what ought to be said. By the time he had left the Tories over Tariff Reform in 1905, I had become a socialist, and frankly Liberals and Tories were all the same to me: I was against them both and they had too much in common for me to care which of them Churchill belonged to.

During the First World War, as I have said, I took a favorable view of Winston. He was probably the only member of Asquith's Cabinet who had a grasp of strategy. Asquith himself had none.

He showed the same strategic grasp in the Second World War. His policy of exploiting our success in Africa and of striking at what he called the soft underbelly of the Axis power was sound. It was entirely in line with the strategic lessons of our past. We had succeeded by exploiting British sea power.

The Tories, of course, pretended to be furious with Winston at the time of the First World War because of the mishandling of the Gallipoli campaign. In fact, what they were knocking him for then, and ever since, was his defection from the party. If the Gallipoli issue had not coincided with Asquith's crack-up, and the subsequent squabble over how many Tories should be included in the new government, Winston's reputation would probably not have suffered anything like so badly.

On the other hand his policy of attacking the Soviet government in 1919 was in disregard of all the lessons of history. Extreme pressure always consolidates a revolutionary regime by evoking patriotism.

I became strongly anti-Winston during the events that led up to the general strike of 1926. Winston, of course, was held up as the hammer of the unemployed. In my view, a lot of this was nonsense. Winston's feelings toward the miners were much more sympathetic than those of some of the Tories who made sorrowful speeches about them. After the strike was over, he was outraged by the way some of the mine owners behaved to the miners.

What Winston felt about the workers was easily misinterpreted. Take, for instance, what happened when Asquith managed to call off the railway strike. Asquith was standing with some members of the Cabinet, congratulating himself on having ended the strike, when suddenly his face fell. "Somebody has got to break it to Winston that it's off," he said. There were no offers. "You'd better go," he said to Lloyd George. "He's *your* friend." Lloyd George displayed no enthusiasm, but dutifully went round to the Home Office.

He found Winston up in his room, on all-fours, with large-scale plans of various railway stations and goods yards spread in front of him, and small blocks of wood, representing troops, being moved in and put into position. "It's off, Winston," said Lloyd George. "Bloody hell!" said Winston, or words to that effect: then he got up and kicked the troops and the maps across the room. Winston had become so enthused about his job that he wanted to go ahead and finish it. Animosity against the strikers had nothing to do with it.

He must be held responsible for the disastrous return to the gold standard in 1925. Winston knew very little economics, and was completely out of his depth with finance. I think he regarded both subjects as tiresome and unnecessary intrusions into the real business of politics. He often said that he was led astray by his financial advisers at the Treasury and the Bank of England.

Our next area of conflict was India in the mid-thirties. Dominated by his memories of India in the late nineties, he was incredibly—almost comically—obscurantist about conditions in India in the thirties. He used to have a certain amount of first-hand information and advice about what was going on, but he used to get it from an extraordinarily blind and prejudiced group of Muslim reactionaries.

He suffered, as many others did, from the idea, which at one time may well have been true, that you could divide India's races into two, those races who would fight and those who would not—the "fighting" races, and the "nonfighting" races of India. Winston got it into his head that all the politicians of India came from the second group. He seemed to think that only the Muslims could fight.

He made a number of grave errors when it came to judging Indian men and affairs. But he *could* learn—though sometimes he *wouldn't* learn—and if he decided to eat his words he would do it without rancor or resentment. At a meeting of the commonwealth prime ministers at Buckingham Palace once, it occurred to me that he and Nehru had never met.

I said to King George VI, who relished this kind of thing,

"Here's a bit of fun: two Old Harrovians who haven't met each other—Winston and Nehru, I'm going to introduce them." "Go ahead," said the king. I introduced them, and they got on splendidly. Winston said how he had admired Nehru's courage in standing up to rioters and Nehru said he had enjoyed reading Winston's book. They chatted most amicably and something like mutual confidence was established, and to the best of my knowledge never diminished.

While on the subject I ought to say that when I became prime minister Winston gave me a great deal of trouble on India, and displayed to the full what I think was a serious defect: he was always rather a mischief maker. When this streak in him was involved with a feeling that the wrong thing was being done, he could behave irresponsibly. When he knew what I was contemplating for India in 1947, he began to say in public that I was going to scuttle out of India and that I was refusing to take the advice of people like the viceroy. As a matter of fact, at the time, Lord Wavell was advising me to make a complete military evacuation. I had made up my mind *not* to take this advice.

I thought it would be a good thing to tell Winston all about this, because I did not want him to cause difficulties for us through lack of knowledge or make a fool of himself. I asked him to come and have a couple of secret talks, giving him access to our information and advice. He came along and took full advantage of them. To my surprise and considerable disappointment, in spite of the understanding that this was all secret, he made speeches in Parliament quite at variance with the facts of which he had been told.

This put me in perhaps the most embarrassing situation of my whole career, since I could not divulge in detail all the facts of the matter, and therefore could not give the lie to Winston.

I find it very hard to forgive him for this. The extraordinary thing is that I *can* forgive him. Winston could get away with this. In any other man it would be damnable and utterly unpardonable.

Of less importance, but in the same vein, was his fury when he heard that I had asked Lord Mountbatten to go out as viceroy. He accused me of trying to exploit the royal family politically, and trying to saddle a member of it with the responsibility of a withdrawal. Winston was very angry about this. I am glad to say that the Mountbattens did not share his view, and his grousing did not prevent them from rendering Britain, India, and the commonwealth a glorious service.

Rather than have access to information that might cause him to change his mind about something, Winston would sometimes prefer to be left in ignorance. He would rather give full rein to his prejudices than advocate a cause which, however well based, he did not personally care for. In other cases, even when the facts were made available to him, for some reason or other he seemed not to grasp them. He was very obtuse, for instance, before and during the abdication crisis.

There, of course, his emotions were involved. Compassion again. He was deeply concerned about the emotional plight of King Edward VIII, felt strongly that it was not right to keep him from the woman he wanted to marry, and equally deeply that Britain should not lose a monarch of outstanding gifts. Winston acted in a way that upset a great many political leaders, but it should be understood clearly that he made not the slightest attempt to make party politics of the occasion.

To my mind, he seemed terribly blind to public opinion. He did not understand, in spite of what the commonwealth prime ministers said, that whatever their personal sympathies, public opinion was opposed not only to the king having Mrs. Simpson as his queen, but to the idea of a morganatic marriage.

This was one of the occasions on which Winston's name was linked with that of Lord Beaverbrook. A great many people have commented, at one time or another, on the curious bunch of friends, advisers, and hangers-on who at one time or another gathered around Winston. Some of them have been great men in their way, and in their field. Some have been, frankly, third-rate on any assessment. "What," I have often heard statesmen of great penetration and understanding ask, "could Winston see in *him*?" "What did Winston get out of *him*?"

The answer was, in the first place—a *kick*! Above all, he valued *stimulus* in another person—the stimulus of a fine brain, perhaps, of good looks, of mutual remembrance of exploits half a century ago in youth, of laughter, skill, courage—many things. But they all came down to—stimulus. And to those people who *had* stimulated him, encouraged him, stood by him, however long ago, Winston remained loyal.

Unfortunately, Winston, in the course of taking his stimulus from some of these people, took other things as well, things that they were much less qualified to give. Beaverbrook is an excellent example. Winston liked Beaverbrook because he stimulated him. But he also took Beaverbrook's advice. Beaverbrook gave Winston advice at the time of the abdication crisis. He told Winston what the public felt. Of course, he was quite wrong.

Beaverbrook continued to offer advice from time to time, and again, so far as I know, he was usually wrong. It was Beaverbrook, as is well known, who advised Churchill on how to conduct his election campaign in 1945. I would not go so far as to say that Churchill could have won that election, though I think he *might* have, if he had gone about it properly. What I am certain about is that Beaverbrook ruined his chances.

I do not think that even Winston's regard for Lord Beaverbrook's political sagacity survived this final assault. During the campaign, I remember Winston giving me a lift. "Well," he said, sinking back into his seat. "I've tried 'em with pep, and I've tried 'em with pap, but I don't know what it is they want."

If he had taken a broad view of what the Conservatives should offer the electors in 1945, he would have done considerably better. But he chose to tighten the noose which the prewar Tories had already put around his neck. His natural combativeness led him, once the campaign had taken shape, to press on with typical Churchillian élan down the road to defeat. As I have said, he was not a good judge of public opinion, and I think that he was sufficiently out of date in his knowledge of the man in the street in peacetime to believe that the kind of nonsense he talked about police state versus Conservative freedom would work.

Churchill often underestimated how much the voter was affected by bread-and-butter considerations, by fears for the security of his wife and children, health and education, and so on. But it wasn't that Winston did not care about these things. Otherwise, he could not have helped Lloyd George build the welfare state. Those people who claim that, as wartime premier, he was opposed to the Beveridge Report are either unfair to him or, more likely, do not know what they are talking about.

Churchill was not "anti-Beveridge." He kept, so to speak, pushing the report away from him, because he wanted to get on and win the war. For this reason, since Winston and the Defence Committee were concentrating on the military aspects of the war, and since, as he himself says in his war memoirs, John Anderson, Arthur Greenwood, and I looked after nearly everything else, the Labour Party was very much more equipped to put the Beveridge Report into effect.

I notice that Sir John Wheeler-Bennett, in his book on King George VI,* observes that when the prospect of having Churchill for prime minister was mooted in 1940, a number of Labour leaders were averse to accepting Churchill because he had called out the troops against the miners in Tonypandy in 1910. Dr. Hugh Dalton, Sir John says, and some other Labour leaders would have preferred Lord Halifax as prime minister, with Mr. Churchill as minister for defense. He adds that King George VI certainly would have preferred this.

I was certainly not among those Labour leaders who would have preferred Lord Halifax. To my mind, at that juncture, one requirement was imperative and overrode every consideration: we had to win the war. I was convinced that Winston Churchill stood head and shoulders above any other possible prime minister. I personally was relieved when I knew that he could have the job if he wished it. My own experience of the First World War, and my readings in history, had convinced me that the prime minister should be a man who knew what war meant, in terms of the personal suffering of the man in the line, in terms of high strategy, and in terms of that crucial issue—how the generals got on with their civilian bosses. I saw nobody around who could qualify except Winston. And I felt that he qualified superbly.

This does not mean that I cared for everything he did as a war leader or would have tried to do it as he did, even if I had thought I could have succeeded at it. It also does not mean that he was a very easy man to work with. On the contrary, he was difficult. Nor does it mean that I subscribe to the view that he did everything, and in the manner, which his adulators have claimed for him. He did not always display a galaxy of virtues. Some of his weaknesses were prominent.

I think Winston thought himself superior to anybody he had ever met, with one exception—Lloyd George. Of course, Winston

* Sir J. W. Wheeler-Bennett, *King George VI* (London, 1958). [ed.]

always talked as though he were superior to Lloyd George, too. He never spoke of himself as Lloyd George's young lieutenant, but as his coadjutor. But I do not think Winston ever deceived himself. I once said something to Lloyd George to the effect that he was the only man I knew who could handle Winston. Lloyd George smiled. "You see," he said, "I *know* him so well." That, of course, is the real secret of power at the very top.

Winston frequently used to lighten our work by flashes of humor. I recall something ecclesiastical coming up. There were a number of keen young churchmen in the government. Winston said brightly: "This all right with the Church Lads' Brigade?" Another instance was when a former Conservative stood as a Liberal at a by-election. Said Winston: "The only instance on record of a rat swimming *toward* the sinking ship." But on the whole, he was tolerant. I think the comradely way in which he treated Herbert Morrison,* who frequently rubbed up against him, was a good instance of this. Churchill, in spite of their clashes, felt much more warmly about Herbert than many people on Herbert's own side.

I think it was a pity that Winston could not have retired when he had won the war. I had seen enough of him during the war to be sure that unless there was a war on he would not make much of a prime minister. What Britain required when the war was over was an architect, somebody who could build new parts into our society, and repair damage. If he had not been so inveterate a politician, so imbued with political pugnacity, I think he would have seen this. And if he had seen it, I think he would have acted on it.

I see no point in discussing him as a peacetime prime minister. As an administrative prime minister he was so far inferior to Peel, the greatest of them, that comparson is futile. He was miles behind Asquith as a peacetime prime minister. His postwar premiership, in fact, was a mistake from every point of view, and it is saying a great deal for the rest of his life that his record does not suffer from this enormous anticlimax.

* Herbert Morrison, the son of a policeman, was an important Labour politician, home secretary during the war, and a member of the war Cabinet. This statement probably reflects Attlee's own dislike of his second-in-command. [ed.]

By any reckoning, Winston Churchill was one of the greatest men that history records. If there were to be a gallery of great Englishmen that could accommodate only a dozen, I would like to see him in. He was brave, gifted, inexhaustible, and indomitable. "Talk not of genius baffled, genius is master of man. Genius does what it must. Talent does what it can." These lines describe him.

Energy, rather than wisdom, practical judgment, or vision, was his supreme qualification. For energy I do not know who will rank with him outside Napoleon, Bismarck, and Lloyd George. However, though his energy alone puts him in this class, it is not the full story of what he did to win the war. It was the poetry of Churchill, as well, that did the trick. Energy and poetry, in my view, really sum him up.

Without Churchill, Britain might have been defeated. I do not say we would have been defeated. But we might have been. He was so perfectly suited to fill a particular need, the need was so vital, and the absence of anybody of his quality was so blatant that one cannot imagine what would have happened if he had not been there. I dare say we would have got along without him. There were certainly plenty of leaders whose nerves were as steady as his, had just as much belief in Britain's cause, and were just as ready to fight to the bitter end. But there was no need of them because Winston was there.

He was, of course, above all, a supremely fortunate mortal. Whether he deserved his great fate or not, whether he won it or had it dropped into his lap, history set him the job that he was the ideal man to do. I cannot think of anybody in this country who has been favored in this way so much, and, into the bargain, at the most dramatic moment in his country's history. In this, Winston was superbly lucky. And perhaps the most warming thing about him was that he never ceased to say so.

GORONWY REES

Churchill: A Minority View

When the trumpeter had blown the last reveille, when the gun carriage had discharged its burden on the quay and the journalists had exhausted all their treasuries of special prose; then, surely, the time had come when one might reasonably wonder what it had all been about. Yet it seemed almost blasphemous to ask such a question. For a week we had been encompassed by so vociferous a cloud of witnesses to Churchill's greatness; obituaries had been furbished up at the last moment to ensure that no possible extravagance had been omitted from their praise; the television had luxuriated in funeral tributes, the dead man's literary agent, his valet, his detectives, had scraped the barrel of memory for the last threadbare fragments of reminiscence. A large and

From "After the Ball Was Over," by Goronwy Rees, *Encounter,* November, 1965, pp. 3–9.

lucrative industry had been founded on his death. Special supplements rolled from the presses; new editions of his works proliferated; the voice of Dimbleby* was loud in the land. And to crown it all there had been the marvelous ceremony of his funeral, the tight blue-and-white square of the naval escort drawing the gun carriage, the guardsmen bowed over their reversed rifles, the voices and the trumpets echoing in the dome of St. Paul's, the tiny launch that carried him away from it all down the river. There had never been such a wake since Valentino's. How could one have any doubt what it all meant?

For the answer was surely obvious. It was generally agreed that Churchill was the greatest, as Englishman, statesman, orator, writer, historian, artist; most of all it would seem, *als Mensch:*

> Soldier, scholar, sportsman he,
> As 'twere all life's epitome.

But even such lines would hardly have satisfied Churchill's panegyrists. They might have suggested that Churchill was in some way human, whereas what was wanted was to show that he was of another order of nature from the pygmies who had surrounded him, truly a Colossus who had bestridden the petty world; one expected some new planet, fiery and luminous, to blaze out in the heavens when he was translated into immortality.

The *Times,* to its own satisfaction, in its memorial supplement almost struck the required note: "He belongs to the country; he belongs to the Commonwealth; he belongs to the world; now he belongs to the ages." Almost, but not quite. "Universe," for "world," and "Eternity" for "ages" would really have captured the Pecksniff touch.

If all the wonderful entertainments that the Earl Marshal has in his repertoire, ready for every occasion, from a cricket match to a coronation, had included a ceremony of canonization, it would surely have been produced at this moment. It would have been all the more appropriate because canonization is apt to provoke just those symptoms of collective hysteria that were displayed in the week following Churchill's death and culminated on the day of his funeral.

* A famous broadcaster, particularly known for his rich descriptions of royal events. [ed.]

To anyone who has even the slightest resistance to hyperbole, it was precisely those symptoms that gave a slightly sinister and creepy quality to the whole proceedings. One could not help feeling that so public an extravagance of grief and mourning could not really have been inspired by one man, that it was not Churchill the nation was burying, but a part of their own history, not a statesman but an Empire, not a hero but themselves as they once were and never would be again.

Fortunately, amid the spate of reminiscences, lamentations, funeral orations, memorial tributes, which Churchill's death, or its approach, inspired, there were a few that were worthy of their subject. It was, for instance, an admirable idea to republish, in book form, Isaiah Berlin's essay on *Mr. Churchill in 1940,* which first appeared in 1949 in *The Atlantic Monthly* and *The Cornhill Magazine* as a review of the first volume of Churchill's war memoirs. Written primarily for an American audience and while Churchill was still alive, it does not fall short of the hyperbole to which he was condemned when dead; but with more justification because it captures exactly the feeling of admiration, gratitude, almost reverence that Churchill inspired in Britain at the one period of his life when he performed an indispensable service to his country.

Churchill in 1940 was indeed a phenomenon that is not likely to be repeated in our history; for 1940 was perhaps the last time that Britain would ever exercise an independent and decisive role in world affairs, and in Churchill a man was found who rose to the occasion with all the formidable force and energies of his nature. For that moment at least, an indestructible bond was forged between himself and the British people; each trusted each other completely; both knew exactly what part they had to play in the crisis they faced together. The mourning provoked by Churchill's death was very largely inspired by grief that such a moment would never occur again; it was a nation mourning for his and its own past greatness.

Isaiah Berlin does not take account of the possibility that it was the nation and the moment that made the man, and not *vice versa.* Such hypotheses are unprofitable and in any case were not necessary to his purpose. What he admirably and vividly expresses is how, at a particular moment of time, the British people found the man they wanted and the qualities in the man that enabled him to respond to all the demands that were made upon him. So remarkable a conjuncture of events, so striking a personality, the sense of a world at a turning point in history, stir Isaiah Berlin as they stirred the subject of his essay. He expresses this feeling so vividly, with so much *brio* and eloquence, with so much imagination tempered by fine and acute analysis, that he really makes one feel for a moment what the world looked like through Churchill's eyes.

But he also notices, almost in passing, one aspect of Churchill that is frequently overlooked. He contrasts Roosevelt's "gay and apparently heedless abandon" with "a dimension of depth" in Churchill, "evidences of seasons of agonized brooding and slow recovery," and "a corresponding sense of tragic possibilities, which Mr. Roosevelt's lighthearted genius instinctively passed by." It is perhaps on this, rather than on his more flamboyant and superficially more attractive qualities, that one might found a real claim to greatness for Churchill; yet, strangely enough, it was precisely this that for the greater part of his political career created an almost unbridgeable gulf between him and the overwhelming majority of his fellow countrymen.

Isaiah Berlin is justified in writing as he does about Churchill in 1940, with such generous and exalted enthusiasm, because he is writing about a triumph, for a man and for a country in which they were so closely identified that it would be impossible to distinguish what part each played in it. But in fact this identification was only momentary; it persisted indeed to a degree, throughout the war, though never agan at so intense a pitch, yet at the same time the British electorate, under the pressure of the war, was slowly formulating political conclusions which were at the opposite pole to Churchill's and led to his abrupt fall from power in 1945.

Thus Churchill in 1940 was at a wholly exceptional point in his life, and exceptional most of all in the relationship that he established with his countrymen. For the most striking feature of Churchill's long political career is that, for all his brilliant qualities, or perhaps because of them, he was repeatedly and for long periods rejected by the British people, that, until the Second World War, he never won their love or trust, and that his political following was confined to a small group of personal friends for the most part of no great weight or significance. Neither the nation nor a party acknowledged him as a leader. When, as at the moment of his death, one was invited to regard him as a great national statesman, hero and father in one, it was difficult to remember that for the greater part of his career he had been an object of suspicion, mistrust, or indifference, and that up to the war it had been singularly barren of any solid or permanent political achievement.

As a spur to memory one could not do better than to read Lady Violet Bonham Carter's *Winston Churchill as I Knew Him*. It is brilliantly written, so well indeed as to make one regret that Lady Violet during her long life has not written more and talked less. And if Isaiah Berlin's essay is written in a spirit of hero worship, Lady Violet's book is the story of a love affair, and like all true love affairs it reveals rather more about both the lover and the loved one than its author might suspect. Like all love stories, also, it is a story of youth, in the years when Lady Violet was a young girl whose father was prime minister of Britain and Churchill a brilliant young politician on the make. Lady Violet endows her story with all the glamour and charm of young love seen with the nostalgic hindsight of the old; moreover, the glamour and charm suffuse, like a golden glow, her vividly painted picture of the society, and the age, in which her passionate devotion was formed. Sometimes one feels as if one were reading a novel by Ouida.

It is an essential feature of its plot that her hero, on his first appearance, is already a man who in his childhood and youth has had the bitter experience of being rejected. No man ever had a father who was more a man after his own heart than Churchill. The brilliant, turbulent, immensely gifted Lord Randolph Churchill, who revolutionized British politics between 1870 and 1880, and then guttered out like a spent candle, had all the qualities that Churchill himself admired, together with a personal charm that he himself never possessed; courage, audacity, loyalty, a formidable capacity for hard work, a kind of recklessness that carried him like a meteor across the political sky. Yet such a man, made for a boy's love and devotion, treated his son as if he were a stranger, and with a chilly disapproval that amounted to contempt. "He seemed," Churchill wrote, "to have the key to everything, or nearly everything worth having. But if I even began to show the slightest idea of comradeship, he was immediately offended; and when I once suggested that I might help his private secretary to write some of his letters, he froze me into stone."

Yet all his father's coldness could not kill Churchill's love and devotion. "The icy detachment and indifference of Lord Randolph," writes Lady Violet, "failed to destroy the proud and passionate allegiance of his son," and she touchingly describes Churchill's reaction to the remarkable intimacy in which she lived with her own father and to the views he confided to her on persons, policies, and events. "He sometimes asked me with a kind of wishful envy: 'Your father told you that? He talks to you quite freely? I wish I could have had such talks with mine.' And sometimes he added: 'But I should have had them if he lived. It *must* have come.' "

The pattern of rejection that Churchill experienced in his childhood and youth was to repeat itself consistently during his political life. Lady Violet emphasizes that despite her father's own affection for Churchill, and acute appreciation of his brilliant intellectual gifts, Churchill was never able to win the trust or confidence of his colleagues in the great Liberal government of 1906, or the confidence of the Liberal Party. He was like some brightly colored bird of paradise, whose gaudy plumage made him suspect to birds of a more sober hue. Sometimes his antics made him almost a joke. "He is full of the poor," wrote Charles Masterman, "whom he has just discovered. He thinks he is called by Providence to do something for them."

And when, after the fall of Lloyd George, Churchill, through principle or lack of principle, deserted the Liberals and rejoined the Conservatives, they received him, even though they gave him office, with equal hostility and mistrust. Their feelings were appropriately expressed in a popular biography, published in 1931, entitled *The Tragedy of Winston Churchill,* in which he is depicted as a brilliant politician brought to ruin by his own faults, of overweening ambition, lack of principle, personal disloyalty, irretrievable egotism; *Punch* caricatured him trying on one of his eccentric hats before a mirror and remarking: "As usual, it's too small."

Lady Violet reminds us again and again how deeply the solid core of the Conservative Party hated and mistrusted Churchill, as they had hated and mistrusted his father; they would have been glad if he had suffered the same political extinction, and at one time it seemed likely that he might. They pursued him with a venom and vindictiveness only equaled by the sycophancy of their adulation in his declining years. In the thirties any Conservative politician with an eye to power regarded Churchill as an incorrigible advocate of lost causes, out of touch with the electorate and with the people, doomed forever to sterile opposition. One of the most striking features of Churchill's career up to the war is that he was never able to organize, either within or outside the Conservative Party, a solid and coherent body of public opinion in support of his policies.

Outside the Conservative Party, indeed, he was regarded with just as much mistrust as within, though he won the sympathy and admiration of a fragment of the Labour Party by his hostility to Hitler and to National Socialist Germany. But for most of the Left, a policy of rearmament was all the harder to swallow precisely because Churchill advocated it; he was, after all, a man of blood, the man of Gallipoli, of intervention in Russia, of Tonypandy, of the *British Gazette*; now that he advocated arms and the covenant, it could only be for the wrong reasons, in the cause of war and not of peace.

We are not to suppose that such feelings, of doubt, suspicion, mistrust, and downright hostility, disappeared overnight when war came and Churchill rejoined the government. There were many Conservatives who never forgave Churchill for opposing the policy of appeasement, or for supplanting their shabby angel of peace, Neville Chamberlain, who, strangely enough, was capable of inspiring the most intense loyalty and devotion in his followers. And when, finally, in 1940, Churchill became prime minister, it was not as a leader whom the entire nation had summoned unanimously to power as the only possible savior of an apparently ruined cause; it was simply because Halifax was unwilling to undertake the burden of the premiership and Churchill was the only other Conservative politician under whom Labour would serve in a coalition government. If there had been any other available, he would, from the point of view of the nation as a whole, have done just as well at that moment.

The attempt, at the time of his death, to represent Churchill as a kind of father of his people is essentially a falsification of his entire political career and especially of his long and complicated relationship both with the British electorate and with the political parties of which he was alternately a member. The election of 1945, with, once again, its total rejection of Churchill, was evidence that, even though he retained the nation's gratitude for his wartime achievements, it was not sufficient to secure the return of him and his party to power; moreover, during the election, Churchill himself did not fail to reveal one of his most striking political weaknesses. For if, for most of his political life, the British people profoundly mistrusted Churchill, he on the other hand never understood them; by nature he had none of that instinctive sense of a nation's deepest emotions, wishes, aspirations, prejudices, which is commonly taken to be one of the marks of greatness in a statesman, and in this respect he completely lacked the mysterious insights of a Lincoln, a Roosevelt, a Lloyd George, or a Hitler.

Isaiah Berlin calls Roosevelt, as compared with Churchill, "frivolous." But he also makes one realize that Roosevelt's enormous sensitivity to the moods and feelings of the masses, and his capacity to give them concrete political expression, conferred on his policies a kind of moral authority to which Churchill, as a peacetime politician, could never aspire. And when Churchill was returned to power, it was not as a result of a gift of national leadership, or as a statesman of genius, but purely and simply as a party politician presiding over a singularly undistinguished administration.

Lady Violet Bonham Carter, for all her adoration of Churchill, makes it clear that the kind of blindness Churchill showed toward the deepest needs and wants of his countrymen in the mass applied equally in his personal relationships. He did not easily inspire affection or even liking, except in a very limited circle, which included, among his closest friends, such very unpleasant characters as Lords Birkenhead and Beaverbrook. His obsessive concentration on whatever concerned him most at the moment was one of his most remarkable gifts; but it was also an effective barrier to communication with others or to any understanding of their problems and difficulties, unless they happened to coincide with his own. Lloyd George, exasperated by Churchill's obsession with his "blasted ships," once said to him, according to Lord Riddell: "You think we all live in the sea, and all your thoughts are devoted to sea-life, fishes, and other aquatic creatures. You forget that most of us live on land."

This unawareness of the needs, the interests, the legitimate preoccupations of others, was a weakness in Churchill as a man and, more seriously, as a politician and a statesman. It reflected an egotism that could see nothing outside the blinkers of his own imagination, which, if it was intense, was also surprisingly narrow and often superficial; it made intolerable demands on anyone who had to work with him and reduced discussion with him to a not always inspired monologue. Under the fierce and unremitting pressure of the war it created strains upon his colleagues that were hardly to be borne; in Lord Alanbrooke's diaries it is possible to trace a feeling toward Churchill which is something more than dislike. Any fair assessment of Churchill's wartime administration would have to take into account the question whether Churchill's incessant bullying of his military advisers, and his interference in spheres where his judgment was singularly fallible and erratic, did not in fact hinder rather than assist the efficient conduct of the war.

It would be easy, of course, to see these faults as simply the reverse side of Churchill's greatness, the inevitable consequence of his implacable concentration on the matter in hand, of his consciousness of superior intellectual powers and spiritual energies that were perfectly adapted to the crisis which he had to meet and master. In the same way, it would be easy to accept Churchill's long exclusion from power simply as yet another example of men's unfortunate habit of failing to recognize manifest genius, and to see in Churchill, during his years in the wilderness, another prophet who was not without honor save in his own country, another stone which the builders rejected but became the head of the corner. Yet this would be, once again, to falsify the evidence of Churchill's political career; it would be to suggest that, in refusing their confidence to Churchill, the British people and the British political parties had in some way been grievously in the wrong, whereas the truth is that, over a long period, Churchill had been guilty of a series of such gross errors that it was almost impossible to take him seriously as a politician, much less a statesman.

It is not necessary to go back to Gallipoli, though Mr. Robert Rhodes James is perhaps right to remind us now that Churchill must take a large part of the blame for that disaster, both in its planning and its execution. But he was also wrong about intervention in Russia; he was wrong about the return to the gold standard; his antics in the general strike were such that, if his colleagues in the government had imitated him, it might have developed into civil war; he was wrong about India; he was wrong about Mussolini, about Spain and, initially, even about Hitler; he was absurdly wrong about the abdication. No British politician in the interwar years had so consistent a record of error and misjudgment; and if this was partly redeemed by his opposition to Hitler, when once he had realized what a danger German rearmament was to Britain, it was a part of the tragedy of the thirties, of what he himself called the "Unnecessary War," that Churchill was unable to persuade others to accept his views largely because he had been proved so utterly and demonstrably wrong on almost every other important political issue with which he had concerned himself.

Nor is it possible to see in Churchill's political errors, of which some at least had disastrous political consequences for the country, any rational or coherent political philosophy that, however unpopular at the time, might under other circumstances prove its essential worth; they were at best the reflection of a purely personal attitude to life and to politics that was strangely divorced, except in one single and important respect, from the realities of his time, and this no doubt helps to explain why, up to 1939, he was so singularly unsuccessful in organizing any solid and powerful body of public opinion behind him. The truth was that, except in the one crucial case of Germany, he did not have any policies that were relevant to the situation in which Britain found herself between the wars.

It might be generally agreed that, on the eve of the war, Churchill was, as a politician, a failure, indeed a quite spectacular failure, given his exceptional qualities both of intellect and character; one who, with every gift and every opportunity, after nearly sixty years of public life, of which thirty had been spent in high office, had no great legislative or administrative achievement to his credit, enjoyed the trust and confidence neither of his party nor his countrymen, and seemed doomed to spend the remainder of his days in futile and discredited opposition. It is less generally agreed, or at least avowed, that this failure was of his own making.

How, then, are we to explain his sudden transformation, almost overnight, in the eyes of his countrymen and of the world, into the colossal figure whom the nation mourned at his death, the equal, it would seem, of the almost mythical heroes of the past, an Alexander, a Caesar, a Napoleon, all these with an extra touch of humanity thrown in; in Isaiah Berlin's words, "a mythical hero who belongs as much to legend as to reality."

It is sad to think that for some time to come we are not likely to have a study of Churchill that will prefer the reality to the legend. But if it were to be written, perhaps its author would notice, as affording some explanation both of Churchill's failure and his triumph, that one of Churchill's most absorbing interests, perhaps, indeed, the most absorbing interest of his life, was one that to most of his contemporaries was profoundly distasteful and repugnant; that is to say, war. It was one that had been with him from his earliest youth, when he had looked so avidly for some *frischer und fröhlicher Krieg* to which he could attach himself; it was deepened by the, for him, exhilarating experience of the First World War and by his historical studies for his life of Marlborough; when the Second World War came, it was for him, as he himself confesses, a relief and a liberation, not only because the great dangers that he had apprehended for so long were now obvious to all but because he felt, rightly, that he was the man, perhaps the only man, who was fully equipped, mentally, morally, psychologically, to face and overcome the appalling problems that war creates.

It would not be unfair to Churchill to say that, both on national and personal grounds, he welcomed the war; he could have said with some truth that it was both the country's and his own last chance. This is not to say that Churchill was ever blind or insensitive to the misery, suffering, and cruelty of war; or that the policies he advocated were intended to provoke war rather than to preserve peace; or that, war having come, he ever wished to wage it for its own sake. But he would have found it perfectly natural to say, with Robert E. Lee, that it is a good thing we know how terrible war is, or we should grow too fond of it. And also he believed in war as a perfectly legitimate weapon of national policy, which should be kept in reserve for the last emergency but nevertheless should be always brightly furbished and ready for use; and he believed that, bad as war is, there are other things which are worse.

Moreover, war was not, for all its horrors, something that filled him personally with dismay and despair. He was like an athlete who had trained all his life for some supreme contest, and when at last it came, he rejoiced in the opportunity to show, to himself and to others, how well equipped he was to meet it, how ready for all its contingencies, even its disasters. If it had not come he would have been disappointed, like some championship contender who has been cheated of a title fight. If there was one particular gift he gave his countrymen in 1940, and which no one else could have given, it was to inspire them with something of his own exhilaration that at last a moment had come that would demand of them everything they had. Lincoln spent half the Civil War looking for a general who would fight and enjoyed fighting. Even among generals such men are rare; in Churchill, in 1940, Britain found such a man.

And, as such men do, he succeeded, for a time, in conveying to his countrymen the extraordinary sensation of actually enjoying "blood, sweat and tears," of facing total defeat and all the sufferings and sacrifices that were necessary to overcome it. This is not, of course, a sensation that men often enjoy, or for long; they go to war like Siegfried Sassoon's soldiers:

> Most went glumly through it
> Dumbly doomed to rue it.

In this sense, Churchill was abnormal. Though he saw and felt as deeply as anyone the terrible issues, the waste, suffering, and destruction, involved in war, he also saw it, as Peter Pan saw life, as "an awfully big adventure." Churchill himself was aware of his abnormality and of how much it isolated him from others; Lady Violet Bonham Carter quotes him as confessing, with a certain feeling of guilt, during the First World War, that though for others the war meant universal suffering, he could not help admitting that he was enjoying himself intensely at the Admiralty.

To say this of Churchill now is unfashionable, because in this generation war has become a dirty word, and to say of anyone that he enjoys it is rather like accusing him of being a psychopath. But it is significant that from the beginnings of his political career this is precisely what people tended to feel about Churchill; it alarmed and bewildered them; it made them feel that he was a man who might lead them into irresponsible adventures; it was the basis of the mistrust that he almost universally inspired. In popular speech, in the press, this feeling was often expressed by calling Churchill a warmonger. This was unjust; he cared for peace as much as any man; but he believed that peace could be preserved and, if necessary, restored, by force of arms, and this reading of history had no terrors for him. Popular feeling was given a more sophisticated expression in 1929 by John Maynard Keynes, reviewing the fourth volume of *The World Crisis.*

> With what kind of feelings does one lay down Mr. Churchill's two thousand pages? . . . Admiration for his energies of mind and his intense absorption of intellectual interest and elemental emotion in what is for the moment the matter in hand—which is his best quality. A little envy, perhaps, for his undoubting conviction that frontiers, races, patriotism, even war, if need be, are ultimate realities for mankind, which lends for him a kind of dignity and even nobility to events which for others are only a nightmare interlude, something to be permanently avoided.

"Only a nightmare interlude, something to be permanently avoided. . . ." Either in 1929, or now, there are probably few people who would disagree with Keynes's description of war as a phenomenon of the twentieth century. In such a view war belongs to a past in which life was anyhow nasty, brutish, and short, and, in our own more advanced civilization, cannot be taken seriously except as a brutal and momentary invasion of the condition of peace which is the norm of civilized life. And with war they would classify other irrational factors like frontiers, races, patriotism, all parts of the same nightmare, "something to be permanently avoided."

As a hope and an inspiration, such a view has every attraction; as a statement of fact, it is extravagantly wide of the mark. It dismisses war as violent, irrational, degrading to the human being, something that really has no business to belong to the history of our own time; it also ignores the ugly fact that war has shaped and determined the lives of men and women in the twentieth century more than any other historical phenomenon. Indeed, one might reasonably say that it was both the most important and the most characteristic feature of the age through which we have had to live. Far from war being a "nightmare interlude," it is peace that has been a slow convalescence between the fierce and repeated agonies of war, in which nations have enjoyed the somewhat illusory comforts of soldiers returned to base to be rehabilitated for the front line.

Such a view is of course intensely antipathetic to the spirit of the age; there is something inexpressibly faded and out of date about it, it belongs to the world of Gobineau and Carlyle and Nietzsche and Spengler and other prophets who look rather tawdry today in their tattered robes. Yet as a realistic view of what has happened, and is happening, in the history of our time, it has more to commend it than the liberal and progressive optimism of someone like Keynes. It was Churchill's merit as a politician, which also gave him his claim to greatness as a statesman, precisely that from youth upward he instinctively understood that war was the determining factor in the history of the twentieth century and had the courage to face and accept the consequences.

To say this so soon after his death may be taken by many people as a slur upon his memory, especially because his panegyrists have already done so much to falsify that memory out of all recognition. For it would have been shocking for the British public to be told, at the moment of his death, that their grief and mourning, the somber beauty of his funeral, were all for a man whose true greatness lay in his unalterable conviction that war, in our time, is indeed the ultimate reality and that nothing had happened in his lifetime to modify this belief. Yet it is precisely this that gave to Churchill that "dimension of depth—and a corresponding sense of tragic possibilities" to which Isaiah Berlin refers. Yet even he dissembles some of the truth of his own insight. He tells us, for instance, that whereas more typical politicians derive their inspiration from the present or the future, Churchill derived his from the past, and somehow this may leave one with the impression that Churchill's view of war was also a thing of the past, a romantic nostalgia for vanished glories, an imaginative sympathy for "old, unhappy, far off things and battles long ago." In fact, Churchill's acceptance of war as the ultimate reality of our time came from a profound and tragic insight into the present; in this he was more modern than any of his contemporaries, and it is this above all that distinguishes him from all the other democratic statesmen of his age.

ANTHONY STORR

The Inner Man

THE PSYCHIATRIST who takes it upon himself to attempt a character study of an individual whom he has never met is engaged upon a project that is full of risk. In the exercise of his profession, the psychiatrist has an unrivaled opportunity for the appraisal of character, and may justly claim that he knows more persons deeply and intimately than most of his fellows. But, when considering someone who has died, he is deprived of those special insights that can be attained only in the consulting room, and is, like the historian, obliged to rely upon what written evidence happens to be available. In the analytical treatment of a patient, the psychiatrist is able to check the validity of the hypotheses that

---

From *Churchill Revised: An Assessment,* by A. J. P. Taylor, Robert Rhodes James, J. H. Plumb, Basil Liddell Hart, and Anthony Storr. New York: The Dial Press, 1969, pp. 229–74.

he proffers by the patient's response, and by the changes that occur in the patient as a result of his increased comprehension of himself. The psychiatrist may often be wrong or premature in his interpretation of his patient's behavior and character; but, as the long process of analysis continues, errors will gradually be eliminated and the truth recognized by both parties in the analytical transaction. Deprived of this constant appraisal and reappraisal, psychiatrists who attempt biographical studies of great men are apt to allow theory to outrun discretion: with the result that many so-called psychoanalytic biographies have been both bad biography and bad psychoanalysis. The disastrous study of Woodrow Wilson by Freud and Bullitt is a case in point.

In this essay, I advance a hypothesis about Churchill, which I think is warranted by the facts. But what I have to say must be regarded as tentative, for the possibilities of error in this complicated field are very great. Although Churchill himself provided many autobiographical details, especially in *My Early Life,* these are not the kind of details that are of much service to the psychiatrist. For Churchill showed as little interest in the complexities of his own psychology as he did in the psychology of others; and would have been the first to dismiss this essay as both futile and impertinent. Moreover, as C. P. Snow remarks in his essay in *Variety of Men,* Churchill's character was "abnormally impenetrable to most kinds of insight." His deeds, speeches, and career have been lavishly and repeatedly recorded, but very little of what has been written about him reveals anything of his inner life. Although Churchill can be rated as an artist, both as writer and painter, he was not, like many artists, introspective or concerned with his own motives. Indeed, if he had been, he could scarcely have achieved what he did, for introspection is the accomplice of self-distrust and the enemy of action.

Winston Churchill is still idolized, not only by those of us who remember his speeches in 1940, and who believe, as I do, that it was to his courage that we owe our escape from Nazi tyranny, but by men and women all over the world, to whom he has become a symbol, a personification of valor. But Churchill was also a human being, with the same needs, instincts, hopes, and fears that pertain to all of us. It is no disservice to a great man to draw attention to his humanity, or to point out that, like other men, he had imperfections and flaws. Churchill, in spite of his aristocratic birth and social position, started life with disadvantages that he never wholly conquered, although his whole career was an effort to overcome them. Without these disadvantages he would have been a happier, more ordinary, better-balanced, and lesser human being.

But had he been a stable and equable man, he could never have inspired the nation. In 1940, when all the odds were against Britain, a leader of sober judgment might well have concluded that we were finished. Political leaders are accustomed to dissimulation. Even when defeat at the polls is imminent, or the policies that they support have been shown to be futile, they will, until the eleventh hour, continue to issue messages of hope to their supporters. In 1940, any political leader might have tried to rally Britain with brave words, although his heart was full of despair. But only a man who had known and faced despair within himself could carry conviction at such a moment. Only a man who knew what it was to discern a gleam of hope in a hopeless situation, whose courage was beyond reason, and whose aggressive spirit burned at its fiercest when he was hemmed in and surrounded by enemies, could have given emotional reality to the words of defiance that rallied and sustained us in the menacing summer of 1940. Churchill was such a man: and it was because, all his life, he had conducted a battle with his own despair that he could convey to others that despair can be overcome.

For Winston Churchill, like his ancestor the first Duke of Marlborough, suffered from prolonged and recurrent fits of depression; and no understanding of his character is possible unless this central fact is taken into account. His own name for depression was "Black Dog": and the fact that he had a nickname for it argues that it was all too familiar a companion. For great sections of his life, Churchill was successful in conquering his depression; but old age and the narrowing of his cerebral arteries in the end undermined his resistance. The last five years of his protracted existence were so melancholy that even Lord Moran draws a veil over them. It was a cruel fate that ordained that Churchill should survive till the age of ninety; for the "Black Dog," which he had controlled and largely mastered in earlier years, at last overcame his fighting spirit.

Churchill is, of course, not a lone example of a great man suffering from recurrent depression. Goethe was of similar temperament; so were Schumann, Hugo Wolf, Luther, Tolstoi, and many others. The relation between great achievement and the depressive temperament has yet to be determined in detail, but there can be little doubt that, in some natures, depression acts as a spur. When depression is overwhelming, the sufferer relapses into gloom and an inactivity that may be so profound as to render him immobile. To avoid this state of misery is of prime importance; and so the depressive, before his disorder becomes too severe, may recurrently force himself into activity, deny himself rest or relaxation, and accomplish more than most men are capable of, just because he cannot afford to stop. We do not know how many men of exceptional achievement have this tendency toward depression, for it may often be well concealed. That some do, and that Churchill was one of them, admits of no possible doubt.

There is still dispute as to how far the tendency to suffer from recurrent depression is the product of heredity, and how much it is the result of early conditioning. Until the science of genetics is further advanced than it is at present, we shall not be able to answer this question fully. In Churchill's case, it is safe to assume that both factors played their part. For we know that at least two of Churchill's most distinguished ancestors were afflicted by swings of mood of some severity; and there is some evidence to suggest that they were not the only members of the family to be afflicted in this way. A. L. Rowse, writing of the first Duke of Marlborough, says:

> Marlborough was *sensible* in the French sense, a most sensitive register of all the impressions that came to him. An artist by temperament in his ups and downs—the depression he got before the precipitant of action, the headaches that racked him at all the obstructions he had to put up with, and the self-control he exercised so habitually that it became second nature to him. It exacted its price.[1]

In 1705, the Duke wrote "I have for these last ten days been so troubled by the many disappointments I have had that I think if it were possible to vex me so for a fortnight longer it would make an end of me. In short, I am weary of my life." This weariness is

1. A. L. Rowse, *The Early Churchills* (London: Macmillan, 1956), pp. 227–28.

a recurrent theme in his letters: "I am extremely out of heart"; "My dearest soul, pity me and love me." Although it may be argued that many men might write like this in times of stress, Rowse is not the only historian to observe that the first Duke of Marlborough alternated between optimism and depression in a way that some people would not expect in one of England's most famous military commanders. Winston Churchill himself observed: "Sometimes he was overdaring and sometimes overprudent; but they were separate states of mind, and he changed from one to the other in quite definite phases."

The other Churchill forebear who exhibited the same kind of temperament was Lord Randolph, Winston's father. A. L. Rowse writes of him:

> Though a very quick and piercing judge of a situation, his judgment was not really reliable. He was self-willed and impulsive, above all impatient. If he had only had patience all the rest would have come into line. But he had the defect of the artistic temperament, what we in our day of psychological jargon diagnose as the manic-depressive alternation—tremendous high spirits and racing energy on the upward bound, depression and discouragement on the down. This rhythm is present in a more or less marked degree with all persons of creative capacity, particularly in the arts. And clearly this strongly artistic strain we have observed in the stock came out in him, as it has done again in his son.[2]

Rowse is wrong in thinking that the manic-depressive alternation is present in all creative persons, some of whom belong to a very different temperamental group; but he is obviously right in his diagnosis of the Churchill family.

One other member deserves mention in this connection, the Winston Churchill who was father of the first Duke of Marlborough. An ardent royalist, he retired to his country seat in East Devon after the king's forces had been defeated in the civil war. Here he occupied himself by writing history: *"Divi Brittanici:* being a Remark upon the Lives of all the Kings of this Isle." Although we are not informed in detail of his temperamental constitution, A. L. Rowse describes him as follows: "Sunk in glum resentment, he had, at any rate, the consolation that intelligent

2. A. L. Rowse, *The Later Churchills* (London: Macmillan, 1958), pp. 287–88.

people have who are defeated and out of favour: reading and writing . . . His spirit was not defeated: it burns with unquenched ardour in what he wrote."[3] The later and more famous Winston adopted the same policy when he was out of office; and we may be thankful that creative activity can and does provide an effective defense against the depression that threatens to overwhelm those who possess this temperament when they are neither occupied nor sustained by holding a position of consequence.

Brendan Bracken, quoted by Moran, says five of the last seven dukes of Marlborough suffered from melancholia; but it is difficult to confirm this even from Rowse's books, which Bracken alleges are the source of his information. There seems little doubt, however, that the cyclothymic temperament, that is, the tendency to rather extreme swings of mood, was part of the Churchill inheritance.

Before leaving the question of Churchill's heredity, we must take a glance at his physical endowment. It is probable, though not certain, that physique and character are intimately connected, and that the structure and shape of the body reflect genetic rather than environmental influences. A man's cast of mind is largely influenced by the way he is brought up and educated. His physical endowment, though modifiable to some extent, is more likely to be a datum of heredity.

It is clear that Churchill was possessed of enormous vitality. He survived to the age of ninety; and, by the age of eighty, he had surmounted a heart attack, three attacks of pneumonia, two strokes, and two operations. He habitually ate, drank, and smoked as much as he wanted, and this much was a great deal. Until he was seventy, he hardly ever complained of fatigue. Yet, this extraordinary constitution was not based upon natural physical strength of a conventional kind. Indeed, he started life with considerable physical disadvantages. As Lord Moran puts it: "I could see this sensitive boy, bullied and beaten at his school, grow up into a man, small in stature, with thin, unmuscular limbs, and the white delicate hands of a woman; there was no hair on his chest, and he spoke with a lisp and a slight stutter."[4]

3. Rowse, *The Early Churchills,* p. 29.
4. Lord Moran, *Churchill: Taken from the Diaries of Lord Moran* (Boston: Houghton Mifflin, 1966), p. 621.

Winston Churchill himself, in a letter from Sandhurst written in 1893, claimed: "I am cursed with so feeble a body, that I can scarcely support the fatigues of the day; but I suppose I shall get stronger during my stay here." His height was only five feet six and a half inches; and his chest measured but thirty-one inches, which, by Sandhurst standards, was quite inadequate. When the poet Wilfred Scawen Blunt met Churchill in 1903, he described him as "a little square-headed fellow of no very striking appearance." The physical courage that he consistently, and sometimes rashly, displayed was not based upon any natural superiority of physique but rather upon his determination to be tough in spite of lack of height and muscle. His search for physical danger in early youth, and his reckless self-exposure in France, even though his behavior put others in danger, bears witness to the fact that his courage was not something that he himself took for granted but rather something that he had to prove to himself—a compensation for inner doubts about his own bravery.

No man is immune from fear; but those who have been endowed by nature with exceptionally powerful physiques are generally less disturbed by physical danger than most of us. Churchill was uncommonly brave; but his courage was of a more remarkable and admirable variety than that which is based upon an innate superiority of physical endowment. He never forgot that, at his second preparatory school, he had been frightened by other boys throwing cricket balls at him and had taken refuge behind some trees. This, to him, was a shameful memory; and, very early in life, he determined that he would be as tough as anybody could be. When he was eighteen, he nearly killed himself, when being chased by his cousin and brother, by jumping from a bridge to avoid capture. He fell twenty-nine feet, ruptured a kidney, remained unconscious for three days and unable to work for nearly two months. There is no doubt whatever that Churchill's physical courage was immense; but it rested upon his determination to conquer his initial physical disadvantages, much as Demosthenes's skill in oratory is said to have been the consequence of his will to overcome an impediment in his speech.

There have been many attempts to discern a relationship between physique and character, of which W. H. Sheldon's is both the most detailed and the most successful. Sheldon claimed that he could discern three main components in a man's physical makeup, to which he gave the somewhat awkward names of endomorphy, mesomorphy, and ectomorphy. He also constructed a scale of temperament comprising three sets of twenty basic traits, which were generally closely allied to the subject's physique. The three main varieties of temperament are known as viscerotonia, somatotonia, and cerebrotonia.

When one comes to examine Churchill, it is obvious that his physique was predominantly endomorphic. His massive head, the small size of his chest compared with his abdomen, the rounded contours of his body, and the small size of his extremities were all characteristic. So was his smooth, soft skin, which was so delicate that he always wore specially obtained silk underwear. One would expect a man with this physique to be predominantly viscerotonic in temperament: earthy, unhurried, deliberate, and predictable. Churchill actually does rate high on eleven out of the twenty viscerotonic traits; but he also scores almost equally high on somatotonia—that is, the temperament which is allied to the powerful and athletic frame of the mesomorph. According to Sheldon, men whose temperament differs widely from that which accords with their physique are particularly subject to psychological conflict, since they are at odds with their own emotional constitution.

Churchill was a very much more aggressive and dominant individual than one would expect from his basic physique. His love of risk, of physical adventure, his energy and assertiveness are traits which one would expect to find in a heavily muscled mesomorph, but which are unexpected in a man of Churchill's endomorphic structure.

In other words, we have a picture of a man who was, to a marked extent, forcing himself to go against his own inner nature: a man who was neither naturally strong nor naturally particularly courageous, but who made himself both in spite of his temperamental and physical endowment. The more one examines Winston Churchill as a person, the more one is forced to the conclusion that his aggressiveness, his courage, and his dominance were not rooted in his inheritance but were the product of deliberate decision and iron will. "I can look very fierce when I like," he said to his doctor.[5] But the expression of bulldog defiance that appears in his most

5. *Ibid.*, p. 621.

popular photographs was not evident upon his face before the war, and, as Moran hints, is likely to have been assumed when declaiming speeches in front of the looking glass, and thenceforth used on appropriate public occasions.

Before turning from the question of inherited physical and psychological characteristics to consideration of the environmental influences that shaped Churchill's character, it is worth glancing at one more typology. The Swiss psychiatrist C. G. Jung was responsible for introducing the terms "extrovert" and "introvert" into psychology; most people are familiar with the broad outlines of what is meant by these two terms. The extrovert is a person whose chief orientation is toward the events and features of the external world. The recesses of his own soul are not of much concern to the predominantly extroverted person, nor is he much concerned with abstractions, ideas, or the subtleties of philosophy. The main interest of the extroverted person is in action, not in thought, and when troubled, he seeks to do things to distract himself rather than to explore his inner life to determine the cause of his distress. Churchill was undoubtedly highly extroverted. He showed little interest in philosophy and none in religion, and he dismissed psychology as irrelevant.

Jung's further subdivision of types into thinking, feeling, sensation, and intuition has not been widely accepted; but his delineation of the extroverted intuitive in *Psychological Types* fits Churchill so accurately that it ought to persuade people to take another look at the book. Jung writes:

> Wherever intuition predominates, a particular and unmistakeable psychology presents itself. . . . The intuitive is never to be found among the generally recognized reality values, but is always present where possibilities exist. He has a keen nose for things in the bud pregnant with future promise. . . . Thinking and feeling, the indispensable components of conviction, are, with him, inferior functions, possessing no decisive weight: hence they lack the power to offer any lasting resistance to the force of intuition.

Hence, according to Jung, the intuitive's lack of judgment and also his "weak consideration for the welfare of his neighbours." The intuitive is "not infrequently put down as a ruthless and immoral adventurer," terms often applied to Churchill in his youth, and yet "his capacity to inspire his fellow-men with courage, or to kindle enthusiasm for something new, is unrivalled."

In his extremely interesting essay on Churchill, C. P. Snow refers to his lack of judgment. In fact, he says that it was "seriously defective." He goes on:

> Judgment is a fine thing: but it is not all that uncommon. Deep insight is much rarer. Churchill had flashes of that kind of insight, dug up from his own nature, independent of influences, owing nothing to anyone outside himself. Sometimes it was a better guide than judgment: in the ultimate crisis when he came to power, there were times when judgment itself could, though it did not need to, become a source of weakness.
>
> When Hitler came to power Churchill did not use judgment but one of his deep insights. This was absolute danger, there was no easy way round. *That* was what we needed. It was an unique occasion in our history. It had to be grasped by a nationalist leader. Plenty of people on the left could see the danger: but they did not know how the country had to be seized and unified.[6]

I think that the kind of insight to which C. P. Snow is referring might equally well be called intuition. Intuition is in many respects an unreliable guide, and some of Churchill's intuitions were badly wrong. In the First World War, his major strategic conception, the invasion of Gallipoli, was a failure, but his idea of the development of the tank, although it was not properly used at the time, was certainly a success. It is worth noting that as early as 1917 he described a project for making landing craft for tanks and also for something very like the transportable harbors used in the 1944 invasion of France. His intuition was at least as often right as it was wrong, and in his anticipation of the menace of Hitler, and later of the threat of Russian domination of Europe, he was intuitively right where others, who had better judgment than he, failed to see the important point.

Jung's description of the extroverted intuitive has much that applies to Churchill. As Jung points out, this type is lacking in judgment. Churchill could never think for long at a time. Although he had brilliant ideas, he was hardly susceptible to reason and could not follow a consecutive argument when presented to him by

6. C. P. Snow, *Variety of Men* (London: Macmillan, 1967), p. 125.

others. His famous demand that all ideas should be presented to him on a half sheet of paper is an illustration of this point. Alanbrooke, in his wartime diary, wrote of him: "Planned strategy was not his strong card. He preferred to work by intuition and by impulse. . . . He was never good at looking at all the implications of any course he favoured. In fact, he frequently refused to look at them."[7] It is also true that he was, in many respects, deficient in feeling. He had little appreciation of the feelings of others. On three separate occasions, Churchill had promised Alanbrooke the supreme command of the Allied forces. Yet, when it was finally decided that the invasion of Europe should be entrusted to the command of an American, Churchill showed little appreciation of the bitter disappointment which Alanbrooke experienced. "Not for one moment did he realize what this meant to me. He offered no sympathy, no regrets at having had to change his mind, and dealt with the matter as if it were one of minor importance."[8] As Jung says, "Consideration for the welfare of his neighbours is weak."

All those who worked with Churchill paid tribute to the enormous fertility of his new ideas, the inexhaustible stream of invention that poured from him, both when he was home secretary and later when he was prime minister and director of the war effort. All those who worked with him also agreed that he needed the most severe restraint put upon him, and that many of his ideas, if they had been put into practice, would have been utterly disastrous.

In Jungian terminology, Churchill was an extroverted intuitive. In W. H. Sheldon's classification, he was predominantly endomorphic, with a strong secondary mesomorphic component. In terms of classical, descriptive psychiatry, he was of cyclothymic temperament, with a pronounced tendency to depression. These descriptive classifications, though overloaded with jargon, are still valuable as an approach to character, but they reveal very little about the dynamics of a person's inner life. What follows will be an attempt, necessarily speculative, to examine something of Churchill's psychological structure in so far as this is possible.

Let us begin with a further consideration of Churchill's "Black Dog." Lord Moran, who, more than most people, realized the im-

7. Arthur Bryant, *The Turn of the Tide* (London: Collins, 1957), p. 25.
8. *Ibid.*, p. 707.

portance of depression in Churchill's psychology, first mentions this in the following passage from his book:

> August 14th 1944.
>
> The P.M. was in a speculative mood today.
>
> "When I was young," he ruminated, "for two or three years the light faded out of the picture. I did my work. I sat in the House of Commons, but black depression settled on me. It helped me to talk to Clemmie about it. I don't like standing near the edge of a platform when an express train is passing through. I like to stand right back and if possible to get a pillar between me and the train. I don't like to stand by the side of a ship and look down into the water. A second's action would end everything. A few drops of desperation. And yet I don't want to go out of the world at all in such moments. Is much known about worry, Charles? It helps me to write down half a dozen things which are worrying me. Two of them, say, disappear, about two nothing can be done, so it's no use worrying, and two perhaps can be settled. I read an American book on the nerves, *The Philosophy of Fate*; it interested me a great deal."
>
> I said: "Your trouble—I mean the Black Dog business—you got from your forebears. You have fought against it all your life. That is why you dislike visiting hospitals. You always avoid anything that is depressing."
>
> Winston stared at me as if I knew too much.[9]

Later in the book, Lord Moran quotes a conversation with the dying Brendan Bracken:

> You and I think of Winston as self-indulgent; he has never denied himself anything, but when a mere boy he deliberately set out to change his nature, to be tough and full of rude spirits.
>
> It has not been easy for him. You see, Charles, Winston has always been a "despairer." Orpen, who painted him after the Dardanelles, used to speak of the misery in his face. He called him the man of misery. Winston was so sure then that he would take no further part in public life. There seemed nothing left to live for. It made him very sad. Then, in his years in the wilderness, before the Second War, he kept saying: "I'm finished." He said that about twice a day. He was quite certain that he would never get back to office, for everyone seemed to regard him as a wild man. And he missed the red boxes awfully. Winston has always

9. Moran, p. 167.

> been wretched unless he was occupied. You know what he has been like since he resigned. Why, he told me that he prays every day for death.[10]

Many depressives deny themselves rest or relaxation because they cannot afford to stop. If they are forced by circumstances to do so, the black cloud comes down upon them. This happened to Churchill when he left the Admiralty in May, 1915, when he was out of office during the thirties, when he was defeated in the election of 1945, and after his final resignation. He invented various methods of coping with the depression that descended when he was no longer fully occupied by affairs of state, including painting, writing, and bricklaying; but none of these was wholly successful. In order to understand why, we must venture some way into the cloudy and treacherous waters of psychoanalytic theory.

It is widely appreciated that psychoanalysis is chiefly concerned with the effect of environment, especially the very early environment, upon adult character. It is less generally realized that the psychoanalytic standpoint is not incompatible with the typological or constitutional approaches which we have hitherto adopted in our psychiatric scrutiny of Churchill. The two viewpoints are complementary, rather than contradictory. A man's genetic inheritance may predispose him to depression, but whether he actually suffers from it or not is likely to depend upon his early experiences within the family. Psychoanalysis does not assume that all individuals are born alike and would react in precisely the same way to the influences of the environment. There is no blueprint for an ideal upbringing, since no two individuals are the same. What psychoanalysis does assume, however, is that the psychological disturbances from which people suffer are related to the whole emotional climate in which they were reared, and that neurosis and psychosis in adult life are explicable in terms of a failure of the environment to meet the needs of the particular individual under scrutiny, at a time when those needs were paramount.

One salient characteristic of adults who suffer from depression is their dependence on external sources to maintain self-esteem. Of course, we are all dependent on externals to some extent. If a perfectly normal man is taken suddenly from his family, his job, and his social circle, and put into a situation of uncertainty and

10. *Ibid.*, p. 745.

fear, he will become profoundly depressed. The Russian secret police know this well: which is why they arrest a suspect in the middle of the night without warning, place him in solitary confinement, and refuse him any communication with the outside world or any information about his future. It takes but a few weeks of solitary imprisonment in these circumstances to reduce most people to a state of profound dejection, an apathetic stupor in which both hope and pride disappear. We all need some support from the external world to maintain our sense of our own value.

Nevertheless, most of us can tolerate disappointments in one sphere of our existence without getting deeply depressed, provided the other spheres remain undamaged. Normal people may mourn, or experience disappointment, but because they have an inner source of self-esteem, they do not become or remain severely depressed for long in the face of misadventure, and are fairly easily consoled by what remains to them.

Depressives, in contrast to these normal folk, are much more vulnerable. If one thing in the external world goes wrong, they are apt to be thrown into despair. Even if people attempt to comfort them, they are likely to dismiss such efforts as futile. Disappointment, rejection, bereavement may all, in a depressive, pull a trigger which fires a reaction of total hopelessness; for such people do not possess an inner source of self-esteem to which they can turn in trouble, or which can easily be renewed by the ministrations of others. If, at a deep internal level, a person feels himself to be predominantly bad or unlovable, an actual rejection in the external world will bring this depressive belief to the surface; and no amount of reassurance from well-wishers will, for a time, persuade him of his real worth.

Psychoanalysis assumes that this vulnerability is the result of a rather early failure in the relationship between the child and his parents. In the ordinary course of events, a child takes in love with his mother's milk. A child who is wanted, loved, played with, cuddled will incorporate within himself a lively sense of his own value and will therefore surmount the inevitable setbacks and disappointments of childhood with no more than temporary sorrow, secure in the belief that the world is predominantly a happy place, and that he has a favored place in it. And this pattern will generally persist throughout his life.

A child, on the other hand, who is unwanted, rejected, or disapproved of will gain no such conviction. Although such a child may experience periods of both success and happiness, these will neither convince him that he is lovable nor finally prove to him that life is worthwhile. A whole career may be dedicated to the pursuit of power, the conquest of women, or the gaining of wealth, only, in the end, to leave the person face to face with despair and a sense of futility, since he has never incorporated within himself a sense of his value as a person; and no amount of external success can ultimately compensate him for this.

> On one of his birthdays a few years before, in answer to my sister Diana's exclamation of wonderment at all the things he had done in his life, he said: "I have achieved a great deal to achieve nothing in the end." We were listening to the radio and reading the always generous newspaper eulogies. "How can you say that?" she said. He was silent. "There are your books," I said. "And your paintings," Diana followed. "Oh yes, yes there are those." "And after all, there is us," we continued. "Poor comfort we know at times: and there are other children who are grateful that they are alive." He acknowledged us with a smile. . . .

Sarah Churchill, in her book *A Thread in the Tapestry,* begins her portrait of her father with these sentences; and it is surely percipient of her to do so. For she, and other members of the family, must have realized, in those last sad years, that in spite of the eulogies, the accolades, the honors, Winston Churchill still had a void at the heart of his being which no achievement or honor could ever completely fill.

It is interesting to compare this passage with another written by Churchill himself, emanating not from his old age but from his early manhood. *Savrola,* Winston Churchill's only novel, was the first book upon which he embarked, though it was actually the third to be published. Though half-completed in 1897, it was not in print till 1900, since *The Story of the Malakand Field Force* and *The River War* intervened. Savrola, the orator and revolutionary, is, it has often been observed, a picture of Churchill himself. We are introduced to him in his study, surrounded by Gibbon, Macaulay, Plato, and Saint-Simon.

> There were still some papers and telegrams lying unopened on the table, but Savrola was tired; they could, or at any rate, should wait

> till the morning. He dropped into his chair. Yes, it had been a long day, and a gloomy day. He was a young man, only thirty-two, but already he felt the effects of work and worry. His nervous temperament could not fail to be excited by the vivid scenes through which he had lately passed, and the repression of his emotion only heated the inward fire. Was it worth it? The struggle, the labour, the constant rush of affairs, the sacrifice of so many things that make life easy, or pleasant—for what? A people's good! That, he could not disguise from himself, was rather the direction than the cause of his efforts. Ambition was the motive force and he was powerless to resist it.

"Was it worth it?" The question recurs again and again in the lives of people who suffer from depression. At the end of *Savrola,* the query is reiterated. The revolution has been successful, but "A sense of weariness, of disgust with struggling, of desire for peace filled his soul. The object for which he had toiled so long was now nearly attained and it seemed of little worth. . . ." Savrola has to go into exile, and looks back on the city he has liberated, now partially destroyed by shell fire. "The smoke of other burning houses rose slowly to join the black, overhanging cloud against which the bursting shells showed white with yellow flashes.

"'And that,' said Savrola after prolonged contemplation, 'is my life's work.'"

Even more interesting is the passage in which Savrola, "weary of men and their works," ascends into his observatory to "watch the stars for the sake of their mysteries." He contemplates the beauty of Jupiter:

> Another world, a world more beautiful, a world of boundless possibilities, enthralled his imagination. He thought of the future of Jupiter, of the incomprehensible periods of time that woud elapse before the cooling process would render life possible on its surface, of the slow steady march of evolution, merciless, inexorable. How far would it carry them, the unborn inhabitants of an embryo world? Perhaps only to some vague distortion of the vital essence; perhaps further than he could dream of. All the problems would be solved; all the obstacles overcome; life would attain perfect development. And this fancy, overleaping space and time, carried the story to periods still more remote. The cooling process would continue; the perfect development of life would end in death; the whole solar system, the whole universe itself would one day be cold and lifeless as a burnt-out firework.

> It was a mournful conclusion. He locked up the observatory and descended the stairs, hoping that his dreams would contradict his thoughts.

The underlying despair, so characteristic of the depressive temperament, could hardly be better demonstrated. However successful Savrola is, he is still left uncertain as to the value of his achievement. His fantasy of life attaining "perfect development" in some far-distant future is automatically canceled by his belief that the universe must finally cool to a lifeless stop. The man who, a few years before his death, said to his daughter, "I have achieved a great deal to achieve nothing in the end," is displaying an absolutely consistent emotional pattern, already evident in early manhood.

What were the childhood origins of Churchill's depressive disposition? Any answer must necessarily be partly a matter of guesswork, but certain obvious factors present themselves for consideration, of which parental neglect is the most striking.

Winston Churchill was a premature child, born two months before he was expected. No one can say with certainty whether prematurity has an adverse effect upon future emotional development, but we do know that the way in which a baby is nursed and handled affects the rate of its physical and mental progress, and that even the youngest child is sensitive to the environment. A premature child is unexpected and, therefore, something of an embarrassment. We know that preparations for Winston Churchill's appearance were incomplete, for there was a lack of baby clothes; and a first child, in any case, is apt to be somewhat of an anxiety to an inexperienced mother. How was Churchill handled as a baby? All we know is that, in accordance with the custom of those days, he was not fed by his mother, but handed over to a wet nurse about whom we know nothing.

His mother, Lady Randolph, was only twenty when Winston was born. She was a girl of exceptional beauty, far too engaged in the fashionable social life of the time to be much concerned about her infant son. Lord Randolph, deeply involved in politics, would not have been expected to take more than a remote interest in his son and heir, and he more than fulfilled this expectation. In fact, Churchill received remarkably little affection or support from either parent in the vital years of early childhood. The person who saved him from emotional starvation was, of course, Mrs. Everest, the nanny who was engaged early in 1875 within a few months of his birth, and who remained his chief support and confidante until her death when Churchill was twenty. Her photograph hung in his room until the end of his own life. She is immortalized as the housekeeper in *Savrola,* and although Randolph Churchill makes use of the same quotation in his biography of his father, it is worth repeating here, since it reveals something of Winston Churchill's attitude to love.

> His thoughts were interrupted by the entrance of the old woman with a tray. He was tired, but the decencies of life had to be observed; he rose, and passed into the inner room to change his clothes and make his toilet. When he returned, the table was laid; the soup he had asked for had been expanded by the care of his housekeeper into a more elaborate meal. She waited on him, plying him the while with questions and watching his appetite with anxious pleasure. She had nursed him from his birth with a devotion and care which knew no break. It is a strange thing, the love of these women. Perhaps it is the only disinterested affection in the world. The mother loves her child; that is maternal nature. The youth loves his sweetheart; that too may be explained. The dog loves his master; he feeds him; a man loves his friend; he has stood by him perhaps at doubtful moments. In all there are reasons, but the love of a foster-mother for her charge appears absolutely irrational. It is one of the few proofs, not to be explained even by the association of ideas, that the nature of mankind is superior to mere utilitarianism, and that his destinies are high.

Churchill's concept of "disinterested affection" is worth comment. For it is surely not as astonishing as he implies that a nurse should love her charge. A nanny is a woman without children of her own, and without a husband. What could be more natural than that she should devote herself to the child who is placed in her care, and give him all the affection and love for which she has no other outlet? In the passage quoted above, Churchill is showing surprise at being loved, as if he had never felt that he was entitled to it. In the ordinary course of events, a small child receives from his mother and father love that he neither questions nor doubts. And he will generally extend his expectation of love to nannies, relatives, and other members of the family circle. As he grows up, he will find that not everyone loves him as he has come to expect; and this may surprise and disappoint him. But his surprise will surely be evoked by the discovery that some people do *not* love him, rather than by the fact that people other than his parents *do* love him.

Happy children do not ask *why* their mothers or anybody else love them; they merely accept it as a fact of existence. It is those who have received less than their early due of love who are surprised that anyone should be fond of them, and who seek for explanation of the love that more fortunate children take for granted. People who suffer from depression are always asking themselves why anyone should love them. They often feel entitled to respect, to awe, or to admiration; but as for love, that is too much to expect. Many depressives only feel lovable insofar as they have some achievement to their credit, or have given another person so much that they feel entitled to a return. The idea that anyone might give him love just because he is himself is foreign to the person of depressive temperament. In showing astonishment at Mrs. Everest's disinterested love, Churchill is surely revealing what one would expect from his emotional disposition, that he had not experienced from his parents that total, irrational acceptance which we all need and which is given by most mothers to a wanted baby. And although Mrs. Everest's affection made up for what was missing to some extent, it could not replace the love of parents.

We cannot now obtain as much information as we would like about Churchill's very early childhood, but that his parents were neglectful is undoubted. As Randolph Churchill says in his biography:

> The neglect and lack of interest in him shown by his parents were remarkable, even judged by the standards of late Victorian and Edwardian days. His letters to his mother from his various schools abound in pathetic requests for letters and for visits, if not from her, from Mrs Everest and his brother Jack. Lord Randolph was a busy politician with his whole interest absorbed in politics; Lady Randolph was caught up in the whirl of fashionable society and seems to have taken very little interest in her son until he began to make his name resound through the world. It will later be seen how neglectful she was in writing to him when he was for three years a subaltern in India and when his father and Mrs Everest were dead. His brother Jack, more than five years younger, could

not be a satisfactory correspondent and Winston was to feel exceptionally lonely and abandoned.[11]

We are, I believe, entitled to assume that Winston Churchill was deprived by parental neglect of that inner source of self-esteem upon which most predominantly happy persons rely, and which serves to carry them through the inevitable disappointments and reverses of human existence. What were the ways in which he endeavored to make up for his early lack and to sustain his self-esteem in spite of lack of parental affection?

The first and most obvious trait of character which he developed as a response to his deprivation was ambition. As he himself wrote of Savrola, "Ambition was the motive force and he was powerless to resist it." And in a letter to his mother, written in 1899 in India, he writes: "What an awful thing it will be if I don't come off. It will break my heart for I have nothing else but ambition to cling to. . . ."[12] Children who have been more loved and appreciated than Winston Churchill do have something other than ambition to cling to. Ambition is, of course, a perfectly "normal" trait, to be expected in any young man reared in the competitive climate of Western civilization. But Churchill's ambition was certainly inordinate; and it made him unpopular when he was young. Sir Charles Dilke is reported as writing that Rosebery was the most ambitious man he had ever met; but later he amended this opinion by writing alongside it, "I have since known Winston Churchill."

Ambition, when, as in Churchill's case, it is a compulsive drive, is the direct result of early deprivation. For if a child has but little inner conviction of his own value, he will be drawn to seek the recognition and acclaim that accrue from external achievement. In youth, especially, success, or even the hope of success, whether financial, political, or artistic, can be effective in staving off depression in those who are liable to this disorder. It is the inevitable decay of hope as a man gets older that accounts for the fact that severe attacks of depression become more common in middle age. It may be argued that very able people are always ambitious, since it is natural enough for a gifted man to require scope for his abilities and to want those ambitions to be recognized. In Lord

11. Randolph Churchill, *Winston S. Churchill,* Vol. 1, *Youth: 1874–1900* (London: Heinemann, 1966), p. 45.

12. *Ibid.,* Vol. 1, p. 441.

Reith's phrase, to be "fully stretched" is a pleasure in itself. But the compensatory quality of Churchill's ambition is not difficult to discern. Even his famous remark to Lady Violet Bonham Carter, "We are all worms. But I do believe that I am a glowworm," is revealing, in that it combines self-abasement and self-glorification in a single phrase.

Extreme ambition, of the Churchillian variety, is not based upon a sober appraisal of the reality of one's gifts and deficiencies. There is always an element of fantasy, unrelated to actual achievement. This may, as it did with Churchill, take the form of a conviction that one is being reserved for a special purpose, if not by the Deity, then at least by fate. One of the most remarkable features of Churchill's psychology is that this conviction persisted throughout the greater part of his life, until, at the age of sixty-five, his fantasy found expression in reality. As he said to Moran, "This cannot be accident, it must be design. I was kept for this job." If Churchill had died in 1939, he would have been regarded as a failure. Moran is undoubtedly right when he writes of "the inner world of make-believe in which Winston found reality." It is probable that England owed her survival in 1940 to this inner world of make-believe. The kind of inspiration with which Churchill sustained the nation is not based on judgment, but on an irrational conviction independent of factual reality. Only a man convinced that he had an heroic mission, who believed that, in spite of all evidence to the contrary, he could yet triumph, and who could identify himself with a nation's destiny could have conveyed his inspiration to others.

The miracle had much in common with that achieved by a great actor, who, by his art, exalts us and convinces us that his passions are beyond the common run of human feeling. We do not know, and we shall never know, the details of Churchill's world of make-believe. But that it was there, and that he played an heroic part in it, cannot be gainsaid. Before the invention of nuclear weapons, many a schoolboy had dreams of military glory that are hardly possible today. To be a great commander, to lead forces in battle against overwhelming odds, to make an heroic last stand, to win the Victoria Cross are ambitions which have inspired many generations in the past. Churchill was born in an age when such dreams were still translatable into reality; and he sought to realize them in his early career as a soldier. But, unlike many soldiers, he did not become disillusioned. Even as an old man, it was difficult to restrain him from deliberately exposing himself to risk when he went out to France after the second front had been embarked upon. The schoolboy's daydream persisted: and his search for danger was not simply a desire to prove his physical courage, a motive which was undoubtedly operative in early youth. It also rested upon a conviction that he would be preserved, that nothing could happen to a man of destiny—a belief that he shared with General Gordon, who likewise, throughout his life, exposed himself deliberately to death, and who inspired others by his total disregard of danger.

The conviction of being "special" is, in psychoanalytic jargon, a reflection of what is called "infantile omnipotence." Psychoanalysis postulates, with good reason, that the infant has little appreciation of his realistic stature in the world into which he is born. Although a human infant embarks on life in a notably helpless state, requiring constant care and attention in order to preserve him, his very helplessness creates the illusion that he is powerful. For the demands of a baby are imperious. A baby must be fed, cleaned, clothed, and preserved from injury, and, in the normal course of events, these demands are met by a number of willing slaves who hasten to fulfill them. As the child matures, he will gradually learn that his desires are not always paramount, and that the needs of others must sometimes take precedence. This is especially so in a family where there are other children. The hard lesson that one is not the center of the universe is more quickly learned in the rough and tumble of competition with brothers and sisters. Only children may fail to outgrow this early stage of emotional development; and, although Winston Churchill was not an only child, his brother Jack, born in 1880, was sufficiently younger for Winston to have retained his solitary position during five crucial years. Paradoxically, it is children who are deprived as well as solitary who retain the sense of omnipotence. A failure to meet a child's need for total care and total acceptance during the earliest part of his existence leaves him with a sense of something missing and something longed for; and he may, in later life, try to create conditions in which his lightest whim is immediately attended to, and resent the fact that this is not always possible.

In Churchill, this characteristic was evident. During one of his illnesses he required two nurses. His wife told Lord Moran: "Winston is a pasha. If he cannot clap his hands for a servant he calls for Walter as he enters the house. If it were left to him he'd have the nurses for the rest of his life. He would like two in his room, two in the passage. He is never so happy, Charles, as he is when one of the nurses is doing something for him while Walter puts on his socks."[13] Churchill's arrogance, impatience, and lack of consideration for others must have made him extremely difficult to live with; but these traits were softened by his magnanimity. How did so egocentric a man inspire devotion in those who served him, whose immediate needs he seldom considered, who might have to stay up till all hours to suit his own peculiar timetable, and who were often exposed to his formidable temper? It is not an easy question to answer; but it is often true that men who demand and need a great deal of attention from others are manifesting a kind of childlike helplessness, which evokes an appropriate response, however difficult they may be. His wife recorded that the only time he had been on the Underground was during the general strike. "He went round and round, not knowing where to get out and had to be rescued eventually." As with a small child, omnipotence and helplessness went hand in hand. There are a good many characters in public life who would be totally nonplussed if they had to get their own meals, darn their own socks, or even write their own letters.

The fact that Churchill was an aristocrat must have been of considerable service to him. However neglected he was by his parents, there was Mrs. Everest to minister to him; and she was later succeeded by his wife, his valet, his doctor, and innumerable attendants and servants. Those of us who are old enough to remember the days in which the aristocracy and the upper middle class took it for granted that the ordinary details of living, food, clothes, travel, and so on would be taken care of by some minion or other, and who have since adapted to fending for ourselves, can without difficulty recall that the existence of servants did minister to our sense of self-esteem. Churchill was not rich in early life. He had to make his living by his pen. But he knew nothing of the

13. Moran, p. 433.

lives of ordinary people, and, like other members of his class, grew up with the assumption that he was a good many cuts above the general run of the population. This assumption has stood many of his ilk in good stead.

The English upper class has been notorious for handing over its children to the care of servants, and, in the case of boys, disposed to send them to boarding schools at an absurdly early age. The sense of belonging to a privileged class is some mitigation for the feeling of early rejection; and the Churchill family was, of course, of particular distinction within that privileged class. The young Winston Churchill may have felt lonely and unloved, but it cannot have been long before he became conscious that he was "special" in another, less personal sense: the scion of a famous house with a long line of distinguished ancestors behind him. The fact that he chose to write biographies both of his father and of the first Duke of Marlborough shows how important this was to him.

When a child's emotional needs are not met, or only partially met, by his parents, he will generally react to this frustration by hostility. The most "difficult," badly behaved children are those who are unloved; and they tend to treat all authority as hostile. Winston Churchill was no exception. But even the most rebellious and intransigent child retains, in imagination, a picture of the parents he would have liked to have. The negative image of authority as rejecting, cruel, and neglectful is balanced by a positive image of idealized parents, who are invariably loving, tender, and understanding. And the less a child knows or has intimate contact with his real parents, the more will this double image persist. Real parents are real people: sometimes loving, sometimes impatient; sometimes understanding, sometimes imperceptive. The child reared in the intimacy of an ordinary family soon amalgamates the images of "good" and "bad," and comes to realize that, in other human beings as in himself, love and hate, goodness and badness, are inextricably intermingled. Psychiatrists have often observed that delinquent and emotionally disturbed children, who have parents who are actually neglectful or cruel, still maintain that these "bad" parents are really "good," and blame themselves for the parents' faults. This idealization of parents serves a defensive and protective function. A small child, being weak and defenseless, finds it unbearable to believe that there are no adults who love, support, and guide him; and if there are not, he invents them.

Winston Churchill showed this idealization very clearly. Of his mother, he wrote: "She shone for me like the Evening Star. I loved her dearly—but at a distance." This romantic view of his mother gave way to a more realistic appraisal of her when, as a young man of twenty-three, he was compelled to recognize her financial irresponsibility and to write to her about her extravagances. But the images formed in childhood are not so easily dispelled; and Churchill, at least in his early years, retained a romantic view of women, which was derived from his idealization of his beautiful mother. Violet Bonham Carter draws attention to this:

> This inner circle of friends contained no women. They had their own place in his life. His approach to women was essentially romantic. He had a lively susceptibility to beauty, glamour, radiance, and those who possessed these qualities were not subjected to analysis. Their possession of all the cardinal virtues was assumed as a matter of course. I remember his taking umbrage when I once commented on the "innocence" of his approach to women. He was affronted by this epithet as applied to himself. Yet to me he would certainly have applied it as a term of praise.

Like many another romantic, Churchill was in youth somewhat awkward in his approach to women, although he was emotionally involved with at least three girls before he married. In his latter years he took little notice of women, and indeed would hardly speak to them. But the romantic vision persisted, attaching itself to the figure of Queen Elizabeth II. When contemplating the queen's photograph, he is reported as saying: "Lovely, inspiring. All the film people in the world, if they had scoured the globe, could not have found anyone so suited to the part." Royalty never lost its magic for him; and, like his ancestor in the time of the civil war, he remained an ardent royalist throughout his life, despite the declining popularity of the monarchical principle among the sophisticated. When Churchill spoke of himself as a servant of the queen, he undoubtedly felt that he was. His idealization of the monarchy, which extended itself to the kings and queens of other states besides Britain, meant that he seldom saw royalty as creatures of flesh and blood, any more than he saw his parents as human beings. It is a characteristic that he shared with many others in Great Britain.

Winston Churchill's idealization of his father was even more remarkable. It is not surprising that a small boy should see so beautiful and elegant a young mother as a fairy princess. But his father, though a notable public figure, and a highly gifted man, was so consistently disapproving of, or uninterested in, his small son, that Churchill's hero worship of him can be explained only in terms of the psychological mechanism outlined above. As Violet Bonham Carter writes: "The image remained upon its pedestal, intact and glorious. Until the end he worshipped at the altar of his Unknown Father." And his father remained entirely unknown to him, never talked intimately with him, and seldom wrote to him, except to reprove him. After Lord Randolph's death from general paralysis of the insane, when Winston Churchill was twenty, he learned large portions of his father's speeches by heart, and, in 1906, published a two-volume biography of him. Filial devotion could hardly go further; but it was devotion to an image, not to a real father whose life he had shared.

Children whose emotional needs have been insufficiently satisfied by their parents react to the lack by idealization on the one hand and hostility on the other. Winston Churchill's obstinacy, resentment of authority, and willfulness were manifest very early in his life. He was sent to boarding school before his eighth birthday; and it is evident from his earliest reports that the school authorities became the recipients of the hostility which he must have felt toward his parents but which was never manifested because of his idealization of them. He was repeatedly late. "No. of times late. 20. very disgraceful." From being described as "a regular pickle" in his earliest report, he is later designated as "troublesome," "very bad," "careless," "a constant trouble to everybody," and "very naughty." He remained at this school from November, 1882, till the summer of 1884, and himself recorded how much he hated it. It is likely that he was removed because of the severe beatings he received, for the headmaster was a sadistic clergyman who would inflict as many as twenty strokes of the birch upon the bare buttocks of the little boys under his care, and who clearly enjoyed this exercise of his authority. But savage punishment failed to cow Winston Churchill, and probably served to increase his intolerance toward authority.

It is interesting to note that, in his early letters from school, he did not complain, but reported himself as happy; although, as he later admitted, this was the very opposite of the truth. Small boys who are miserable at boarding school very frequently conceal the fact from their parents. Ignorance of what the world is really like may lead them to suppose that ill-treatment and lack of sympathetic understanding is the expected lot of boys; and that, if they are unhappy, it is a sign of weakness and their own fault. This is especially true of those with a depressive tendency, for the hostility they feel toward parents and other authorities easily becomes turned inward against themselves. They therefore report themselves as happy because they feel they ought to be so, and easily deceive imperceptive parents who are not concerned to discover the truth.

There is, indeed, an intimate connection between depression and hostility, which was not understood until Freud had unraveled it. The emotionally deprived child who later becomes prey to depression has enormous difficulty in the disposal of his hostility. He resents those who have deprived him, but he cannot afford to show this resentment, since he needs the very people he resents; and any hostility he does manifest results in still further deprivation of the approval and affection he so much requires. In periods of depression, this hostility becomes turned inward against the self, with the result that the depressive undervalues himself or even alleges that he is worthless. "I have achieved a great deal to achieve nothing in the end."

It is this difficulty in disposing of hostility that drives some depressives to seek for opponents in the external world. It is a great relief to find an enemy on whom it is justifiable to lavish wrath. Winston Churchill was often accused of being a warmonger, which he was not. But there is no doubt that fighting enemies held a strong emotional appeal for him, and that, when he was finally confronted by an enemy whom he felt to be wholly evil, it was a release which gave him enormous vitality. Hitler was such an enemy; and it is probable that Churchill was never happier than when he was fully engaged in bringing about Hitler's destruction. For here, at last, was an opportunity to employ the full force of his enormous aggressiveness. Here was a monstrous tyranny, presided over by an arch-demon who deserved no mercy, and whom he could attack with an unsullied conscience. If all depressives could constantly be engaged in fighting wicked enemies, they would never suffer from depression. But, in day-to-day existence, antagonists are not wicked enough, and depressives suffer from pangs of conscience about their own hostility.

It is not decrying Churchill to state that his magnanimity and generosity to his many enemies rested upon this basis. People with Churchill's kind of early background know what it is to be insulted and injured; and, in spite of their internal store of hostility, they retain a capacity to identify with the underdog. It is unlikely that Churchill would have ever felt anything but hatred for Hitler, had the latter survived. But he showed an unusual compassion for the other enemies he defeated. Brendan Bracken reports that when Churchill sued Lord Alfred Douglas for making defamatory statements about him, he was not elated when he won the case. Indeed, he appeared depressed; and this was because he could not bear the thought of his defeated opponent being sent to prison. Although Churchill relished being in action against the enemies of England, compassion for them was equally in evidence, and he did not hesitate, at the age of twenty-three, to criticize Kitchener for the "inhuman slaughter of the wounded" at Omdurman and to attack him in print for having desecrated the Mahdi's tomb.

This alternation between aggression and compassion is characteristic of persons with Churchill's character structure. No one could have had more pride in the British Empire; and yet, when Churchill was twenty-seven, he was writing of "our unbridled Imperialists who have no thought but to pile up armaments, taxation and territory." This criticism was prompted by his reading of Seebohm Rowntree's book *Poverty,* which engaged his compassion for the underfed working class, neglected by imperialist politicians. Churchill was highly aggressive, and in many ways insensitive, but he was far from ruthless, and when he could imaginatively enter into the distress of others he was genuinely concerned. This was especially so in the case of prisoners, with whom he could closely identify himself. Churchill's period of office as home secretary was notable for the improvements that he introduced in the treatment of "political" prisoners, in his day the suffragettes; for the reform that allowed "time to pay" in the case of those who would otherwise have been imprisoned for the nonpayment of fines; and for the introduction of measures that reduced the number of young offenders sent to prison. He also advocated the introduction of lectures and concerts to prisoners, and insisted upon the provision of books for them.

Churchill's compassionate concern with prisoners originated in part with his generalized capacity to identify himself with the underdog, which we have already discussed. It also had a more particular root, which sprang from his personal experience. During the Boer War he was captured by the Boers and incarcerated as a prisoner of war. Although his period of imprisonment was very brief, for he was caught on November 15 and escaped on December 12, this experience made an ineradicable impression upon him. In *My Early Life* he writes of his imprisonment as follows:

> Prisoner of War! That is the least unfortunate kind of prisoner to be, but it is nevertheless a melancholy state. You are in the power of your enemy. You owe your life to his humanity, and your daily bread to his compassion. You must obey his orders, go where he tells you, stay where you are bid, await his pleasure, possess your soul in patience. Meanwhile the war is going on, great events are in progress, fine opportunities for action and adventure are slipping away. Also the days are very long. Hours crawl like paralytic centipedes. Nothing amuses you. Reading is difficult; writing impossible. Life is one long boredom from dawn till slumber.
>
> Moreover, the whole atmosphere of prison, even the most easy and best regulated prison, is odious. Companions in this kind of misfortune quarrel about trifles and get the least possible pleasure from each other's society. If you have never been under restraint before and never known what it was to be a captive, you feel a sense of constant humiliation in being confined to a narrow space, fenced in by railings and wire, watched by armed men, and webbed about with a tangle of regulations and restrictions. I certainly hated every minute of my captivity more than I have ever hated any other period in my whole life. . . . Looking back on those days, I have always felt the keenest pity for prisoners and captives. What it must mean for any man, especially an educated man, to be confined for years in a modern convict prison, strains my imagination. Each day exactly like the one before, with the barren ashes of wasted life behind, and all the long years of bondage stretching out ahead. . . .
>
> Dark moods come easily across the mind of a prisoner. . . .

Not all persons react to imprisonment like this. There are some who actively seek prison as a refuge from the troubles of this world.

Others spend their time more or less contentedly reading or engaged in solitary reflection. It is those who are liable to depression who most suffer pangs of the kind that Churchill described; for, deprived of the outside sources of stimulation that sustain them and the opportunity for adventure and excitement that is a defense against their innate tendency, they relapse into that state above all which they most fear.

Churchill was never happy unless he was fully occupied, asleep, or holding the floor. He had no small talk. It is impossible to imagine him being cozily relaxed. He had to be perpetually active, or else he relapsed into "dark moments of impatience and frustration," as Violet Bonham Carter describes his moods. As early as 1895 he was writing to his mother from Aldershot:

> I find I am getting into a state of mental stagnation when even letter writing becomes an effort and when any reading but that of monthly magazines is impossible. This is of course quite in accordance with the spirit of the army. It is indeed the result of mental forces called into being by discipline and routine. It is a state of mind into which all, or nearly all, soldiers fall. From this slough of despond I try to raise myself by reading and re-reading Papa's speeches, many of which I know almost by heart. But I really cannot find the energy to read any other serious work.

Army discipline and routine had a constraining effect upon him, not unlike that of prison; and the realization that he became depressed as a result may have contributed to his decision to seek political, rather than further military glory.

We have already mentioned Churchill's dislike of standing near the edge of a railway platform. He also admitted to Moran, while staying at Claridges, that he disliked sleeping near a balcony. "I've no desire to quit this world," he said with a grin, "but thoughts, desperate thoughts come into the head." He was also apprehensive about traveling by air, and was fond of quoting Dr. Johnson on sea travel: "Being in a ship is being in a jail, with the chance of being drowned." An underlying preoccupation with death, so characteristic of the depressive temperament, is easily detectable. In early youth, he was convinced that he would die young, as his father had. We can attribute this in part to an identification with his idealized father; but a conviction that time is short and an early realization of the ephemeral nature of human life is typical. His dislike of visiting hospitals belongs in this category of preoccupation, and so does his early tendency to hypochondriasis. Lucy Masterman reports of him in 1910: "He thought he had got every mortal disease under heaven, and was very much inclined to dine off slops and think about the latter end." When Admiral Pound died, Churchill said: "Death is the greatest gift God has made to us." It is not argued here that Churchill was ever suicidal—there is no evidence on that point. But it seems likely that death had a kind of fascination for him against which he had to defend himself. Men who have to be hyperactive in order to protect themselves against depression generally have a secret longing for total peace and relaxation; and the garden of Proserpina, "where even the weariest river winds somewhere safe to sea," has a special appeal that has to be fought against.

Churchill at first reacted to authority by intransigent disobedience. This rebelliousness was not only a way of discharging his hostility, but a means of self-assertion—probably the only way of self-assertion available to a boy who, at that stage, felt himself to be weak physically, and who showed no disposition to excel in any school subject except history. Soon, however, another means of preserving, or rather gaining, self-esteem presented itself. Although he continued to perform inadequately in most school subjects, certainly far less well than his intelligence warranted, he discovered that he had a gift for words, a gift which became his principal asset and which stood him in good stead throughout his life.

Before the use of words became his chief vehicle of self-expression, he had, at the age of eleven, shown a desire to learn the cello. Had this desire been granted, it is possible that music might have become important to him; for, as many musicians know, the world of sound can be a never-ending source of solace, and the ability to play an instrument is both a means of self-expression and a source of self-esteem. But Churchill's early interest in music was not encouraged, and soon died out; and his musical taste remained at the level of Sullivan and music-hall songs.

Churchill's attitude to words and the use of them is of interest psychologically. When he first met Violet Bonham Carter, he asked her whether she thought that words had a magic and a music quite independent of their meaning. For Churchill, they undoubtedly did. The magic of words became part of his inner world of make-believe. Sartre, in his autobiography, has recorded a similar process:

> A Platonist by condition, I moved from knowledge to its object; I found ideas more real than things, because they were the first to give themselves to me and because they gave themselves like things. I met the universe in books: assimilated, classified, labelled and studied, but still impressive; and I confused the chaos of my experience through books with the hazardous course of real events. Hence my idealism which it took me thirty years to undo.

All through his life Churchill was a voluble fount of ideas. Smuts said of him: "That is why Winston is indispensable. He has ideas." His imagination was really creative; and it expressed itself in rhetoric, in an ornate phraseology that soon soared above the sober and often intransigent facts of reality. This was why he was always having to be restrained by his advisers; by his civil servants when he was home secretary; by his chiefs of staff, especially Alanbrooke, when he was prime minister.

The literary style that first attracted him was that of Gibbon, whom he frankly imitated: and he also owed much to Macaulay. It is not surprising that these authors appealed to him. Of the two, Gibbon is the wittier, the more realistic, and the better balanced. His sentences, beautifully constructed, have a strong appeal to the musical ear. The remarkable thing is that Gibbon did not abuse his literary gift to distort history or advance his own prejudices, with the possible exception of his intolerance toward Christianity. Gibbon's *Decline and Fall* remained a standard work for many years. The same cannot be said of Macaulay, who used the magic of words to persuade his readers of views that were often highly subjective.

Churchill knew that his imagination could mislead him into false appraisals, but he could always be brought back to reality, although it might take hours of argument to do so. Churchill's grasp of military strategy was considerable, but it was liable to be interfered with by his romantic imagination, which often led him to disregard the logic of the possible. And the fact that he could clothe his ideas in magnificent language must have made those ideas even more convincing to him. He was able to inspire himself as well as others by the magic of words, which indeed can take on a life of their own.

Artists and philosophers create worlds that may be, and often are, substitutes for the disappointing and stubborn facts of human existence. Had Churchill not been born into an aristocratic and political family, he might have become a writer of a different kind. Since his interest in other human beings was minimal, and his grasp of human psychology negligible, it is unlikely that he would ever have been a novelist of character. But he could have written good adventure stories, and did so in *My Early Life,* which, although true autobiography, has in places the pace and dash of a thriller. But Churchill's imagination was captured by dreams of military glory and of political power; and so, although he can be rated as a literary artist, his creativity also found expression in imaginative schemes of social reform, in military inventions like the tank, and in strategic conceptions like Gallipoli, for the failure of which he was made a scapegoat.

Even as an orator, Churchill remained essentially literary. As he said himself: "I am not an orator, an orator is spontaneous." [14] In youth, his chief ambition was to be master of the spoken word, but it was an ambition that he never completely realized. Although some of his phrases, especially in his 1940 speeches, have become immortal, his was a literary rather than an oratorical talent. His speeches were carefully written out and often learned by heart; and, in youth, he was extremely nervous before delivering them. He lacked the common touch that great orators like Lloyd George possessed; and his diligence in preparing his speeches is another example of his extraordinary determination to conquer his natural disadvantages, and to succeed in spite of, rather than because of, his native endowment.

One of the most successful of modern writers, Georges Simenon, says: "Writing is not a profession, but a vocation of unhappiness." Not all artists are depressive by temperament; but those who are habitually use their skill to ward off the "Black Dog," and commonly go through a period of depression directly they have completed a new work. During this interval, before they can get

14. *Ibid.,* p. 429.

started again, they often believe that they are finished, and that they will never have another original idea; but, in time, the creative impulse generally reasserts itself. It is likely that Churchill used his writing as a defense against the depression that invariably descended upon him when he was forced to be inactive. This psychological mechanism is clearly evident when we come to consider his painting. He did not start to paint until he was forty, and what initiated this new departure was a period of despair. Several observers have attested the severity of Churchill's depression after the failure of the Dardanelles expedition, which he had initiated and which led to his resignation from the Admiralty in 1915. Violet Bonham Carter records: "He took me into his room and sat down on a chair—silent, despairing—as I have never seen him. He seemed to have no rebellion or even anger left. He did not even abuse Fisher, but simply said, 'I'm finished.' " Churchill himself wrote of this period:

> I had long hours of utterly unwonted leisure in which to contemplate the frightful unfolding of the war. At a moment when every fibre of my being was inflamed to action, I was forced to remain a spectator of the tragedy, placed cruelly in a front seat. And then it was that the Muse of Painting came to my rescue—out of charity and out of chivalry, because after all she had nothing to do with me—and said, "Are these toys any good to you? They amuse some people."

And from that time onward, painting became a great resource to Winston Churchill: something to which he could always turn in time of trouble, something that would invariably engage his interest and provide a perpetual challenge.

Psychoanalysis has long recognized the relation between aggression and depression, and the difficulty that the depressed person has in the disposal of his aggressive impulses. Although creative activity frequently contains an aggressive component, this is not always easy to discern; nor do we habitually think of painting a picture or composing a symphony as an aggressive activity. Those who find my thesis unconvincing should turn to Churchill's own account of his approach to a canvas in his book *Painting as a Pastime*:

> Very gingerly I mixed a little blue paint on the palette with a very small brush, and then with infinite precaution made a mark about

> as big as a bean upon the affronted snow-white shield. It was a challenge, a deliberate challenge, but so subdued, so halting, indeed so cataleptic, that it deserved no response. At that moment the loud approaching sound of a motor-car was heard in the drive. From this chariot there stepped swiftly and lightly none other than the gifted wife of Sir John Lavery. "Painting! But what are you hesitating about? Let me have a brush—the big one." Splash into the turpentine, wallop into the blue and the white, frantic flourish on the palette—clean no longer—and then several large, fierce strokes, and slashes of blue on the absolutely cowering canvas. Anyone could see that it could not hit back. No evil fate avenged the jaunty violence. The canvas grinned in helplessness before me. The spell was broken. The sickly inhibitions rolled away. I seized the largest brush and fell upon my victim with berserk fury. I have never felt any awe of a canvas since.

He later compares painting a picture to fighting a battle. Indeed, this little book is one of the most revealing things he ever wrote about himself.

Churchill's predilection for rather grandiose, highly colored language was related to the need of his romantic imagination to lighten the gloom into which he was apt to descend. His choice of color in painting is strictly analogous:

> I must say I like bright colours . . . I cannot pretend to feel impartial about the colours. I rejoice with the brilliant ones, and am genuinely sorry for the poor browns. When I get to heaven I mean to spend a considerable portion of my first million years in painting, and so get to the bottom of the subject. But then I shall require a still gayer palette than I get here below. I expect orange and vermilion will be the darkest, dullest colours upon it, and beyond them there will be a whole range of wonderful new colours which will delight the celestial eye.

In psychoanalytic jargon, this is a "manic defense." The counterpart to the gloomy, subfuse world of the depressive is a realm of perpetual excitement and action, in which colors are richer and brighter, gallant deeds are accomplished by heroes, and ideas expressed in language replete with simile, ornamented with epithet, and sparkling with mellifluous turns of phrase. In his book on painting, Churchill gives us a delightful glimpse into his inner world of make-believe: a world where every prospect pleases, but which is just as remote from reality as is the downcast, hopeless hell of the man who feels useless and "finished."

Churchill's need of this manic realm is equally reflected in his choice of friends. Holders of the Victoria Cross were immediately attractive to him, irrespective of their personalities; for they were real live heroes who coincided with those in his inner world. So were ebullient, energetic adventurers, like Lord Birkenhead and Lord Beaverbrook. Churchill was a poor judge of character. The sober, steadfast, and reliable seldom appealed to him. What he wanted were people who would stimulate, amuse, and arouse him. Lord Moran notes that he was unimpressed by many of the quietly distinguished doctors who were sent to see him, but easily fell for the near-charlatans, the men with the gift of the gab who were unrestrained by scientific caution. The flamboyant extrovert is life-enhancing, although exhausting; he brings zest and vitality to life. Men like Birkenhead helped Churchill to find and to sustain the manic side of his own personality.

In an earlier passage we have taken note of the fact that persons with Churchill's type of psychological structure find it hard to learn that they are not the center of the universe. Because of the lack of intimate relations, first with parents, and later with other people, they remain egocentrically oriented: narcissistic. Every baby starts life in a predominantly solipsistic state; most progress to a more mature emotional condition in which it is realized not only that other people have desires and needs, but also that one's own desires and needs interact with them in such a way that one can both satisfy and be satisfied simultaneously. The child who is early deprived forms no such conception, with the result that he makes inordinate demands on other people but has little idea of being able to give them much. Churchill was generous to defeated enemies, but remained extremely demanding and insensitive to the requirements of others. His principal love object remained himself, because that self had never, in childhood, been satisfied.

Psychoanalysts describe such a character as "oral," because it is through the mouth that the baby's earliest needs are met; and, when they are not met, oral traits of character persist, both literally and metaphorically. It is interesting that, in one of his earliest school reports, Churchill is described as greedy; and it is also recorded that he was beaten for stealing sugar. All through his life, he needed feeding at frequent intervals; he was dependent on, though not necessarily addicted to, alcohol, and was a heavy smoker of cigars. He was also greedy for approval. His intimates knew that, if he showed them a manuscript of what he was writing, what he wanted was praise unadulterated with any tinge of criticism. "You are not on my side" was the reproach leveled at friends who ventured any adverse comment upon his ideas or his creations. The part of him that still demanded the total and uncritical acceptance, which he had never had as a child, still divided the world into black and white, so that friendship and disagreement were regarded as incompatible. Because of this characteristic, his own relationship to friends was also uncritical. He was intensely loyal. As Brendan Bracken said, "He would go to the stake for a friend"; and this was what he expected from his own friends. He remained hungry—hungry for fame, for adulation, for success, and for power; and although he gained all these in full measure, the end of his life showed that he never assimilated them into himself, but remained unsatisfied.

It was often said of Churchill that he "lacked antennae," that is, that he was insensitive where other people were concerned. There are several anecdotes which reveal that, quite unwittingly, he gave offense to other people on social occasions by neglecting them or taking no notice of them. This imperviousness to atmosphere is characteristic of the narcissistic person, who, like a small child, is still living in a private world that takes little account of other people except in so far as they provide what the child wants. We expect that small children will be "selfish," intent on their own satisfaction, with little regard for what others are feeling. Churchill retained this characteristic in adult life; and it was directly related to his early deprivation. For the "selfish" are those who have never had enough. It is only the child whose emotional needs have been satisfied who is later able to give as much as he takes. Churchill said of himself, quite accurately, "I have devoted more time to self-expression than to self-discipline." Had he been less egocentric, he would not have achieved so much; had he been more self-disciplined, he would have been less inspiring.

We have discussed in some detail the methods that Churchill employed to prevent himself from relapsing into the depression which dogged him, and against which, as Lord Moran said, he was fighting all his life. Perhaps the most remarkable feature of Churchill's psychology is that, on the whole, the defenses he employed against depression proved so successful. Although in youth he suffered long periods of depression, his various methods of dealing with this disability seem to have had the result that, in later life, he could generally extricate himself from the slough of despond and never let himself be overwhelmed by it until his old age. Those who knew him intimately during his years in the political wilderness may report differently. There are some hints that he drank more heavily during this period. But on the written evidence at present available, the success with which he dealt with his own temperament is quite extraordinary. Indeed, it is quite likely that some of those who were comparatively close to him never realized that he was liable to depression at all.

At the beginning of this essay, I suggested that the relation between great achievement and the depressive temperament was worth more attention than has yet been bestowed upon it. In psychiatric practice, it is not at all uncommon to come across men of great ability and dynamic force who have achieved far more than the common run of success and who are generally supposed by their contemporaries to be, if not necessarily happy, at least free from any kind of neurotic disability. On the surface, such men appear to be more confident than the average. They often inspire those who serve them, set an example by their own enormous appetite for work, and appear to possess inexhaustible vitality. Those who follow in their wake regard such leaders as being superhuman, and merely envy their energy without stopping to inquire what it is that drives them. Yet, anyone who has himself ventured along the corridors of power knows that the extremely ambitious are often highly vulnerable, that the tycoon may be lost if his luck deserts him, and that the personal and emotional relationships of those who pursue power are often sadly inadequate. Ambition, taken in isolation, may be a trait of character that merely reflects a man's desire to find adequate scope for his abilities. It can also be a demonic force, driving the subject to achieve more and more, yet never bringing contentment and peace, however great the achievement. The degree to which the highly successful are able to conceal, both from themselves and from others, that they are tormented beings, is extraordinary; and it is often only in the consulting room that the truth emerges. Alanbrooke, weary of the war and the enormous responsibility he carried, was content to lay down his burden and retire to domestic happiness and bird watching. Churchill, on the other hand, was extremely reluctant to abandon power, although, as early as 1949, after his first stroke, some medical opinion considered that he should no longer pursue high office. There is no doubt in my mind as to which of the two men was the happier and the better balanced. Yet Alanbrooke, as he would himself have been the first to admit, could never have inspired the nation as did Churchill.

The end of Churchill's long life makes melancholy reading. It is indeed a tragedy that he survived into old age. Moran records that, after his retirement in April, 1955, "Winston made little effort to hide his distaste for what was left to him of life," and adds that "the historian might conclude that this reveals a certain weakness in moral fibre." Any historian who does so conclude will merely reveal his ignorance of medicine. For cerebral arteriosclerosis, with which Churchill was seriously affected, not only saps the will, as Lord Moran says. It also makes impossible the mechanisms of defense with which a man copes with his temperamental difficulties. In old age, most people become to some extent caricatures of themselves. The suspicious become paranoid, the intolerant more irritable, and the depressives less able to rouse themselves from the slough of despond.

Moran brings his story to a close five years before Churchill's death because he "thought it proper to omit the painful details of the state of apathy and indifference into which he sank after his resignation." I think he was right, as a doctor, to do so. He records that Churchill gave up reading, seldom spoke, and sat for hours before the fire in what must have amounted to a depressive stupor. To dwell upon the medical and psychiatric details of Churchill's end would have exposed Moran to even more criticism from his medical colleagues than he received in any case. But the fact that the "Black Dog" finally overcame an old man whose brain could, because of an impaired blood supply, no longer function efficiently, merely increases our admiration for the way in which, earlier in life, he fought his own disability. For he carried a temperamental load that was indeed an exceptionally heavy burden.

It is at this point that psychoanalytic insight reveals its inadequacy. For, although I believe that the evidence shows that the conclusions reached in this essay are justified, we are still at a loss to explain Churchill's remarkable courage. In the course of his life he experienced many reverses—disappointments that might have embittered and defeated even a man who was not afflicted by the "Black Dog." Yet his dogged determination, his resilience, and his courage enabled him, until old age, to conquer his own inner enemy, just as he defeated the foes of the country he loved so well.

We have often had occasion to comment upon Churchill's "inner world of make-believe" in which, as Moran says, he found reality. At one period in his life, he was fortunate. For, in 1940, his inner world of make-believe coincided with the facts of external reality in a way that very rarely happens to any man. It is an experience not unlike that of passionate love, when, for a time, the object of a man's desire seems to coincide exactly with the image of woman he carries within him. In 1940, Churchill became the hero that he had always dreamed of being. It was his finest hour. In that dark time, what England needed was not a shrewd, equable, balanced leader. She needed a prophet, a heroic visionary, a man who could dream dreams of victory when all seemed lost. Winston Churchill was such a man; and his inspirational quality owed its dynamic force to the romantic world of fantasy in which he had his true being.

Bibliographical Note

THE MOST IMPORTANT BOOKS by Churchill himself are indicated in his brief biography printed at the beginning of this collection. Twenty-one volumes of his speeches have also been published. Books and articles by and about Churchill are almost without number. Churchill's own writings are listed in Frederick Woods's *A Bibliography of the Works of Sir Winston Churchill* (Toronto, 2nd ed., 1969).

Every book of history that touches on the period from 1900 to 1955 will include some discussion of Churchill, and of course this is particularly true of all books on modern England. Any political biography or autobiography covering the long period during which Winston Churchill was an active politician will shed light upon him, and most will have considerable material about him. The list of books and articles that deal directly with him is immense itself, although the number of monographic studies in articles or book form is not as large as one might expect. Here I can only hope to indicate some of the more obvious sources, as well as a few of the more interesting obscure ones. Most of the many general lives, all too frequently written for the "young" reader, will be omitted.

The most thorough biographical source, when completed, will be the official life, with its companion volumes of documents. The first three volumes have appeared; the first two were written by Winston Churchill's son, Randolph Churchill: *Youth 1874–1900* (Boston, 1966) and *Young Statesman 1901–1914* (Boston, 1967). Because of Randolph Churchill's death, the third volume (*Winston S. Churchill: 1914–1916* [Boston, 1971]) was written by Martin Gilbert, who will also prepare the later ones as well.

To place Churchill within his times, the reader should investigate four excellent accounts of twentieth-century England: Alfred F. Havighurst, *Twentieth-Century Britain* (New York, 1962); T. O. Lloyd, *Empire to Welfare State* (New York, 1970); Charles Loch Mowat, *Britain Between the Wars 1918–1940* (Chicago, 1955); A. J. P. Taylor, *English History 1914–1945* (New York, 1965).

Notable collections of important articles and memoirs on Churchill include: *The Atlantic* (March, 1965); A. J. P. Taylor *et al., Churchill Revised* (New York, 1969); Maurice Ashley, ed., *Tributes Broadcast by the BBC* (London, 1965); Charles Eade, ed., *Churchill by His Contemporaries* (London, 1953); Brian Gardner, *Churchill in Power As Seen by His Contemporaries* (Boston, 1970); Bruce Ingram, ed., *An Eighteenth Year Tribute to Winston Churchill: Illustrated London News* (London, 1954); Sir James Marchant, ed., *Winston Spencer Churchill* (London, 1954); and Observer, ed., *Churchill by His Contemporaries* (London, 1965). *Churchill,* edited by Martin Gilbert (Englewood Cliffs, N.J., 1967), is an anthology that also includes selections by Churchill himself.

There are important longer studies, of which the following might be mentioned: Maurice Ashley, *Churchill as Historian* (London, 1968); Dennis Bardens, *Churchill in Parliament* (London, 1967); Mary C. Bromage, *Churchill and Ireland* (Notre Dame, Ind., 1964); Violet Bonham Carter, *Winston Churchill: An Intimate Portrait* (New York, 1965); R. MacGregor Dawson, *Winston Churchill at the Admiralty* (Toronto, 1940); V. W. Germains, *The Tragedy of Winston Churchill* (London, 1931); Captain A. D. Gibb, *With Winston Churchill at the Front* (London, 1924);

Trumbull Higgins, *Winston Churchill and the Dardanelles* (New York, 1963); Ronald Hyam, *Elgin and Churchill at the Colonial Office 1905–1908* (London, 1968); Robert Rhodes James, *Lord Randolph Churchill* (London, 1959) and *Gallipoli* (New York, 1965); Lord Moran, *Churchill: The Struggle for Survival* (London, 1966); A. MacCallum Scott, *Winston Churchill* (London, 1905) and *Winston Churchill in Peace and War* (London, 1916); George Malcolm Thomson, *Vote of Censure* (London, 1968); and Kenneth Young, *Churchill and Beaverbrook* (London, 1966).

The following are more popular accounts that provide an overview of Churchill's life: Lewis Broad, *Winston Churchill 1874–1952* (London, 1952); Virginia Cowles, *Winston Churchill* (New York, 1953); Philip Guedella, *Mr. Churchill: A Portrait* (London, 1941); A. L. Rowse, *The Churchills, from the Death of Marlborough to the Present* (New York, 1958); Malcolm Thompson, *The Life and Times of Winston Churchill* (London, 1945); and Fred Urguhart, ed., *W.S.C.: A Cartoon Biography* (London, 1955). John Connell's *Winston Churchill* (2nd ed., London, 1965) is a valuable pamphlet on his writings.

There are innumerable articles, sections, or chapters on him in scores of journals and books. The following struck this editor as particularly valuable, although not completely suitable for inclusion in the present collection: Earl of Birkenhead, *Contemporary Personalities* (London, 1924); R. D. Blumenfeld, *All in a Lifetime* (London, 1961); Collin Brooks, *Devil's Decade: Portraits of the Nineteen-Thirties* (London, 1948); F. Lauriston Bullard, *Famous War Correspondents* (Boston, 1914); Angus Calder, *The People's War* (London, 1969); H. S. Commager, "Winston Churchill: An Appreciation" (*American Mercury,* August, 1945); R. H. S. Crossman, *The Charm of Politics* (London, 1958); Viscount D'Abernon, *Portraits and Appreciations* (London, 1930); Vladimir Dedijer, "Participants as Historians" (*Times Literary Supplement,* May 30, 1968); John Ehrman, "Lloyd George and Churchill as War Ministers" (*Transactions of the Royal Historical Society,* London, 1961); A. G. Gardiner, *Prophets, Priests and Kings* (London, 1908) and *Pillars of Society* (London, 1913); A Gentleman with a Duster, *The Mirror of Downing Street* (New York, 1921); P. J. Grigg, *Prejudice and Judgment* (London, 1948); Philip Guedella, *The Liberators* (London, 1942); F. H. Hinsley, "Mr. Churchill's The

Second World War" (*The Cambridge Journal,* April, 1951); J. M. Keynes, *Essays in Biography* (London, 1933); Bryan Magee, "Churchill's Novel" (*Encounter,* October, 1965); Lucy Masterman, "Churchill: The Liberal Phase" (*History Today,* November and December, 1964); A. L. Rowse, *The English Spirit* (London, 1944); Arthur Salter, *Personality in Politics* (London, 1947); Herbert Sidebotham, *Pillars of the State* (London, 1921); C. P. Snow, *Variety of Men* (New York, 1967); Lord Swinton, *Sixty Years of Power* (London, 1966); Watchman [Samuel V. Adams], *Right Honourable Gentlemen* (London, 1939); Reed Whittemore, "Churchill and the Limitations of Myth" (*Yale Review,* December, 1954); Woodrow Wyatt, *Into the Dangerous World* (London, 1952).

Contributors

CLEMENT ATTLEE (1883–1967), later Earl Attlee, was educated at Haileybury and Oxford. He became leader of the Labour Party in 1935, was deputy prime minister in the wartime government, and prime minister of the Labour government of 1945–51.

ISAIAH BERLIN was educated at St. Paul's and Corpus Christi College, Oxford, and is president of Wolfson College, Oxford, and professor of humanities at the City University of New York. An intellectual historian, Sir Isaiah is the author of several books, including *Karl Marx* (1939), *The Hedgehog and the Fox* (1953), and *Four Essays on Liberty* (1969). He was with the British Embassy in Washington from 1942 to 1945.

JOHN COLVILLE, who attended Harrow and Trinity College, Cambridge, served Churchill as his assistant private secretary, 1940–41 and 1943–45, and as his joint principal private secretary, 1951–55.

He was also private secretary to Neville Chamberlain, the prime minister before Churchill, and to Clement Attlee, who succeeded Churchill as prime minister.

A. G. Gardiner (1865–1946) was a very prolific author and journalist, and a firm supporter of the Liberal Party. He wrote with insight about Churchill in *Prophets, Priests and Kings* (1908) and *Pillars of Society* (1913), as well as in the essay reprinted in this volume.

Ronald Hyam is a member of the history faculty at Cambridge University. His book *Elgin and Churchill at the Colonial Office, 1905–1908* is mostly devoted to an excellent discussion of the accomplishments and difficulties experienced by the Earl of Elgin, the colonial secretary in Sir Henry Campbell-Bannerman's Liberal government of 1905–8, and by his under-secretary, Winston Churchill. The section extracted here, with footnotes eliminated, deals with the relationship of the two men and provides a telling glimpse of Churchill's personality and his ways of working. Readers may also wish to consult Hyam's perceptive review-essay "Winston Churchill Before 1914" (*Historical Journal,* March, 1969, pp. 164–73).

Robert Rhodes James is the director of the Institute for the Study of International Organisation at the University of Sussex. Educated at Sedbergh School and Worcester College, Oxford, he has been a clerk to the House of Commons, a Fellow of All Souls, Oxford, and is the author of several biographical and political studies, most recently *Ambitions and Realities* (1972).

B. H. Liddell Hart (1895–1970) was the author of numerous books of military history and theory. An early proponent of mechanized warfare, he was one of the most influential—and tardily understood—military critics of the twentieth century.

John Gibson Lockhart (1891–1960) served in both world wars, was a publisher, and wrote several short biographies, as well as books on the sea.

Arno J. Mayer, educated at the City College of New York and Yale University, is professor of history at Princeton University and is the author of *Political Origins of the New Diplomacy* (1959), which won the Beer Prize of the American Historical Association, and *Politics and Diplomacy of Peacemaking* (1967).

GORONWY REES is a journalist, critic, and novelist; he was also principal of the University College of Wales, Aberystwyth. The controversial article reproduced here was refuted in *Encounter,* by A. L. Rowse ("Churchill Considered Historically," January, 1966, pp. 45–50) and by Kenneth Younger ("Off the Ball," February, 1966, pp. 94–96).

G. W. STEEVENS (1869–1900) met Churchill when they traveled together on their return from the Battle of Omdurman. During the Sudan campaign, Steevens was a well-known correspondent for the *Daily Mail,* where the essay included here was first published.

ANTHONY STORR is an English psychiatrist and author. He was educated at Winchester and Christ's College, Cambridge, and has written *The Integrity of the Personality, Sexual Deviation,* and *Human Aggression.*

PETER WRIGHT was on the British staff of the Supreme War Council during the First World War, and wrote about his experiences in *At the Supreme War Council* (1921). The essay included here is taken from his second book, *Essays and Criticism* (1925).

WOODROW WYATT is a prominent Labour politician and writer. He has been a Member of Parliament from 1945 to 1955, and from 1959 on.

Peter Stansky studied at Yale University and King's College, Cambridge, and received his Ph.D. from Harvard University in 1961. He was the recipient of Harvard University's Jay Prize in 1961, and of a Guggenheim Fellowship in 1966–67. Professor Stansky, currently Associate Professor of History at Stanford University, has written articles and reviews for scholarly journals and magazines both in the United States and abroad, and is co-author, with William Abrahams, of *The Unknown Orwell.* His previous books include *Ambitions and Strategies: The Struggle for the Leadership of the Liberal Party in the 1890s* (1964); with William Abrahams, *Journey to the Frontier* (1966); as editor, *The Left and War: The British Labour Party and the First World War* (1969); and *John Morley: Nineteenth Century Essays* (1970).

Aïda DiPace Donald, General Editor of the World Profiles, holds degrees from Barnard and Columbia and a Ph.D. from the University of Rochester. A former member of the History Department at Columbia, Mrs. Donald has been a Fulbright Fellow at Oxford and the recipient of an A.A.U.W. fellowship. She has published *John F. Kennedy and the New Frontier* and *Diary of Charles Francis Adams.*